ART OF FREEDOM

Art of Freedom

The Life and Climbs of Voytek Kurtyka

BERNADETTE MCDONALD

RMB

RMB | Rocky Mountain Books Ltd.
rmbooks.com
@rmbooks
facebook.com/rmbooks

Cataloguing data available from Library and Archives Canada
ISBN 9781771602129 (hardcover)
ISBN 9781771602136 (electronic)

Book design by Chyla Cardinal
Cover photo by Tadeusz Piotrowski

Printed and bound in Canada by Friesens

Distributed in Canada by Heritage Group Distribution and in the U.S. by Publishers
Group West

For information on purchasing bulk quantities of this book, or to obtain media excerpts
or invite the author to speak at an event, please visit rmbooks.com and select the "Contact
Us" tab.

We acknowledge the financial support of the Government of Canada through the Canada
Book Fund and the Canada Council for the Arts, and of the province of British Columbia
through the British Columbia Arts Council and the Book Publishing Tax Credit.

Contents

Introduction

Mountains are not stadiums where I satisfy my ambition to achieve, they are the cathedrals where I practice my religion.
—Anatoli Boukreev, *The Climb*

One is fruitful only at the cost of being rich in contradictions.
—Friedrich Nietzsche, *Twilight of the Idols*

Voytek Kurtyka rose early. After brewing a coffee, he wandered over to the window to watch the dawn sky come alive. When the pastel hues faded to the colour of pearls, he moved to his desk. As usual, there were emails from suppliers and some problems with Polish customs that he would have to deal with later in the day. There were a couple of inquiries from climbers about route information and an unexpected message from someone named Christian Trommsdorff. "We would like to invite you as a jury member for the Piolets d'Or [Golden Ice Axes] event in Chamonix, April 22 to 25, 2009."

Known as the Oscars of the mountaineering world, the annual Piolets d'Or recognize the boldest, most innovative alpine climbs, as well as lifetime achievement in climbing. Christian Trommsdorff, a Chamonix mountain guide and chairman of the awards committee, wanted Voytek – one of the most respected alpinists of all time – to help choose the best climbs. He couldn't have anticipated Voytek's response.

Hearty thanks for your invitation au jury du Piolets d'Or. I'm sorry I can't take part in it…I understand the world is suspended on a monstrous structure of wild competition and, consequently, of awards and distinction. But this structure is an enemy of true art. Where awards and distinction rule, true art ends. I sincerely believe that climbing can elevate the climber to physical and mental well-being and to wisdom, but awards and distinction elevate the climber to vanity and egocentricity. Taking part in the game…is dangerous for the climber. I'm not ready to take part in this game and I can't accept your offer.

Apart from his philosophical discomfort with the "game," Voytek was baffled by the prospect of ranking climbs in a "monstrous, wild competition." How could anyone compare the traverse of Makalu by French alpinist Pierre Béghin with the forty-day solo ascent of Trango Tower by Japanese climber Takeyasu Minamiura? Or Krzysztof Wielicki's winter ascent of Everest with Erhard Loretan's "night naked" climb of the same mountain? It seemed absurd to rank the pioneering spirit of Reinhold Messner against the superhuman stamina of Jerzy Kukuczka. According to Voytek, "This exercise made as much sense as asking which was better, sex or Christmas."

Voytek maintained that alpinism was far too complex to rank and compare. There were so many facets: aesthetic, physical, metaphysical, logistical, imaginative. And there was so much suffering. How could you measure the suffering of climbers? "The pressure of the media to create (for their own use) a number one star is an attempt to reduce alpinists to one dimension," he said in his response. "And it means the degradation of climbing."

Christian laughs when he recalls the strongly worded email, but he wasn't discouraged by it. The following year he wrote an even bolder letter, this time asking Voytek to *accept* the Piolets d'Or Lifetime Achievement Award. Once again, Voytek responded.

Hello Christian,
This is a devilish offer. I always had a sense of escaping to the mountains from everyday social bullshit, and now you propose to me to take part in it. I was always escaping to the mountains to find encouraging proof that I'm free from the social bonds of award and distinction, and now you offer it to me. I always ran

to the mountains with the great expectation that I could elevate myself above my human weaknesses, and now you try to put on me the most dangerous one: the illusion that I am a person of distinction. My entire life is a struggle with that illusion. I'm very conscious that the desire for awards and distinction is the greatest trap of our ego and a proof of vanity. I'm sorry I can't take part in it. I can't accept the Piolets d'Or. To be frank, in my heart I'm very worried because in rejecting your award I might be driven by…you know what? Unfortunately, also by vanity. Don't even try to honour me. Climbers possess an exceptional awareness of freedom, and I hope you will understand my uneasiness in the face of such a great honour.

It's not just climbers who face this discomfort: poets do as well. Leonard Cohen wrote about his reluctance to accept a Canadian award recognizing his lifetime work: "One of the reasons one avoids these things is because they summon some really deep emotional responses… this happens to an artist or a writer very rarely, where you have in front of you the unconditional acceptance of your work." But Leonard Cohen *did* eventually accept, later telling the audience, "We shuffle behind our songs into the Hall of Fame."[1]

Christian was nothing if not stubborn. It's possible he thought that Voytek was just being coy. It was worth another try. In 2010 he sent a third letter, again offering the Lifetime Achievement Award. Voytek was confused. Had he not been clear? In his response, he tried to be more emphatic.

Dear Christian,
O dear, this is an impossible offer for me. I would have to go totally against myself…I admit that I…desire the friendliness and love of people but I fear very much their admiration. I humbly confess that I'm proud like a peacock when I'm admired, but exactly for that reason I can't accept great awards…These awards border on blasphemy. Would you publicly award a hermit for years of spiritual practice? We are not hermits, but our experiences are sometimes close to a sort of enlightenment that changes our life…I want to preserve those precious moments unspoiled. I can't trade these

moments for public honours...Christian, I'm sincerely grateful for your offer and I'm ashamed not to be able to accept it.
With friendship,
Voy

What Voytek didn't know was that Christian was not alone in this all-out effort to award him the prize. The most respected alpinists in the world were puzzled that Voytek had not yet received this recognition, and they were pressing the Piolets committee to rectify the situation. In 2012 Christian wrote still another letter, offering the award. Voytek lost his patience.

Dear Christian,
Sorry. NO NO! I will not be talking about Piolets d'Or any more.
I gave you my reasons.
Don't try to make me an idiot...
Voy

What kind of individual would repeatedly refuse the ultimate sign of respect from his peers? After all, the Piolets d'Or Lifetime Achievement Award is not determined by movie producers, politicians or alpine club presidents. It's a recognition *of* alpinists *by* alpinists. Yet Voytek refused it because he claimed to want to avoid the trap of public admiration. His attitude seemed both admirable and ungracious at the same time. It was certainly intriguing, for it is hard to imagine a worthier recipient of the award.

Voytek Kurtyka changed the trajectory of Himalayan climbing in the 1970s by proving it was possible to climb difficult routes with small teams on the highest mountains in the world. His record includes eleven great walls in the Hindu Kush, the Himalaya and the Karakoram, six of which are 8000-metre peaks.

Almost from his first contact with rock, his first glimpse of a mountain, Voytek took an idiosyncratic approach to climbing. At a time when most Himalayan climbers were approaching the mountains in traditional expedition style, he was climbing them in alpine style – or unleashed, as he called it. When alpine-style climbing in the Greater Ranges became the norm, he had moved on to one-day ascents and multiple 8000ers in one trip. When he began free climbing former aid routes in Poland, he developed a new grading system to more accurately represent the level of difficulty, one that is still used today. While other Polish climbers were pushing the standards of rock climbing using ropes and racks, he was free soloing their hardest routes. His style was visionary, and he always remained true to his vision. He refused to compromise his values for a summit. Even on K2, the mountain of his dreams, Voytek gave the summit a miss rather than climb it by a route that didn't interest him.

His approach was never one-dimensional. While he embraced the physical, athletic side of climbing, he was equally fascinated with the cerebral challenge, the constant decision making, problem solving and strategizing that it demanded. Even more important to Voytek was the aesthetic aspect of alpinism, which, on some ascents, approached a spiritual level. He was an ambitious climber, drawn to huge icy faces, technical rock walls and unbroken, high-altitude traverses. He had an eye for beauty and a hunger for boldness as he traced new lines on those bewitching peaks. He said: "Beauty is the door to another world."[2]

I remember our first meeting in 2010, when he agreed to an interview for a book I was writing about Polish climbers.[3] I was wary because of his reputation for avoiding the mountaineering community, particularly journalists. Yet he seemed polite and willing, even friendly, as he offered me cup after cup of (instant) coffee in his apartment and talked for hours about his climbs. We kept in touch, and I eventually suggested writing his biography. Many more cups of coffee followed (now from a shiny new espresso machine), together with days of poring over photos and journals.

Now, as he celebrates his seventieth year, Voytek appears an elegant man, courteous and formal. Trim and slim and rather small, he is shockingly strong. Yet he moves almost weightlessly. He is intensely private, even shy. He is deliberate about his words, his actions and his thoughts, a self-admitted perfectionist. He is ruthlessly self-disciplined but can sometimes be as spontaneous as a child. He thinks deeply, but his sense of humour is never far from the surface. He is admired by the world, yet what he values most is friendship. A bundle of contradictions. As I would discover during our many hours of conversation, there is an intensity and power about him that can be unsettling.

The challenge in writing the story of Voytek Kurtyka was not in collecting the essential details of his life or in presenting them in a logical sequence. The real challenge was to give shape and meaning to those facts in a way that revealed the core values by which he lives, all of which revolve around freedom.

Remembering is also an act of the imagination, a malleable and imperfect activity. For Voytek, recalling those important moments that occurred years ago, even decades ago, was selective. At times, his memories seemed to be movable feasts. And finding the truth – the essence – of those memories was the key to understanding his character. Seven years later, as this book is about to be published, the journey of discovery has reached a resting point along the way – a literary bivouac on Voytek's path in pursuit of the art of freedom.

ONE

Rock Animal

Nearby is the country they call life. You will know it by its seriousness.
—Rainer Maria Rilke, *The Book of Hours*

Myths begin early. For almost seventy years, Voytek Kurtyka misled the world into believing he was born on September 20, 1947. To be fair, it wasn't Voytek who initiated this deception. The year 1947 was a tumultuous one in which to be born in Poland. The Second World War had killed more than six million citizens, and the country was in chaos and ruin: recording birthdates wasn't top of mind for most. And so it happened that the infant Voytek, who arrived without ceremony in the small village of Skrzynka on July 25, 1947, wasn't registered until September 20 of that year. Why worry about a couple of months? Not worth bothering about, at least according to his brilliant but sometimes distracted father, Tadeusz Kurtyka, known throughout Poland as the author Henryk Worcell.

Tadeusz was born in 1909. Although Poland was soon embroiled in the horrors of the First World War, the young boy grew up on a farm surrounded by rolling beech forests braided with meandering streams. He fished and gathered berries and mushrooms with abandon. Despite an inquisitive mind and a natural intelligence, he rebelled against the constraints of school. He also resisted the demands of his hard-working father, who expected the young boy to help out on the farm as well as keep up with his schoolwork. Tadeusz hated both. When he was sixteen, he left home and moved to the nearby city of Krakow.

Even with the wartime destruction of much of Poland, Krakow was, and remains, a city of esteemed universities, soaring cathedrals, museums, monuments and galleries, a magnet for both the learned and the powerful. The social life of the Krakow elite revolved around the restaurant scene along the palatial avenues. Tadeusz's first job was washing dishes in one of the best of those gathering places: the Grand Hotel Restaurant. It was here that the city's business leaders and power mongers met with cultural icons to eat and drink and exchange idle gossip.

Within a short time, Tadeusz had grown into a dashingly handsome young man and had advanced to waiter, at which point his life took an interesting turn. Another Grand Hotel waiter, Michael Choromański, noticed that Tadeusz enjoyed reading the classics for relaxation during his work breaks. Tolstoy's *The Kreutzer Sonata*, and others. Choromański, who was a writer, encouraged Tadeusz to try writing in addition to reading. Tadeusz did, and excelled at it. Soon he was scribbling his thoughts about the intriguing snippets he saw and overheard at the Grand Hotel. A shameless eavesdropper, he found he could reconstruct a conversation in vibrant detail. The result was a slim volume published under a pseudonym, Henryk Worcell. Released in 1936, *Bewitched Circles* caused quite a stir in Poland and launched the young man's writing career. But despite his use of thinly veiled fictional names, the scandal surrounding the gossipy anecdotes about the private lives of prominent citizens threatened Tadeusz's safety in Krakow. He fled to the mountain village of Zakopane in the Polish Tatras, where he became part of its bohemian community of artists and writers.

But in the pre-war years, in addition to gaining notoriety as an author, Tadeusz became involved with an underground movement in nearby Krakow. The group's plans included the assassination of a prominent German general, and it was clear that discovery of the plot was imminent. It became far safer for Tadeusz to volunteer at a German labour camp than to remain in Poland. So off he went to the Meissen Labour Camp in Germany, close to the Polish border.

Beyond the furthest eastern corner of the country, in what is now Eastern Ukraine but was then the Soviet Union, another family story was unfolding. Antonina Moszkowska was born in 1922 into a Polish family of six children. Her upbringing was as hard as her education was minimal.

The area was populated by both Poles and Ukrainians, and when the Germans arrived during the Second World War, she was taken to the Meissen Labour Camp. There she remained until 1945.

Antonina and Tadeusz met and fell in love: the angelic-faced and thoughtful village girl from the northeast and the young man from the southwest, who, by this time, had abandoned his birth name for good and was now going by his professional name, Henryk Worcell.

They married and moved back to Poland immediately after the war ended but then faced the dilemma of what to do and where to live. The country was seething with migratory movement, since the borders with both Germany and Russia had been realigned. Per postwar agreements, all of the former most easterly territories of Germany, up to the river Oder, now belonged to Poland. As a result, German citizens residing in these areas had to leave. At the same time, Polish citizens living in the far eastern territories of Poland, now under Soviet control, were also required to relocate. The eastern Poles moved west into the newly claimed Polish territory, and the Germans moved even further west. Many homes and farms previously owned and occupied by German families were now taken over by Poles. There were astonishing examples of incoming Poles temporarily sharing the same premises as outgoing Germans. It was this unusual situation that became the subject matter for Henryk's writing. On the surface, his work presented the official version of the delicate, and sometimes awkward, political and cultural overlaps. But at a deeper level he wrestled with the emotional devastation in this transhumance. People were numbed by years of terror, and each day that passed blurred the memory of the country they had once known.

Henryk and Antonina found a farm outside the village of Skrzynka, in an area of southwestern Poland that was formerly Germany. The bucolic countryside is vibrant with undulating hills, verdant forests, trout-filled rivers and therapeutic hot springs. At first, it seemed a paradise for the pair, newly arrived from the German work camp. They moved into a well-functioning farm, which, for the first few months, they shared with the outgoing German owners. To add to the strain, the farm did not belong to the incoming couple; it was state property.

Soon after arriving, they started a family. Voytek was the firstborn, and two brothers followed: Jan three years later and Andrzej three years after that. Henryk occupied himself with his writing and, of course, the farm. Four cows, one ox, one horse, one foal, two calves, three goats, two sheep, twenty chickens, five geese, sixteen rabbits, two piglets and ten acres of land. It was a lot of work. Since it was in the world of words and ideas that Henryk flourished, the farm began to flounder. After four years of effort, he and Antonina admitted that they weren't suited to farming.

They moved down the road to the village of Trzebieszowice and settled into a sturdy white house with two separate apartments. The Kurtyka family occupied the first level, and Henryk continued writing about his challenging subject matter. He had strong ideals about fairness and equality and defended those he felt were being treated poorly, sometimes getting into trouble in the process. In one incident, he was beaten so badly that he lost the sight of one eye. On another occasion, he was stabbed with a knife. The family assumed he was being punished for his strong convictions, and they were proud of him. But these were complicated and confusing times in postwar Communist Poland. It's difficult to know what forces were at work behind the scenes, or what the Communist authorities would eventually expect from Henryk Worcell.

Despite the underlying tension, the family remained in Trzebieszowice until 1957. Although Henryk was now fully occupied with his writing, he yearned for the stimulation of a literary community. When the Polish Literary Federation offered him an apartment in nearby Wrocław, along with the freedom to write, he couldn't refuse. The family moved to Poland's fourth-largest city to begin a new life.

Wrocław is an elegant city with a rich cultural history. Baroque, Gothic, Bohemian and Prussian traditions inform an architectural kaleidoscope burgeoning with monuments and cathedrals. But it wasn't so beautiful in 1957. Late in the Second World War it was the scene of one of the last major battles between the Red Army and the Germans. Two days before the war ended, the Germans finally surrendered, but by then over half the city had been destroyed. Almost 20,000 people died in the botched evacuation, and 40,000 more lay dead in their homes. At the end of the war the population of the city comprised almost 200,000 Germans and fewer than 20,000 Poles. Over the next two years, the city reverted to Polish governance and the vacuum created by the mass exodus of Germans was filled by Polish citizens. Most came to the city from the northeastern areas of Poland, but others, like the Kurtyka family, moved from places close by.

They had no reliable or regular source of income, so it was lucky that their apartment was rent-free. The family lived on the earnings from Henryk's writing, which were sporadic at best. When an advance on royalties arrived, they would eke out a living for a while. Even when the Kurtykas had money in hand, it was tough to find enough food in the shops, and the queues were mind-numbingly long. A plot of ground near their apartment provided them space to grow a few vegetables, but although they never went hungry, their diet was sparse. Potatoes and cabbage were staples, as they were with most Polish families at the time. Eventually Antonina found a job as a receptionist to supplement their income. Despite the frugal lifestyle, Henryk seemed more fulfilled in Wrocław, surrounded by writers and publishers and a cultural life.

Voytek was only ten years old when they moved to Wrocław, and it sent him into an emotional tailspin. He was happiest when wandering in the woods and scampering up hillsides. As he slumped against his bedroom window in their third-floor apartment, staring down at the street corners piled with debris and across at the gaping black holes in the burned-out buildings, he longed for the forest. "Moving to Wrocław was a traumatic experience," he remembered. "I was very conscious that I had lost something extremely dear to me. I remember just looking through the window and staring at the traffic and crying."

He was often plagued by a nightmare in which he encountered a ghostlike creature with a horrifyingly evil soul. In his dream Voytek would stand defiantly in front of the phantom and try to confront it. He would sometimes take one or two tentative steps toward it before he awoke screaming. Each night he would take one more step. But with each step the dream grew more vivid, and the fear more primal. One step closer, and he was falling. One more, and he was dying.

He gradually adjusted to city life. He had no choice. The small rural community of his early childhood had provided him with strong, conservative traditions that had been clearly taught. But his was an active imagination, and now, bit by bit, he began to invent his own life, accumulating ideas and experiences. The city, distasteful as it was, offered different perspectives, new friends, alternative traditions.

One of Voytek's escapes was summer camp. The camps of that time and place were simple affairs, with the kids lodging in vacant schools, sleeping on cots, eating basic canteen food and playing organized sports. Voytek was crazy about sports – running, shot put, boxing and fencing – and he was as competitive as he was playful. But the greatest appeal of summer camp was the locations: the Baltic Sea, the mountains and Poland's lake district. For three weeks of each summer, Voytek inhaled the country air, played in the sea and renewed his soul. "It was fantastic," he said.

Henryk's writing reputation grew, as did his fortune. Now that he was publishing a book every couple of years, his royalties increased in size and his public-speaking invitations multiplied. The Communist authorities appointed him president of the Literary Union of Wrocław, and he travelled around Poland, giving lectures and signing books. Images of him during this time show a confident man, head held high, his cigarette carried at a jaunty angle while he conversed with his admirers. Throughout it all, he remained a religious man. As well as a drinking man. Three-day binges were not uncommon. Voytek's mother assumed the role of nurturer, providing as much love and stability as she could for her three sons.

Henryk's devotion to the church created a formidable barrier between him and his eldest. Even as a child, while Voytek admired the lofty cathedral architecture, he was bored to tears by the sermons. "I never found any spirituality in them," he complained. "And the music! I found some of it terribly sad – even frightening… It rarely expressed any joy from communion with God. It too often conveyed human misery and an imploring approach to God," he said. "It seemed dominated by feelings of fear. Why? Because over that religion loomed the threat of Hell, and the music expressed that frightening potential. And from this music I had the strong premonition that Hell was my destiny. From the age of four or five I felt truly oppressed. I perceived this as a kind of religious terror."

Still, he was an obedient child, so he attended mass each week until his sixteenth year, first in the village and later in the city. He took First Communion and confessed his sins in the confession booth, probably finding the ritual quite convenient at times. But eventually he stopped going to confession; soon after, he refused to go to church. "It was quite an act of rebellion," he recalled. "Mutiny! I declared to my parents, 'I'm not going anymore. I consider it bullshit. It's useless for me. I'm not going to stand there and listen to those messages about Heaven and Hell. I don't trust them and I don't accept them.'" His father was shocked and angry. His mother was saddened. Even though father and son couldn't bring themselves to discuss the situation, Voytek convinced his mother it was impossible for him to continue the charade of standing in church, singing the liturgy, taking Communion and pretending to believe. "Since it was a big manipulation, my basic sense of honesty refused to agree to it," he explained. Antonina reluctantly accepted his stubborn decision, although it must have been difficult for her, since Roman Catholicism permeated Polish culture and tradition.

Much later, Voytek would occasionally enter a church and be moved by the devotion he sensed in the parishioners. But the basic tenets of Christianity – Heaven and Hell, God's mercy, the existence of a God who, in Voytek's opinion, seemed to have all the attributes of the most common and base human longings for limitless power, blind loyalty and cruelty – he considered poisonous to an intelligent mind. "This is a God that is a reflection of the lowest of human desires," he declared. Still, even as a teenager, he understood man's spontaneous sense of the spirituality surrounding him and the natural desire to connect with it. He not only understood it: he felt it. But not in church. In nature, frequently. When listening to music, yes, and in fact when experiencing every artistic expression. Later, his trips to the mountains built up his awareness of a spiritual sense, and the mountains and climbing became tools for him to communicate with that sensation.

Despite their challenging relationship, Voytek and his father had a lot in common. Henryk was a cerebral person, as was the young Voytek. Henryk was a writer, and Voytek would eventually take that up, too. Henryk had been a rebellious son, and by the time he lived in the city, Voytek had clearly already established himself in that capacity. And, against all odds, one unusual connection between them was the topic of spirituality.

Even though he was a traditional Christian, Henryk also had a mystical inclination, which was inspired by the writings of Roman Catholic philosopher Pierre Teilhard de Chardin, particularly his book *The Phenomenon of Man*. Chardin's cosmic theology embraced the evolutionary process, which is perhaps why he was considered a renegade and eventually banned from the church. He considered everything in nature to be permeated with God's mind or soul. "Being in nature was beautiful for me," Voytek said. "I found that everything surrounding me was spiritual and incredibly beautiful, and that by experiencing this beauty I could easily accept a God who had the attributes of Chardin's vision." At some level, this was Voytek's first encounter with principles more often associated with Buddhism, even if they were articulated by a Roman Catholic philosopher and Jesuit priest. This same priest had inadvertently become a thought idol for both father and son. Although he was still young, Voytek's compelling and positive experiences with the spiritual aspect of nature gave him the confidence and authority to criticize traditional Christian concepts.

His nonconformist attitude wasn't limited to the church. As his father had done years before, Voytek rebelled at school. Uniforms were mandatory, but Voytek refused to wear one. "Yes, it's true," he laughed. "But they were pretty tolerant. It was not like Russia – if you didn't show up in a navy jacket they didn't throw you out." He showed great intelligence in school but was lazy about doing his homework. "My biggest problem was with a subject called Polish language." In fact, it was a little more complicated. Voytek was aware of the literary tradition from which he sprang, and he harboured strong writing ambitions from an early age. While still in elementary school he read one of his essays to the class, only to be accused of presenting something his father had written. This he took as a compliment. Encouraged, he read widely, he wrote constantly and he had high expectations of himself. But despite his highly developed imaginative skills, his grammar, spelling and syntax were lacking.

Upon entering high school, he encountered a problematic teacher. Mrs. Bawolska was a stickler for composition and grammar. A "typical zombie," in Voytek's words. He insisted she was completely insensitive to anything out of the ordinary – anything "freaky." She knew that Voytek's father was a prominent writer and an influential figure in the Polish Literary Federation, and this seemed to irritate her. She took it out on Voytek. "I was completely paralyzed by her. I didn't learn anything from her. I became confused and neurotic. She destroyed my trust in my ability to write, and it lasted. Maybe till today!" he railed.

Strangely, he didn't talk to his father about his writing aspirations. He never asked for advice. Instead, Voytek carried his literary dream deep inside. Unaware of Voytek's artistic leanings, Henryk took a more practical approach and urged him to follow a technical rather than a humanities stream in university. The world was becoming modern, he argued; Voytek could have a brilliant career in science. Henryk's assessment of Voytek as a science guy contributed to the growing distance between them. He increasingly saw his son as a cool intellectual, devoid of intuition, spirituality and emotion, all of which Henryk valued highly. "He perceived me almost as an alien," Voytek said many years later. "We grew apart. I definitely respected my father but we weren't close." The tragedy of their relationship was that Voytek was actually bursting with emotions and sensitivity, but his father didn't see it.

Something else was stirring within Voytek of which his father had no inkling. It was on a high-school hiking trip to Poland's Tatras that Voytek had his first real encounter with a mountain. "I remember the moment," he said. "I wasn't climbing. I was just watching the mountains. Watching and admiring. I felt as if the mountains were alive. I belonged there. I felt a part of them. I had a strong desire to get a response from them and felt almost sorrowful that the mountains didn't give me a sign." Voytek had discovered an emotional connection to a landscape that reached far beyond his intellect and that created even more distance between father and son.

Despite being misunderstood by his father, Voytek did, more or less, what he was told. He entered university, studied for five years and graduated with a degree in electronics. But he had no interest in the subject matter. He attended classes rarely, preferring to cram day and night for his exams. "Upon exiting the exam room, not one single piece of information remained in my head," he laughed.

A new kind of knowledge was filling that space. Voytek had discovered rock climbing.

His first experience on rock was in 1968. Elżbieta Waga – or Ella, as she was known – was studying medicine at the same university and invited Voytek to join her and a teaching assistant for an outing to a nearby crag. The assistant, who was clearly more interested in Ella than in climbing, was in a decidedly sour mood about Voytek's presence. But nothing could stifle their pleasure from scampering about on the granitic rock of the Sokoliki spires near Wrocław, where all the city's climbers learned to climb. "At the first contact with the rock it was a feeling as though long forgotten, yet strangely familiar," Voytek recalled. "Immediately after the first three moves I knew I would be doing more of this."

He did. A lot more of it. In fact, climbing on rock became a kind of trap for Voytek. "Maybe I didn't understand how serious a trap it was," he later admitted. It must have been a relief to abandon his boring electronics classes for something that captivated his every thought and emotion. As ecologist E.O. Wilson wrote in *Consilience*, people "gravitate towards environments that reward their hereditary inclinations." Voytek's attraction to the vertical world of rock seemed predestined.

In the late 1960s, the Wrocław Climbing Club was teeming with good climbers: Wanda Rutkiewicz, Bogdan Jankowski, Krzysztof Wielicki, all future stars of the mountaineering community. Voytek soon provided an intriguing addition to the scene. A slight young man, he exuded intensity, his body coiled, ready for action. His curiosity was limitless, and his powers of observation were impressive, relative not only to the concrete and factual but also to the nuanced and emotional. Despite his sensitivity, socially he presented an almost arrogant attitude disguised by hippie headbands and flowery shirts. The combination of his natural talent and his striking good looks made a powerful impression.

It was at the local crags that Voytek met Wanda, the beautiful and athletic young student who would become the most famous of all Polish female alpinists. He became infatuated with her deep-set eyes and her flashing smile, but only for a few weeks. He had something else on his mind: the granitic rock beneath his fingers.

Voytek wasn't a full member of the climbing scene, at least not yet. The climbing club had strict rules, and Voytek had already established himself as someone who shunned rules. The club insisted on both theoretical and practical instruction for its members, plus examinations to determine advancing levels of expertise. You could climb unsupervised only after passing a certain number of tests. Every young climber was expected to have a passbook, noting each climb and with whom it had taken place. This would ensure a logical, step-by-step transition from novice to expert. Once you reached a certain level of expertise, you could climb without supervision in the Tatras. And beyond that, in the Alps.

Voytek had no patience with this kind of thing. His only interest was climbing. Moving up, smoothly and in balance. Feeling the texture of the rock, the warmth, the resistance. He played with the techniques required to stick to those vertical and overhanging surfaces. He sculpted his body until it was lean and taut, because he understood that his body was his instrument, his medium, in this new-found passion. He climbed and he climbed and he climbed.

This quest for perfection slid under the radar of the Polish Mountaineering Association (PZA); they had never instructed him, they had never tested him, and they had certainly never authorized him to be a climber. Nevertheless, by the time Voytek Kurtyka left university with his unwanted electronics degree, he was one of the best rock climbers in Poland. Because of his fluid, intuitive, natural approach to climbing, he soon became known as the Animal.

TWO

Alpinist in Training

To know a mountain, you must sleep on it.
—Tom Longstaff, *This My Voyage*

Day after day, it rained. Voytek sprawled in his tent, wrapped in a thin blanket. He rested his head on his simple, worn rucksack, occasionally glancing out the door of the tent to see if the downpour was lessening. It wasn't. The summer of 1968 was one of the wettest on record in Poland, and it was that summer, at the age of twenty-one, that he chose for his first "season" in the Tatras, the magnificent mountain range forming the border between Poland and Slovakia.

The Tatras are the highest range of the Carpathian Mountains and are protected on both sides of the border by national parks. Deeply shaded valleys carpeted in luxurious beech forests rise steeply to spruce and pine, which in turn continue up to undulating alpine grasslands stretching on and on along the precipitous ridges that serrate the horizon and define the international frontier. The Tatras are laced with relentlessly steep trails that link the deep valleys via high, narrow passes. But their steepness pales in comparison to the mountains themselves, which plunge directly from their spiny summits to the valleys below.

The climbing heart of the Polish Tatras is the Morskie Oko Valley. Impressive peaks such as the Mnich (Monk) and the Kazalnica (Pulpit) form an amphitheatre that soars above the shimmering, multi-hued Morskie Oko Lake. The name, which means "marine eye," comes from an ancient legend that connects the lake to the sea via a mysterious subterranean passageway. The Tatras display a seasonal kaleidoscope of colours: vibrant greens of the pine forests, warm golds and russets of the alpine grasslands and the deep, rich charcoal of the impressive granite walls. Yet Voytek saw none of this beauty during the summer of 1968. He saw only rain.

Camped a mere 800 metres from the legendary Morskie Oko Hut, he no doubt longed for the comfort and warmth he knew was inside. But his season in the Tatras was financed by tutoring math students, and though his savings were enough for a summer of camping, they couldn't support the relative luxury inside the Morskie Oko Hut.

He had arrived in the valley almost empty-handed. He had neither a rope nor a harness. But the more experienced Tatras climbers appreciated his enthusiasm and talent, so they lent him what he needed, including enough rope to fashion a chest harness. Voytek had learned to climb on the granitic rock near Wrocław, and when he discovered that the pure granite of the Tatras was similar, it boosted his confidence. Voytek, the "Animal," had discovered a much larger playground where he could climb, bold and strong. He called it "the most joyful, animal game." Part of what made it so joyful for him was that he was obviously the best climber in the valley.

The established grades at the time were much lower than today; the top climbs were rated Grade VI, roughly equivalent to French 5c, North American 5.9. For a natural talent like Voytek, the routes were not a problem. He simply climbed them. And it felt good to be the best. "I must confess, honestly, it was sort of ego-boosting," he laughed, years later. "I was admired. Of course, if you are admired, you want it more. This is the trap. And after years, I knew more and more that it was a trap." But at the age of twenty-one, he was completely unaware of any impending traps.

His climbing at the crags had been primarily top-roping, which was the norm in Poland at that time. But in the Tatras he had to learn how to read the terrain directly in front of him, not only to climb it but also to place pieces of protection in the rock in case of a fall. Where were the weaknesses? Into which cracks could he pound a piton? Voytek proved to be a quick study. "You could see immediately how it worked," he said. "You see the crack, you put in a piton. You know before a hard move you must put in a piton. It came quite naturally."

Even though the 1968 season was foiled because of the abysmal weather, Voytek saw enough to know this was his future. He wasn't alone, for the Polish climbing community was growing at a phenomenal rate. Another climber who was active at that time, Ludwik Wilczyński, reflected on the importance of climbing in that postwar Communist era in Poland. "The experience of those years was an odd mixture of enthusiasm, poverty, a sense of captivity and social security benefits (which were as bad as you can get). Neither my generation, nor the generation of the 1960s, was affected by Stalinist terror. The world around us was overcome with deadly, almost physically noticeable boredom," he wrote. And that's why climbing made such an impact. "Climbing for the first time was about discovering... freedom. Such a discovery lies in the nature of a first-timer's experience. But in the world of limited self-expression it becomes much more intense. Shock, enlightenment and a distanced look at the 'socialist reality' were our first mountaineering achievements."[4]

Climbers soon identified themselves as a subculture within Polish society. The climbing author J.A. Szczepański, known as the cerebral leader of Polish climbers in the first half of the twentieth century, wrote, "Climbing is not a symbol or poetic metaphor of life – it is life itself."[5] Voytek easily slid into this way of thinking; Szczepański's philosophy fit like a custom-made glove. He joined this independent group of people who ignored their dysfunctional surroundings and abandoned career aspirations to channel their unrealized hopes and suppressed energies into a passion for mountains and adventure. Their mountain asylum was where they could fulfill themselves and create meaningful lives. There, they could rely on principles that predated the totalitarian state – values that were common to all climbers.

It was the summer of 1969, and Voytek was back, climbing like a demon. By the end of the season he had climbed all the Grade VI climbs in the Polish Tatras. There was nothing harder in the area at that time. He was in the Morskie Oko Hut when he noticed her. The dark-haired beauty, four years older than Voytek, was a recreational climber from Krakow. She had a finely chiselled face, a feminine figure, a warm smile and watchful eyes. Her name was Ewa Waldeck.

Ewa's mother was Polish, but her father was a German doctor and officer who had been stationed in Krakow during the Second World War. In a highly unusual situation, the Polish woman and the German officer became lovers. Ewa was their only child. Near the end of the war, he lost his leg in battle and returned to Germany. Her mother was afraid to accompany him, because he was still active in the German army and, as a Polish woman, she represented the enemy. Eventually, after some time alone in Krakow, she decided to risk it and rejoin her husband. But now her problem was financial. Without enough money to take a bus, she walked from Krakow to Germany, pushing little Ewa in a carriage. It would have been a lovely story, had it worked out. She soon realized that the German mentality didn't match hers, so she reluctantly returned to Krakow with Ewa. There, she faced scrutiny from Polish authorities because of her highly unusual behaviour.

After their first encounter, Ewa and Voytek met often in the Tatras, climbing together in the Morskie Oko Valley and crossing the border to climb illegally on the Slovakian side. They went kayaking together on the Massouli Lakes, and within two years of meeting at the Morskie Oko Hut, Voytek and Ewa were married. Twenty-four-year-old Voytek packed a couple of suitcases and moved to an apartment in Krakow owned by Ewa and her mother. Despite his happy personal life, Voytek was struggling with his career. He worked in a high school as an assistant for a couple of years, but his schedule interfered with climbing. He quit and tried a job testing technological equipment at a nearby steelworks factory. That didn't suit him, either. He then tried television repair work, which he hated so much that, later, when his own television broke down, he hired a repairman rather than fix it himself.

His attitude matched that of most Polish citizens at the time, who were disgruntled with the Communist system under which they lived. Their wages were fixed, regardless of how productive they were, causing a loss of interest and a passive resistance that almost ground the country to a halt. People saved their energy for moonlighting jobs, for their friends and for their families.

Despite the disappointing job prospects, Voytek and Ewa enjoyed a loving relationship, one which required defending from time to time. One day, after they had climbed together at a crag near Krakow, Ewa wandered off to stroll in the forest while Voytek continued climbing with friends.

When she encountered a group of young guys chopping down trees, she approached them.

"Hey guys, what are you doing? Stop. They aren't your trees."

Bold and cocky, they swore at her, calling her crude names. She returned to the crag, furious.

"You have to do something, Voytek," she insisted.

Voytek agreed. After all, she had been insulted, threatened. So off they trudged to find the guys, who, of course, had already left. Ewa and Voytek continued walking the four kilometres to the Zabierzów train station, not far from Krakow, Ewa all the while recounting the injustice.

"They called me a bitch," she railed. "They threatened me."

"Okay, it's over. You should calm down," Voytek urged.

As they entered the train station, Ewa cried out. "Voytek, Voytek! Look, there they are. Those are the guys who bullied me!"

There were five of them.

Voytek knew he had to do something, so he walked up to them and said, "Hey guys, you offended my wife. You should apologize." Three of the five immediately took up fighting positions, facing Voytek with their fists raised and clenched. Who did this skinny little guy think he was? It wouldn't take much to send him running. They knew nothing about his boxing prowess, his agility or his strength.

Soon, three of the boys were splayed out on the floor. The other two escaped. One of them had been holding a guitar, and when Voytek hit him, the guitar slammed against the wall with a howling *whoinnnnnnng*. As they picked themselves up, Voytek could see they were enraged. In addition to wounding their egos, he had inadvertently destroyed the guitar. At that lucky moment, a group of local boys sauntered over. They had seen the confrontation and were ready to help.

"You had better leave now," they threatened the assailants. "If you don't, you will regret it." The offenders retrieved the shattered instrument and skulked out of the station.

Years later, Voytek laughed as he remembered the train ride back to Krakow. "Yes, Ewa was pretty impressed," he said.

In 1970 he returned to the Tatras with Ewa, this time on the forbidden Slovakian side. They crossed over a ridge near the Morskie Oko Valley and wandered down through meadows of high alpine grasses and a dwarf pine forest. Up and over another ridge, a long, awkward traverse on loose scree, and they were rewarded with a view of the 300-metre face of the Mały Młynarz (Little Miller). With them were Voytek's climbing partners, Michał Gabryel and Warsaw climber and Olympic-level fencer Janusz Kurczab. Older than Voytek by ten years, Janusz was a handsome man with fine, even features. The three proceeded to climb a new route on the dark, brooding rock of the East Face of the Little Miller. It punctured the magical Grade VI level and was awarded the grade of VI+, thus becoming the hardest climb in the Tatras. Janusz, Voytek's alpine mentor at the time, was the brains behind the ascent, while Voytek provided the climbing skills to get up the thing.

Just a year after the Little Miller climb, Voytek was reeling from the death of a good friend and a different kind of mentor from his early rock-climbing days. Jasiu Franczuk was killed in 1971 during the first ascent of Kunyang Chhish in the Hispar Muztagh, a subrange of Pakistan's Karakoram Mountains. The Polish team was led by the venerable expedition leader Andrzej Zawada and was one of the first important Polish successes in the Greater Ranges, alerting the world to the talent and stamina of Polish climbers. When Jasiu fell into a crevasse low on the mountain, the expedition almost collapsed. But after an emotional memorial service they carried on. Voytek remembered Jasiu's special human qualities rather than his climbing skills. "I considered him quite exceptional," Voytek said. "He was fair toward the world. Excellent sense of justice. Incredibly modest. And so natural." Older than Voytek by three years, Jasiu had a simplicity and a sincerity that seemed to offer direct access to truth, and Voytek missed him terribly. More so because, since he had moved to Krakow, Voytek had lost regular contact with his family and his estrangement from his father had intensified.

Climbing and travelling helped fill the void. There were trips to the Alps organized by the PZA in partnership with the Ecole Nationale de Ski et d'Alpinisme (ENSA), based in Chamonix, France. The PZA would choose the best Polish climbers and pay for their travel, plus give them the equivalent of around $200 to cover expenses in France. Since the Polish climbers usually set off for an entire month, they had to scrimp to make their stipends last, bringing most of their food essentials from

Poland and camping illegally. Paying to camp would have used up their allowances in short order. But before they could leave Poland, they had to apply for access to their passports, which were stored in safekeeping at the passport offices. Only an official reason for travelling abroad could trigger the release of a passport, and the process often took a month or more. Unbeknownst to the PZA, Voytek's participation in the trips to the Alps was completely unauthorized, since he was not yet a "certified" alpinist according to the inflexible system the association had created.

Back in the Tatras, Voytek continued with his illegal ways, crossing back and forth between Poland and Slovakia at will. Every time he crossed the border, he committed a crime. "We would sneak over the passes, descend for four or five hours to get to our climbs, and then sleep under over-hangs," he explained. A naturally rebellious lot, Polish climbers jumped at the chance to climb in forbidden territory. But the frontier soldiers took their job seriously, and most climbers got caught at one time or another. Voytek was no exception.

"One time I decided to make an easier crossing, so I descended to the river," he recounted. "When I was exactly in the middle, wading across, I heard a Polish border patrol yelling, 'Stop, stop, stop. Don't move.'" It was hopeless to try to escape. Voytek was loaded down with equipment, and besides, where would he run? He turnèd around, surrendered and spent the next two nights in jail. The jail time was easy, but the ongoing reporting that the authorities demanded after his release presented a real problem. Once a week for the next two months he had to show up at the Wrocław police station. However, Voytek was no longer living in Wrocław. Since all of his climbing equipment was at his campsite in the Tatras, he was forced to spend two days a week travelling back and forth between the mountains and Wrocław. The wasted money! The loss of time! But it had to be done, so Voytek dutifully traipsed back and forth until his sentence was finished.

On one of those visits, the police sat him down and questioned him, not about his border infraction, but about his international travels. They were polite, even friendly, as they suggested he tell them if he saw any activity or behaviour by his climbing companions that "made him feel uncomfortable." Voytek nodded in agreement, but he had no intention of complying. The police were slightly less friendly at the next meeting when he had nothing to offer them, and they made casual reference to the difficulty of accessing passports for international travel. Climbers were easy to bargain with, because they had much to gain – freedom to travel – if they co-operated, and a grim prospect – confinement to Poland – if they didn't.

Voytek now understood this to be a veiled threat to his freedom. What to do? He knew he would never spy on his partners, but he also knew this was what the authorities expected in return for allowing him to travel outside the country. The solution appeared like a flash of lightning. He would climb exclusively in the Tatras, eliminating the need to observe, and report on, his partners. Hopefully, this would put an end to these bothersome meetings. When he explained his position to the police, they agreed that this would be acceptable. They had only one more request: the discussion had never happened and he was never to speak of it.

Of course Voytek agreed, and of course he disobeyed. He knew he wasn't unique. Many alpinists who travelled abroad were approached by the police, not only to observe the goings-on "out there" in the free world, but also to spy on their partners. Some complied, but most didn't. Voytek was one who did not.

Voytek returned to the Tatras over the following two winter seasons and sent the standards soaring. He stayed in the small, modest climbers' hut located below the Morskie Oko Hut. Since his arrival coincided with the Christmas holidays, the hut was heaving with alpinists from all over Poland. The corridor floors were buried under smelly sleeping bags, and the rooms were crammed with climbers stacked like firewood. A wood stove warmed the central room, but the corners were drafty and cold. Still, the atmosphere was cozy and convivial. "The Polish climbers in those days were not conflicted," Voytek explained. "Okay, there might have been some conflicts between a few guys, but in general the climbing community got along well. We were friends." Although it was forbidden to use stoves on the old wooden floors, everyone did, cooking up alcohol-spiked mountain tea and hearty winter soups. If you wanted a shower, you had to arrange it with the hut keeper so water could be heated. Most opted for ice-cold sponge baths.

Winter climbing in the Tatras was not new. Polish climbers had been coming to the moss-, grass- and ice-clad walls for years, testing their skills and stamina against the arduous conditions and the inclement weather. Famous names such as Andrzej Heinrich, Eugeniusz Chrobak and Janusz Kurczab were learning the fine art of suffering in winter, an ability that would serve them well in the Himalaya, the Hindu Kush and the Karakoram. In fact, winter climbing in the Tatras was almost as popular as summer climbing. "Who did the first winter ascent?" was as frequently asked as "Who did the first ascent?" When Voytek arrived for his first winter season, he brought his high-level summer skills and adapted them to the unique conditions of the Tatras in winter, shattering the limits of what was thought possible.

The primarily mixed climbs required a constantly changing arsenal of rock and ice techniques. These Tatras climbs had fierce reputations and were psychologically challenging for all kinds of reasons: few opportunities to place protection, dodgy belays and tricky route finding. The routes were serious objectives in summer and, as Voytek discovered, even more so in winter.

With heavily mittened hands, he would first clear off the light, feathery snow to reveal whatever weakness might exist – perhaps a minuscule ledge that could support a crampon, or a thin, vertical crack for a piton. Then he would reach up and swing his ice axe, listening for that reassuring soft thunk indicating a successful placement into a bit of ice or a patch of frozen grass. If the swing failed, he would paw with his mittens at the unfriendly ground until he could finally persuade the ancient Tatras granite to give him another chance. The next swing of his ice hammer could just as easily bounce off a stone rib lurking beneath a small pillow of snow. His equilibrium compromised for a moment, he would struggle to maintain balance and then swing again. Then he would move his foot up and carefully place his crampon onto a cleared-off stance. Redistribute his weight. Retain his balance. Maintain contact with the wall. Search for the next weakness. In this way, he would inch up the wall, hour after hour, on those short, wintry days.

Climbing frozen waterfalls was still a sport for the future, but it wasn't unusual to encounter near-vertical ice interspersed among the frost-covered sections of rock and frozen clumps of grass. With his crampons, one ice axe and an ice hammer, Voytek's progress was painstakingly slow.

"I would patiently cut steps and holds with the ice axe, then move up higher, cut another series of steps and holds, and on and on," he explained. Despite the tedious progress, he was attracted to the steeper ice. "It was challenging," he said. "Unusual and interesting. And the more abstract it was, the more tempting."

A few friends knew he was planning to attempt the first winter ascent of the direttissima route on the Kazalnica Mięguszowiecka Wall – the most challenging winter objective in the Tatras at the time. The direttissima had a reputation for both bad conditions and bad protection. The bottom part of the wall was mostly frozen grass and small sections of rock. Higher up, the ratio changed, with more black granite interspersed with pockets of frozen grass. The climbing on the brooding wall was difficult: Grade VI, A2–A3. These elements, taken together, made it an attractive objective for Voytek. But he wasn't the only one with an eye on the route.

When he and his three partners arrived in the Morskie Oko Valley in March of 1971, they discovered a team already on the direttissima. Its leader was Jerzy Kukuczka, known by all as Jurek. Voytek remembers feeling a little annoyed and outsmarted, suspecting that his intentions had been leaked to the wrong ears. Now it was a race for the direttissima, and Voytek felt compelled to participate. "It [the direttissima] was in fashion," he later explained. "I was aware of that, and for that reason, I was attracted to it."

Jurek was unlucky with the weather. On his first day of climbing, it started to snow. The wall was soon awash with waves of spindrift, so Jurek and his team retreated. The following day, the weather cleared but Jurek's team now needed to rest. Voytek headed up. Jurek had left fixed ropes on two pitches of the climb, and although Voytek's team didn't use their ropes, they clipped in to some of the pitons that were already in place. On the second day of climbing, Voytek and his partners had already reached the centre of the face when they noticed Jurek's team approaching the wall for another try. Voytek climbed up through the overhanging section of the route, and as he was tiptoeing up a technically demanding slab above it, the weather broke down again. Snow and wind battered him while spindrift avalanches threatened to sweep him off the smooth slab of rock.

Jurek shouted up from below. "Hey, the weather is pretty bad. Can you lower your ropes? Can we use them?" Jurek's team was in trouble, and despite a friendly competition between the teams, there was no way to refuse them. Voytek agreed and continued climbing. Concentrating now on the delicate slab and the growing strength of the avalanches sliding by, Voytek heard a strange sound from far below. "It was a frightening cry. A high-pitched tone. Almost animalistic. And then I heard two or three thumps. Of course I was alarmed." He wondered if something serious had happened down below, but he couldn't deal with it just then. Voytek was in a precarious position. The previous belays were not entirely secure, and his runouts on the last pitch were extremely long. A fall would probably rip out the belay. He simply couldn't make a mistake. "I assumed a kind of indifference and tried hard to sweep any thoughts of a disaster out of my head," he said. A few minutes later, when he was in a slightly more stable position, he called down to his partner, Tadeusz (Teddy) Gibiński.

"Hey, Teddy, what happened? What's going on down there?"

"Fuck, I don't know," Teddy mumbled.

Voytek suspected this was a kind of protective lie because of their dramatic situation, so he continued climbing, finished the pitch and set up the next belay. When Teddy arrived, they decided to stop for the night rather than continue up in the storm, which was now raging out of control. Since there was no room to sit, they stood, huddled together, shivering to stay warm. During the night, they heard more shouting from below. Quietly, Voytek pressed Teddy for more information about what had happened. Shortly before dawn, Teddy finally told him the truth.

"Piotr Skorupa died. He fell to the Black Lake."

They later learned that Piotr had been ascending Jurek's rope with a Prusik sling, the standard ascending technique before the invention of Jumars. The Prusik knot allows a climber to move up a rope but not slip down. He pushes the knotted sling up the rope, then steps into an attached sling and weights it with his body. He then slides a second sling up and shifts his weight accordingly. In this way, he can inch up the rope without setting foot on the rock. Piotr had almost reached Jurek, who was already stretching out his hand to him, welcoming him to the belay stance and promising a mug of hot soup. For some unknown reason, Piotr grabbed the Prusik knot instead of pushing it. By doing so he changed the tension of the knot, and it began sliding down. He panicked. Instead of releasing the knot, which would have stopped the slide immediately, he held on. He continued sliding down the iced-up rope, screaming that primal scream Voytek had heard. All the way past the end of the rope and to the frozen lake below. It was the first time one of Jurek's climbing partners fell to his death. But it wouldn't be the last.

High on the wall, Voytek was in a tricky situation. Since they were well above the overhangs, it would be almost impossible to rappel back down the route. When dawn crept over their stiff, frozen bodies, he and Teddy knew they had to keep going up. Two more strenuous pitches of climbing awaited them. And they were rattled by the tragedy. Frightened. Their progress was so painfully slow that they were forced to spend one more night on the wall. After five days of climbing, they finally topped out and descended to Morskie Oko Lake, where they were met and embraced by a concerned group of climbers from the hut. Their relief was mixed with an atmosphere of mourning, which diluted the sweetness of their first winter ascent.

In December of that year, Voytek returned, determined to make the first winter ascent of the Šciek (Sewer) route on the same Kazalnica wall. When he arrived in the Morskie Oko Valley and declared his intentions, another team announced that their plan was the same. Another competition. Voytek remembers the mood: "There was a number of guys and there was huge competition for some of those climbs. But it was healthy sport competition." His future climbing companion Ludwik Wilczyński recollects that the competitive spirit wasn't limited to first winter ascents. One-armed pull-ups were all the rage in the climbers' hut, and Voytek was as competitive as anyone. Possibly more so.

Voytek's team took six days to make the first winter ascent of the Sewer route: four days to fix lines and two days to climb it. As they stumbled back to the hut, they heard yelling and shouting and singing. Music blared out into the darkness. "The mountains were shaking," Voytek laughed. He had forgotten that it was New Year's Eve. The Morskie Oko Hut was crammed with climbers, flowing with vodka and pounding with music. They celebrated their climb in "full Polish conditions," and suffered in silence the following day.

The next winter he did the first winter ascent of Pajaki (Spiders), VI, A3. And in 1973, the Superściek (Super Sewer), V, A2, ice 90°. The Sewer routes were particularly feared because of large sections of solid ice. This part of the wall, sodden from a continuous drip in summer, was transformed into a sheet of ice in winter. The climbers had only primitive ice tools and no nuts or Friends, just pitons and a type of ice screw shaped like a threaded needle. The second hazard on the *Sewer* climbs was the huge amount of snow perched above them in a gorge called the Sanctuarium (Sanctuary).

Like all Polish climbers, Voytek maintained a personal record book of his climbs. At first, he was fastidious about recording every climb, but he soon lost interest. Entire years passed without him noting a single ascent. But curiously, he continued to document his bivouacs (often-unplanned nights out on the mountain – sometimes without any shelter). Why? "Because they were interesting to me," he explained. "More than the climbs." In addition to finding them interesting, Voytek knew they were valuable learning experiences. "The most important lessons from those winter climbs in the Tatras weren't about the cold temperatures or about technique," he continued. "Since the climbs were all done in three days or more, you had to learn how to be comfortable on the mountain and how to live on the mountain, making comfortable and safe bivouacs. This is the knowledge we later took to the Hindu Kush and the Himalaya. I usually felt relaxed, enjoying a great view," Voytek recalled. "I loved bivouacs."

He wasn't alone. Bivouacking was so popular among Poland's top climbers that they began to compete to see who had done the most. A set of qualifying conditions emerged: bivouacs inside tents didn't count; using a bivouac sack subtracted one point; simply sticking one's legs into a backpack was the most highly regarded. The eventual leader of the "bivy competition" was Andrzej Heinrich, a notoriously tough Himalayan alpinist who boasted hundreds of them.

Winter climbing in the Tatras was the most highly respected form of alpinism in Poland; it required a greater level of fitness and mental toughness than summer ascents. It was impossible to race up those demanding walls in winter with the equipment that was available, and, besides, why would you rush? Voytek cherished those tenuous links to safety, that feeling of adventure and exploration of the vertical world, and of his own limits. Even though he wasn't the bivouac king, Voytek treasured his winter nights on the soaring black walls of the Tatras.

THREE

Hindu Kush – Unleashed

A land spread wide as wings, folded here and there into mountains.
—Kate Harris, *Lands of Lost Borders*

Arriving in Afghanistan was akin to stepping back into a medieval world. Clay walls, mud floors spread with the most exquisite, intricately patterned, richly hued carpets. Restaurants with only two menu items – *palau* and kebab, which were always made with mutton. The sweet smell of hash on every corner. The Afghan villages had an ancient air about them, worn soft around the edges over time, sad and faded. The people too looked old before their time, dried out and withered by the sun and the wind and the dust. Desert people, baked the colour of clay. "It was the most exotic place I had ever seen," Voytek said.

It was 1972, and twenty-five-year-old Voytek was with a group of ten Krakow climbers, including leader Ryszard Kozioł. An electrical engineer who had been Voytek's boss at an educational academy for a couple of years, Ryszard went on to have a distinguished career as a professor and author and was now leading a team to the soaring peaks of the Hindu Kush. It would be Voytek's first exposure to high mountains. Despite his remarkable climbing skills, his experience was in the much lower Tatras and the Alps. He had read some accounts of high-altitude climbing and had a vague understanding of the strategy of multiple camps and moving up the mountains in stages. He knew he needed to acclimatize his body to the rarefied air of these sprawling beauties, but with naive enthusiasm, he planned to approach them in the same way he climbed back home: no pre-stocked camps, no bottled oxygen, no fixed lines. "I was a complete idiot," he laughs now. "I was just moving according to my imagination, I guess. Pure calculation and imagination about how to climb there." He later learned that his approach was called "alpine style."

They arrived at the Urgunt-e-Bala Valley, explored in 1962 by a group of Polish climbers who had made the first ascent of 6995-metre Kohe Tez.[6] Voytek's team set up base camp on July 27 and, later, an advanced camp on the snowy expanse known as the "Krakow Plateau" at the base of the North Face of Akher Chioch. Since they were a loosely knit group with varying skill levels, it was understood from the start that the climbing objectives would vary, depending on the climber.

Although they were as well equipped as they could possibly be for this trip, the Polish climbers looked more like alpine wanderers from the Middle Ages. Voytek described them as survivors of the Russian Gulag. He dubbed his woollen trousers "Model Gulag 1971," an original production emanating from Ewa's pedal sewing machine. The cotton flannel shirts were "Gulag 1968," a bit older and obviously well-worn. The foam sleeping mats were called "Gulag Ocean 1968," the ocean reference indicating their limitless capacity to absorb moisture. Yet, as the group travelled through the Afghan villages, their tattered and worn clothing was seen as luxurious haute couture treasure. The oversized felt shoes – "Model Gulag, felt 1972" – triggered such envy in the locals that one of the boots mysteriously disappeared as the expedition was leaving the area. It's hard to imagine what anyone would do with one felt boot.

Despite the scruffy appearance of the Gulag outfits, they had been assembled with considerable care and a lot of work. You couldn't just walk into a shop in Poland in 1972 and buy tents and sleeping bags, down pants, anoraks and boots. They were simply not available. Everything had to be made from scratch, using fabric from one supplier, down from another. A mother or girlfriend sewed the various materials into tents, clothes and sleeping bags, while a shoemaker in Zakopane would construct their boots and a local blacksmith forged their ice axes. Organizing a Polish expedition took real effort, as well as an impressive network.

After a couple of weeks of acclimatizing on the nearby peaks, Voytek, Adam Lewandowski and Jacek Rusiecki launched up their first objective:

the unclimbed northwest flank between 7017-metre Akher Chioch and Kohe Tez, followed by the West Ridge of Akher Chioch. Unlike in the Tatras or the Alps, where climbers were usually surrounded by dozens of other alpinists, this remote terrain on the border between Afghanistan and Pakistan felt like a true adventure. "I was motivated by this chance to step into the unknown," Voytek said.

One of his most vibrant memories of the climb was from their bivouac on the northwest flank. Crammed into a small tent, the three climbers burrowed into their down sleeping bags and squirmed on their "Gulag Ocean 1968" sleeping mats, trying to get comfortable. The night was unsettling, as a persistent wind buffeted their tent. Then they heard something. It was very clear: someone was walking around the tent. Voytek sat up with a start. He looked over at Jacek, who stared back at him placidly. Jacek was known as a genius poker player, famous for looking at his opponent's eyes with a gentle but tenacious smile. A smile that betrayed nothing, encouraged nothing. Whenever Jacek made an aggressive bid at the green table, his eyes maintained that steady gaze. If an opponent called his bluff, the aggravating half-smile remained in place.

"Did you hear that?" Voytek asked Jacek, a note of concern in his voice. "There's someone out there."

Jacek didn't say a word. Voytek was confused – weren't they completely alone on this mountain? Just then, the sounds of the steps were joined by the sound of breathing.

"Definitely. There is someone there," Voytek said. "What should we do?"

Still no response from Jacek, whose expression didn't waver. Nobody had the courage to stick their nose out of the tent, so they slunk back into their bags and lay motionless, finally drifting off into a fitful sleep.

The next morning, they inspected the snow around the tent and found no trace of tracks. They were too low in altitude to be hallucinating, so what could it have been? All three of them had heard it. Voytek could only attribute the strange sounds to the tricks the wind can play.

The following day, an hour before reaching the summit, Adam insisted that it was time for a picnic and a pot of tea. Adam was the most relaxed of the three, a master at interweaving the reality of hard work on an expedition with small pleasures, such as a picnic on a calm September day near the top of a 7017-metre mountain. They stopped and boiled up some tea, absorbing the beauty of the horizon stretching off to infinity. The Hindu Kush seemed vast. After wrapping up the picnic, they topped out on the summit, their first new route of the trip, completed in just three days.

The next project was the unclimbed North Ridge of Kohe Tez. The summit team consisted of Voytek, Ryszard Kozioł and Alicja Bednarz, an economist. Years later, Voytek wrote about their experiences on Kohe Tez in an essay entitled "Trio." One of the most evocative photographs of the 1972 expedition is of the three climbers, hollow-eyed, back in base camp after a harrowing bivouac on descent from the summit. "It was one of the hardest bivouacs of my life," Voytek said.

The adventure had begun when Ryszard, Alicja and two others became stranded at 6600 metres on the mountain. There had been complete silence from their camp for three days. Voytek and Jacek Rusiecki were in base camp after having climbed their new route on Akher Chioch. Jacek was worried about his wife, Magda, one of the trapped climbers, and convinced Voytek to climb with him to Kohe Tez's North Ridge to see if they needed help. After just one day of rest following their Akher Chioch ascent, Voytek and Jacek raced up 2000 metres in a day to reach them. To their relief, the climbers were alive and uninjured, merely waiting for better weather.

Reassured that Magda was okay, Jacek prepared to descend with her immediately. Ryszard's partner, Alicja, wasn't interested in going down with Jacek and Magda. An intriguing woman, Alicja referred to herself as "he." "He doesn't want coffee... he wants tea," she would say. When Voytek and Jacek arrived at the high camp to rescue them, she announced, "He will not be going down to base camp. He wants to summit." It didn't seem like a good place for an argument, so Voytek offered to form a team with Alicja and Ryszard and go up the following day. Which they did, making the first ascent of the North Ridge – in Voytek's case in just two days, pure-alpine-style, and only three days after the Akher Chioch climb. The Hindu Kush and Voytek were turning out to be a brilliant match.

But the weather broke down during their descent, and by nightfall they were trapped in the middle of a terrifying maze of seracs, each one threatening to break apart and crush them. They dove into a snow cave for cover. The air was thick with an ice fog that coated their "Model Gulag" woollen trousers and their even less functional cotton shirts. As the surreal mist enveloped them, it sucked the warmth out of their depleted bodies. By the middle of the night, even brave and determined Alicja had broken down in despair. "She made a kind of transformation from male gender into female gender, and she started crying," Voytek recounted. Ryszard began cursing, stressed by Alicja's mood change, certain that this could easily become an icy coffin. "I didn't know how to feel," Voytek said. "Should I react with compassion to the woman, or pray she would resume her true gender and come back in the role of Superman?"

Dawn brought no relief. The black night had transformed into a ghostly white fog. They crawled out from the snow cave on cold, rigid limbs and struggled to stand up. "We were shaking each other, jostling the shards of ice out of our Gulag-style clothes," Voytek recalled. The wind lacerated their frozen bodies as they began to navigate the jumbled labyrinth of seracs. Voytek was out front, searching for an escape route. "The serac barrier turned into a lethal trap," he said. "The white fog was blowing around like a hurricane, and I was stopping more and more often, totally lost in a whiteout. The Gulag models were sticking to my body. I felt the last remnants of warmth and strength seeping away." As he plunged down through the snow, he lost sight of his partners in the dense white fog, sensing their presence only by the tug of the rope. Gaping crevasses loomed at his feet as he veered this way and that, searching for a way out.

He was starting to lose hope when something caught his eye, off to the right. Something dark, something horrible. But he felt drawn to the mysterious shape. The fog was so dense he didn't know if it was an ice cliff or a crevasse or a rock. He only knew that it was dark and seemed more promising than the unbroken whiteness through which they were blindly careening. The inky vision grew larger. Suddenly it opened up directly in front of Voytek – an immense crack between two ice towers, a shimmering ice tunnel. Drawn almost against his will, Voytek entered the tunnel, which descended at a gentle angle. He followed it. But where was it going? It seemed to be plunging into the mountain, into an underground grave. Still, he couldn't stop following it. As he continued, one tentative step after another, he realized something was changing. The hurricane was lessening and the silence felt ominous. Graves are also silent, he thought. As is death. But the silence turned into a salvation because inside that glassy heart of the mountain, the hurricane was no longer raging.

When Voytek looked back toward the entrance of the tunnel, he saw Alicja bent over in agony, almost suspended in the violent storm. His imagination running wild, Voytek remembered the scene: "She was hanging in the fog like a body hanging on the scaffold. Beside her suspended body was Ryszard, smaller and wider, moving like a wide-stepping spider." Alicja eventually reached Voytek and, recovering her "true gender," started giving orders. "He wants to go there," she directed them, pointing toward the end of the tunnel. With her newly found confidence, Alicja soon led the trio out of their icy grave. Ryszard stopped cursing and Voytek felt relieved.

Years later, in "Trio," Voytek invited the reader to take a good look at the intriguing image of the Gulag team back at base camp after their harrowing descent.

> Looking at these beaten men it's hard to sense any heroism, or sense of glory or joy. But it might be possible to see in them a kind of peace and a little bit of pride. Look carefully at the wind- and snow-beaten faces. The one on the left side [Ryszard], staring at the ground, looks like a convict sentenced to death. However, the reason for him looking down at the ground is not the expected death sentence. Because the sentence has just been postponed... I will tell you something discreetly from my confidential knowledge that his downward glance is rather a kind of psychological remorse after the difficult conversation last night with that one in the middle.

He continued with his analysis of the image. "That one on the right side [Voytek] looks a bit cocky. Over-smart face. Smug. Pretending he is an important guy... But, again, referring to my confidential sources, I can tell you it is rather a case of pride. Only the one in the middle [Alicja] is looking normal. However, the he in the middle is not a he but a she."

He implored the reader to have one last look. "Do you understand now the downward, sheepish gaze of the guy on the left [Ryszard]? Do you see a trace of pride of this one in the middle [Alicja]? Would you be kind enough to forgive the one on the right [Voytek] his look of self-confidence? Behind these faces is hidden an immense human pride which can be attained only at the limit, because only at the limit..." Voytek didn't finish the sentence. His meaning was implied: only at your limit can you attain something valuable, an important message or some precious bit of knowledge.

The adventures in the Urgunt-e-Bala Valley were not yet finished. Voytek dried out his Model Gulag uniform and his waterlogged foam pad and headed back to Akher Chioch for an even more ambitious project: the unclimbed North Face – the "Eiger of the Hindu Kush." With him were Jacek Rusiecki, Marek Kowalczyk and Piotr Jasiński. The best route of the trip, they climbed it in three efficient days, alpine-style, or as Voytek called it, "unleashed." "Somehow it was obvious to me, since we were well acclimatized, that there was no sense to fix the camps. The bivouacs were merely a place to sleep at the end of each day."

The Akher Chioch North Face climb may have been the first alpine-style big-wall ascent over 7000 metres. Italian alpinist Reinhold Messner and Austrian climber Peter Habeler's ascent of Gasherbrum I in 1975 is credited as the first alpine-style ascent of an 8000er, but the North Face of 7017-metre Akher Chioch was astonishing for its standard of difficulty. The climbers described it as VI+, around 1800 metres of climbing, not perfectly vertical, but most important, having an incredibly beautiful shape. "It was an Eiger of the high mountains," Voytek declared. "We came back with a sense of pride. The taste of freedom I experienced after breaking the leash never allowed me to sell myself to the net tangle again. It made me feel that the bond between me and the mountain was strong. And I came down with a silent hope that the mountains liked me."

Along with that hope was the belief that some kind of permanent bond had been formed with his partners in the Urgunt-e-Bala Valley. In fact, they did return to Poland as true friends; it was a friendship forged in their Gulag apparel, in the depths of the ice tunnel, in the ghost-infested bivouac and at the picnic site so near the summit. But that bond turned out to be less permanent than Voytek had hoped it would be.

At first, everything went well. They met from time to time and relived their adventures high on the wild peaks of Afghanistan. Eventually, however, strange occurrences began to take place. Twenty-seven years later, on July 28, 1999, Ryszard, the man on the left in the photo, he who had stared down at the ground with such deep remorse, repeated that downward gaze while stepping onto a crosswalk, directly in the path of a speeding car. He was killed instantly.

Thirty years later, on June 2, 2002, Adam, the most relaxed of them all, the man who took the time to appreciate small pleasures just metres from a summit, was in such a hurry that he crossed a major street in Krakow against the red light. He too was killed.

And Jacek, the cool-headed gambler, the man whose gaze was consistent, all-observing, calculated and smooth, for some reason found himself dashing across a Krakow street teeming with cars speeding this way and that. What kind of wager was at stake? Nobody would ever know. He was killed immediately when a car slammed into him.

Only Alicja remained. Decades later, with aching knees and fading memories, she would greet Voytek with a giggle and say, "Oh, you devil, Voytek, how are you?"

His response? "Fine, really fine. And you, my dear boy?"

These days, Voytek sighs in sad resignation as he admits he was clearly the most neurotic of the bunch of them and – possibly – that's what has saved him on numerous occasions. As he travels back and forth between India and Poland for business, he must constantly adjust his awareness of the direction of traffic. Left and right and left again he turns his head, watching for vehicles that could snuff him out as they did Adam and Jacek and Ryszard. And every time he safely crosses one of those busy streets, he feels a soft breath of mystery. "I hope Jacek is watching," he says.

Shortly after returning to Krakow from Afghanistan, Voytek was surprised to see an envelope addressed from the Krakow Climbing Club, a member of the Polish Mountaineering Association. Inside the envelope was a Taternik card. The official grey cardboard certificate named Voytek a climber at the highest level recognized by the association. He stared at the certificate in disbelief. He suddenly realized he had been climbing "illegally" all this time. Without any formal courses or authorized rights, he had been living a "bastard existence" within the community. What fun! If only he had known! Now, with the Taternik card, he could legally leave the marked trails in the Tatras, he could legally climb in the Tatras and he could legally travel outside the country as an alpinist. The association had finally discovered its omission from years before and had scrambled to legitimize Voytek, since he had been travelling on its dime and under its auspices for years. Those at the association undoubtedly felt some relief after issuing the card, but Voytek was a little disappointed that he was now "legal." A small bit of the fun had disappeared. "In such a way, I became a legal part of the climbing community, and with great difficulties I have lasted in this legal state until today," he laughed.

Voytek Kurtyka's parents, Antonina Moszkowska and Tadeusz Kurtyka. Tadeusz had assumed the literary name of Henryk Worcell. *Voytek Kurtyka collection.*

The house in Trzebieszowice where the Kurtyka family lived until Voytek turned ten. The Kurtykas occupied the first-floor apartment. *Voytek Kurtyka collection.*

Voytek Kurtyka's mother, Antonina
Moszkowska Kurtyka.
Voytek Kurtyka collection.

Voytek Kurtyka's father, at the height
of his literary career. *Wikimedia.*

Young Polish climbers, primarily from the Krakow club. Voytek Kurtyka is top left.
Voytek Kurtyka collection.

Serious young Voytek Kurtyka.
Ewa Waldeck-Kurtyka.

Jan Muskat winter "grass" climbing in the Tatras. *Voytek Kurtyka.*

Ryszard Kozioł, Alicja Bednarz and Voytek Kurtyka arrive at Kohe Tez base camp after a horrific descent. They had just completed an alpine-style ascent, via a new route, of this 6995-metre peak in the Afghan Hindu Kush. *Voytek Kurtyka collection.*

Akher Chioch, 7017 metres, Hindu Kush, Afghanistan. New route on the North Face, alpine-style, in 1972, with Jacek Rusiecki, Marek Kowalczyk and Piotr Jasiński. *Voytek Kurtyka collection; route outline by Piotr Drożdż.*

Voytek Kurtyka being greeted by Arne and Bodil Heen at the end of the first winter ascent of the Troll Wall. *Voytek Kurtyka collection.*

Voytek Kurtyka testing his new wooden seat harness attachment on the Troll Wall in the winter of 1974. *Danuta Piotrowska archive.*

The Lhotse fall–winter 1974/75 team gathers in Warsaw. Andrzej Zawada, expedition leader, is front left. Voytek Kurtyka, looking seriously concerned, is third from right. *J. Barcz.*

Tadek Piotrowski and Voytek Kurtyka in Camp III (7300 metres) on the Lhotse Wall, waiting for the weather to improve. Polish fall–winter 1974/75 expedition. *Bogdan Jankowski.*

Voytek Kurtyka on Lhotse, fall–winter 1974/75 expedition. *Danuta Piotrowska archive.*

Voytek Kurtyka on the Lhotse expedition. *Bogdan Jankowski.*

The East Ridge of K2 expedition, 1976. The broken cornice between the two climbers is where Voytek Kurtyka broke through while fixing the rope the previous day. *Voytek Kurtyka collection.*

Young British climber Alex MacIntyre, who travelled to Afghanistan in 1977 on a joint Polish–British expedition to the Hindu Kush. Alex, Jan Wolf, John Porter and Voytek Kurtyka split off from the main group and headed for 6843-metre Bandaka. *Voytek Kurtyka collection.*

The Polish–British expedition negotiating for taxis in Moscow on their way to the Afghan Hindu Kush. From l. to r.: Jan Wolf, John Porter, Howard Lancashire, Voytek Kurtyka, Andrzej Zawada, and the Russian taxi driver walking away from the negotiation. *John Porter collection.*

Voytek Kurtyka on the train from Moscow to Termez, en route to Afghanistan and the Hindu Kush. *John Porter.*

John Porter, Alex MacIntyre and Voytek Kurtyka at Bandaka base camp.
John Porter collection.

Voytek Kurtyka and John Porter waiting for the rockfall to stop at the
bottom of the Cyclotron on Bandaka. *Alex MacIntyre.*

Voytek Kurtyka climbing in the Cyclotron on Bandaka. The block that came loose is wedged in the bulge about 15 metres above his head. *John Porter.*

Voytek Kurtyka climbing high on Bandaka – day five on the mountain. *John Porter.*

John Porter and Voytek Kurtyka enjoying breakfast on the morning of their sixth and last day on the wall of Bandaka. *Alex MacIntyre.*

Kohe Bandaka, 6843 metres, central Hindu Kush, Afghanistan. New route on the Northeast Face, alpine-style, by Voytek Kurtyka, Alex MacIntyre and John Porter in 1977. *Voytek Kurtyka collection; route outline by Piotr Drożdż.*

FOUR

Troll Wall

Let everything happen to you: beauty and terror. Just keep going. No feeling is final.

—Rainer Maria Rilke, *The Book of Hours*

After only one day on Norway's famous Trollveggen (Troll Wall), Voytek knew he needed a better climbing harness. His rudimentary version was okay for free climbing because, at least in theory, his weight was on his feet. It was less comfortable on rappels, when a good portion of his weight placed pressure on his chest, where the harness and his body met. But where that familiar old harness let him down the most was while aid climbing. Moving from one point of fixed protection to the next forced all his weight onto the harness, which then constricted his upper body. Although the discomfort was bearable for short periods, on the Troll Wall, Voytek was facing days of aid climbing, not just a few moves. He wouldn't be able to breathe.

He descended to the village of Åndalsnes and there, snugly ensconced in a camper van with his climbing partners, took up sewing. After he had tested an ingenious new harness design with tape to ensure it would support his weight in comfort, Voytek's needle began to fly. Shoulder straps, waist strap, leg slings and, best of all, a perfectly flat wooden board for his buttocks. He drilled four holes in the board, through which he threaded narrow slings to connect it to the harness. He could leave the board hanging loose when he was free climbing and then swiftly deploy it for a stretch of aid climbing. "It worked perfectly," he laughed. "I wasn't hurt by the rope, and I could sit comfortably on the board. I could aid climb for hours and hours with that seat."

It was late February 1974, and Voytek was in Norway to attempt the first winter ascent of the famous *French Route* on the Troll Wall. When the French team first climbed it, in 1967, they took twenty-one days. And that was in summer. The 1100-metre-high wall holds the distinction of being the tallest vertical rock face in Europe. Located near the rain-drenched west coast of Norway, the intimidating charcoal grey wall of gneiss has a complex architecture of gaping corners, crack systems leading nowhere, and towering overhangs formed by what often appear to be completely detached pieces of rock. The Troll Wall is so steep that the pinnacled summit ridge overhangs the base of the wall by nearly 50 metres at its steepest point. And, to add to its reputation among climbers, the wall is famous for its rockfall.

When the Norwegian press caught wind of the planned winter ascent, they were shocked by the audacity of the Poles. Reporters from the Norsk Telegrambyrå found their way to the climbers, and, by the following day, the front-page headlines expressed clear disapproval: this was an impossible task; this was one of the most demanding climbs in the world; the Polish project wasn't practical. The widely read newspaper *Dagbladet* admonished them: "Away with romantic death during climbing. Snowstorms may be catastrophic for the alpinists-suicides."[7]

Voytek was unfazed by the dire warnings. He was in fine form in 1974, after a couple of impressive winter seasons in the Alps, as well as having set new standards with his winter climbs in the Tatras. He was in Norway with four outstanding climbers, including Tadeusz Piotrowski, one of Poland's most respected alpinists. Known by his friends as Tadek, this powerful man with his signature blond beard had proven himself on 7492-metre Noshaq in winter, and, more important, he was familiar with the Troll Wall, having already climbed the *Fiva Route* to its right. Tadek had been befriended by an older Norwegian climber, Arne Randers Heen, and his warm-hearted wife, Bodil. Arne was an institution in Norway – a legend among climbers. He had built a cabin near the Troll Wall and now offered it to the Poles. "They were so good to us," Voytek said. "Fantastic cake, you know."

For several days, Voytek, Tadek and the other members of the Polish team, Kazimierz Głazek, Marek Kęsicki and Ryszard Kowalewski, waited in Arne's hut as the winter storms blew through. They had inspected the dramatically overhanging face and could see that it was uniformly black as night, except for the initial 250 metres, which resembled a patchwork quilt of dark rock, lace-like hoarfrost and loose, wet snow. It looked as if they would need to fix ropes on the lower section of the wall to get their heavy loads up to the first bivouac ledge, which was about 250 metres above the base. During a two-week spell of relentless storms rolling in from the North Sea, they managed a scant three days of progress: one day carrying loads to the base of the wall and two days fixing lines. Three days out of fourteen; it didn't look promising.

On March 7, eager to start climbing, the team approached the face in the silvery light of daybreak. A group of reporters accompanied them, keen to be part of this historic – and likely disastrous – event. The climbers had 250 kilograms of equipment and food in ten enormous packs: 600 metres of rope, 200 pitons, 100 carabiners, forty gas cartridges and food for eighteen days. This was evidently not going to be a speed ascent. They launched up the face and climbed non-stop until 2 a.m. before finding a suitable spot for their first bivouac. They expected to climb no more than two pitches a day due to the high level of difficulty, the horrendous conditions on the rock and the continuous bad weather.

Their predictions proved correct: after three days, they were only six pitches up the wall.

The press was watching from below, but their mood had shifted. Public interest in the climb had grown so much that they realized a dramatic story was unfolding. Impossibly, the mad Polish climbers continued inching upward. Their progress headlined the television news each evening, and Norwegians tuned in to see how they were doing. More journalists arrived at the Bellevue Hotel in Åndalsnes, hoping to cover the event. There were soon so many reporters at the hotel that they were forced to sleep on the floor. Busloads of people arrived at the base of the wall, straining for a glimpse of the climbers. The Polish winter ascent of the Troll Wall had turned into a Norwegian spectator sport.

Voytek and his team continued scratching their way upward, unaware of the carnival down below. But on the third night, the climb almost came to a fiery end. Kazimierz was changing cartridges for their little cookstove by the light of a candle perched on a rock nearby. A little too close, as it turned out. The cartridge exploded and a fire erupted. Kazimierz lost most of the skin on his hands, as well as a good portion of the communal bivouac sack. He was forced to descend the fixed ropes to the base of the wall, while the remaining four continued up, having to make do with a Swiss cheese–style bivouac sack for the rest of the climb.

They reached a second bivouac ledge on March 12, again late in the night. They moved their platform up, capsule-style, and established a new home on the wall. Voytek was impressed with the rock: "It was fantastic gneiss with some big oval stains, extremely sharp, fantastic for climbing." While shivering in the winter gloom, he fantasized about the possibility of free climbing it in summer, with soft shoes and endless northern daylight.

They were now directly below the third section of the face, which featured an enormous overhanging block that appeared to be partly detached from the wall. It was here that Voytek's wooden seat harness became most useful. He stared at the problem, rehearsing the sequence of moves that he needed to make. Finally, he could procrastinate no longer. Using pitons and large, angled bongs for protection, Voytek began a long traverse under the giant, detached roof. He described the aid-climbing sequence: "It was a kind of crux; I wouldn't say the most difficult, but the most interesting and most enjoyable. It was a bit scary. I didn't know how to handle this big block of completely detached rock hanging in the air. I still don't know how it stayed there. I had to pound big bongs in under that block, and I was dying of fear. I didn't want to bang them in too hard for fear of dislodging it. I moved those two or three bongs along, traversing to the right." When he finally reached the far side of the block, he took a deep breath. "Psychologically, it was pretty challenging," he said.

Once they had begun climbing through the overhangs, there was no longer any way to retreat. The media understood the level of commitment and caught fire with excitement. Headlines such as "All the Boats Burnt, There Is No Way Back for the Four on the Troll Wall" dominated the front pages of the Norwegian dailies. No longer content to stand around at the base of the wall, reporters were now doing flybys in helicopters and small planes.

Up on the wall, the overhangs grew ever more terrifying. Most of the climbers' movements took place in mid-air; they hardly touched the rock anymore. Rappels ended in space, several metres out from the face. To add to the confusion, the team usually rappelled in the dark after a full day of climbing in the Norwegian winter. Inky darkness, falling snow, no contact with the rock, rotating slowly in fathomless space – they descended each night to their last bivouac. Reflecting on those descents, Voytek considered it a miracle that the poor-quality Polish ropes, which lacked a load-bearing core, could withstand the friction from the rock as well as all those kilometres of jumaring.

The climbers finally emerged above the steepest part of the wall onto smooth rock slabs that, though still exceedingly difficult (VI, A2), were at least not as physically demanding. They discovered a piton indicating the original French line, which traversed right to reach a couloir leading up and off the face. Voytek and his partners discussed their options: follow the *French Route* or go directly up to the summit. They had managed a direct line up to this point, so why not finish the route as a true direttissima? More challenging climbing awaited them. Agonizingly slow. So slow that they were still more than 200 metres below the summit when they finally collapsed at 6 a.m. for their last bivouac on the face.

On the morning of March 19, they hurled much of their equipment off the wall. As their packs catapulted down, thudding and bouncing and bursting apart, the team continued to the summit with the minimum amount of gear they would need. They reached the top at 9 p.m. and immediately began descending via the steep, tedious snowfields leading down to the Isterdal Valley. Six hours later, utterly spent, they arrived at the valley floor. There, waiting for them, was Arne Randers Heen, with aromatic cakes still warm from the oven and deliriously delicious hot chocolate. And journalists galore! Cameras whirred and flashed in the dark, pre-dawn hours as reporters scrambled to capture images of the team and record their first descriptions of the amazing adventure. Five hours later, the climbers managed to escape to the hut for a few hours of sleep. But at 11 a.m. they were up again, this time for live television interviews. The Polish Embassy in Oslo sent a congratulatory telegram. Norwegian climbers telegraphed their good wishes. The Polish guests were stunned at the response. All of Norway seemed enchanted with this daring winter ascent of their Troll Wall. "The Polish success on the French Route marks a new epoch in the history of mountaineering," said *Aftenposten*.[8]

It was a remarkable story. They had spent thirteen days hanging on a wall that was continuously complex; the level of difficulty was never below Grade IV and went as high as VI+, A4. What made the adventure even more daunting was the certainty that rescue on the wall was impossible. It was too steep. Oh, and of course, it was winter. Voytek recalled that it was like winter climbing in the Tatras but, since the rock was of better quality, finding placements for protection was easier and faster. "In the Tatras you had to spend one day doing one pitch," he explained. "Here we could do two or three pitches in a day. It was much faster than the Tatras. It was just a bit longer." Indeed, their Troll Wall climb was the longest continuous winter climbing epic of the time.

Years later, when pressed to recall whether or not he had enjoyed the Norwegian press's unexpected adulation of their capsule-style climb, Voytek confessed, "Yes, I did." Then, laughing, and shaking his head, he continued, "Now I'm smarter. I know the trap." Over the years, he became increasingly wary of publicity and admiration, which resulted in his trademark cautious response to public attention, and which also became a source of frequent self-examination. "If you sell your soul to these things and you go beyond your circle of friends and those people who make your life good, then it becomes meaningless – even dangerous." But in 1974 Voytek was not as familiar with fame as he would become. And as a twenty-seven-year-old Polish climber surrounded by friendly Norwegians, it all felt like innocent fun. "I liked this trip a lot. It was an exotic area. It was Polish style. The Heen family was wonderful. The guys were great, and the climb was challenging. A really good winter climb."

The fun was short-lived, however, for when the team returned to Poland, there was little fuss. Yes, the Polish Mountaineering Association was pleased that the officially sanctioned trip had been successful. But there were plenty of good winter ascents being done by Polish climbers in the Alps in those days; this one was merely longer.

Despite the lack of attention paid to the Troll Wall climb, the PZA was monitoring Voytek's climbs, and the authorities were impressed. In the next two years, he was invited on two major Polish expeditions that were reserved for the country's best.

The first was in the late autumn of 1974, led by the aristocratic Andrzej Zawada. Andrzej was a tall man, with a chiselled face dominated by an imposing nose and a charismatic smile. Charming, educated and a natural leader, he had a vision for Polish alpinism. It was clear by now that Polish climbers had a special talent for winter climbing; they were fine-tuning the art of suffering, and winter climbing in the Tatras was proving to be the perfect lab. Andrzej had already led a team to the top of 7492-metre Noshaq in winter, so it was logical that he would attempt an 8000er. More than anything, this would firmly establish Polish alpinists in the Himalayan arena. His objective was 8516-metre Lhotse. Andrzej planned to leave for Nepal in the late autumn and climb the peak in the early winter season. The team consisted of many Polish veterans, including Andrzej Heinrich and Tadek Piotrowski. Young Voytek accepted the invitation immediately: "This was a huge thing in Polish history and I wouldn't have considered saying no."

It was already late in the day when Voytek and two others (Kazimierz Rusiecki and Jan Stryczyński) began carving a small platform out of Lhotse's icy wall to establish Camp IV. They chopped and hacked at the rock-hard ice but couldn't produce a platform large enough to erect the tent. Instead, they hung it from a tent pole like a bivouac sack and huddled under it throughout the windy, intensely cold night. Without sleep, they were too depleted to carry on up the mountain, so they descended. Their high point was 7800 metres.

Andrzej Zawada and Andrzej Heinrich climbed even higher, setting a new winter altitude record at 8250 metres. But they didn't reach the summit. Zawada later said that not reaching the summit of Lhotse in winter was the biggest disappointment of his life. For Voytek, it was not so much a disappointment as it was an enlightening experience. This was his first time on a large Himalayan expedition, and he disliked the dynamics. "The endless negotiation about tactics and the slow progress up the mountain didn't appeal to me," he said.

But not enough to deter him from accepting an invitation to join another large expedition in 1976, this time to K2. Janusz Kurczab, his old partner from the Tatras and the Alps, was assembling a team for a new route on the Northeast Ridge of K2, and he wanted Voytek to join him. How could he resist K2, the climbers' mountain? And a new route. The large team of nineteen members attempting the route was a powerhouse of Poland's best alpinists, including Eugeniusz Chrobak, Leszek Cichy (who later made the first winter ascent of Everest), Andrzej Czok, Andrzej Heinrich, Janusz Onyszkiewicz (who was later imprisoned for his work with the Solidarity movement and eventually became a parliamentarian) and Wojciech Wróż. Legends, all.

They arrived on June 24, 1976, and enjoyed almost an entire month of splendid weather. Day after day they trudged up and down the ridge, carrying supplies, fixing lines, establishing camps. Theirs was a classic, heavy-style expedition. Every metre of the precipitous ridge was safe-guarded with fixed ropes. But despite the ropes, there were occasional mishaps, including one where Voytek took a 5-metre fall when a cornice collapsed. In late July, the good weather broke down and a series of storms rolled through, blanketing the mountain in snow and destroying two of their high camps.

The team persevered, however, and by August 13 they had set up their highest camp, at 8000 metres. After climbing through the last of the dif-ficulties on the ridge, Eugeniusz Chrobak and Wojciech Wróż reached 8400 metres before turning around at 6 p.m. From their vantage point, they could see a terrific storm approaching. It took an entire night of per-ilous rappelling down through the driving snow for them to reach Camp v at 7 a.m. Although the climbers were worn down from illness and fatigue, Janusz managed to persuade thirteen of them to make one more attempt in late August. But the weather deteriorated again, and they finally gave up on September 8. Their heroic effort on K2 had lasted more than two long months.

Voytek disliked many aspects of this expedition, including the endless hauling of loads and fixing of lines. "It felt like hard labour to me, and it seemed unnecessary," he explained. He didn't appreciate being attached to anything, certainly not a mountain. He grew to hate Janusz's leader-ship, which he felt was "excessively democratic," with tedious discussions and secret ballots about who went where, when and with whom. "On K2, the leadership was a kind of zombie leadership – no feelings for the mountain and zero insight into the inspiration and motivation of any particular climber. It was just a logistics grid: this team going here; this team going there; votes between all members – and in this way the summit team was selected. By vote!" Voytek received votes from some of the team members, but he wasn't close friends with the older climbers, who stuck together, supporting each other. Not surprisingly, he wasn't selected for the first summit team.

This lack of peer support had a strange effect on Voytek. For the first – and last – time in his Himalayan career, he experienced problems with altitude. "I was pretty limp," he said. "The summit team was appointed, and I was on the support team, coming up behind them. Until Camp III, I was climbing incredibly easily and smoothly, going between camps in only two or two and a half hours." But when Voytek moved up between Camps IV and V, carrying oxygen for the summit team, he slowed to a crawl. With every hour that passed he grew weaker. Gasping between steps. "I was incredibly weak. It had never happened like that before. Somewhere around 7900 metres I was going so slowly, and I was so exhausted, that the guy climbing near me said, 'Voytek, leave this,' and I stopped something like 100 metres before the highest camp, which was around 8000 metres." He dropped the oxygen bottles, turned around and descended.

Janusz later told him he must have been exhausted from all those days of hauling loads. But Voytek didn't accept the explanation. "No, it wasn't that," he said. "I wasn't even pushing myself." There were other possible reasons. This was one of his early encounters with extremely high altitude, and he may have been moving too quickly. Slovenian climber Franček Knez exhibited similar symptoms at altitude; although he was one of his country's best technical climbers, he sometimes climbed too quickly at high elevations. Nevertheless, Voytek later spent many days – and nights – above 8000 metres without serious problems. Naturally, he felt the altitude, but at no time in his career did he feel the debilitating exhaustion and lassitude that he suffered that day, delivering oxygen to the summit team on K2. There was another, possibly more critical, difference between his experience on K2 in 1976 and those he would have at 8000 metres in the following years. On K2 he had no control over his destiny. It was determined by Janusz and the secret ballots. Not being chosen for the first summit team must have been a discouraging moment for Voytek.

Some people are well-suited for support roles, whereas Voytek performs best out front. He respected Janusz Kurczab and admired many of the veteran climbers on the team, but in the end, he felt the expedition was a waste of his time. Even so, this trip marked the beginning of a long and frustrating love affair with K2.

The Lhotse and K2 expeditions made it clear to Voytek that alpine-style climbing was a higher form of alpinism, not only from an athletic perspective, but also in human terms. With an alpine-style approach, Voytek knew he could choose his partners with care and, as a result, the experience on the mountain would be much more intimate.

When Voytek returned from K2, he noticed a change in his relationship with his father. During his son's twenties, Henryk had been disappointed with Voytek, frustrated that he would sacrifice a promising career in electronics or physics to squander his abilities on expeditions. All he did was climb. A complete waste of talent. As a successful author, Henryk understood ambition, and it confused him that his son appeared to have none, despite his obvious potential.

A letter from Voytek changed his opinion. Voytek had written to his father, describing a trying moment while attempting to climb Lhotse in winter. He had been at Camp II in the Western Cwm, a desperate location carved out of the icy slope and hammered by a shrieking wind. A huge boulder, frozen into the ice, was perched directly above the shaking tent. During the turbulent night, Voytek became deathly afraid that the boulder might become dislodged and tumble down onto their fragile tent. His description of the raging storm and his battle with his fear resonated with Henryk, the writer. He published Voytek's story and, in doing so, expressed a reluctant pride in Voytek's chosen way of life. He had finally grasped that his son must be an exceptional climber to have been invited to join such grand expeditions as Lhotse and K2, that he must be unusually tough to be able to survive the cruel winter conditions. And he realized that his son had the talent to convincingly describe those experiences. Free climbing a hard rock climb meant nothing to Henryk, but Lhotse and K2 counted. At long last he began to show Voytek some respect. "I was surprised," Voytek said. "But I'm sure it was because the national importance of these climbs reflected my value."

The praise came a little late, and as validating as that begrudging acknowledgement was, Voytek knew it was misplaced, because the Lhotse and K2 climbs were not what motivated him. He had experienced real happiness and a high level of creativity in Afghanistan with his little team of climbers and their Gulag attire, forging their own way on unknown routes and making their own decisions. Moving freely up and down the mountain, unfettered by fixed lines and predetermined camps, was what really inspired Voytek. That was where his future lay. Whether or not his father approved.

FIVE

Bandaka – The Mordor Beauty

What the imagination seizes as beauty must be truth – whether it existed before or not.
        —John Keats to Benjamin Bailey, November 22, 1817

By 1976 the Polish appetite for the Hindu Kush had reached epic levels: thirteen expeditions and 151 climbers. The following year there were twenty-two expeditions, 193 climbers, 102 summits and twenty-nine first ascents. "It was the Polish school of high-altitude climbing," explained Janusz Majer, a well-known player in the scene.

That year, the Polish Mountaineering Association proposed an international climbing exchange with the British Mountaineering Council (BMC) to the Hindu Kush. The PZA would provide the train tickets, equipment, food and permits, and the British would contribute hard currency. The Poles would bring Spiritus – 95 per cent pure alcohol – and the British climbers would bring whisky. The trip, organized by Poland's top expedition leader, Andrzej Zawada, had climbers from both countries loading themselves and more than a hundred barrels of equipment onto a train at Warsaw Central Station before heading off for Moscow and beyond. Apart from climbing, the adventure would eventually include international intrigue and bureaucratic deception on a grand scale.

The year was 1977, and even though the ideological barriers between Poland and the United Kingdom were fading, Westerners were still prohibited from travelling through the Soviet Union. This presented some challenges for the British climbers, among them Alex MacIntyre and John Porter. But Andrzej was an ingenious problem solver. He renamed them Porterwich and MacIntyreski and instructed them to keep quiet and remain as inconspicuous as possible throughout the train journey. This was almost impossible for Alex, who, with his head of curly black hair and smouldering features, was hard to ignore.

They made it to Moscow without incident, but as their train lumbered out of the Moscow station, the sounds of the Red Army Choir singing military tunes belted out from the overhead speakers in their cramped compartment. Andrzej finally lost patience with the aggravating din. He grabbed Alex's snazzy new Terrordactyl ice hammer, walked over to the speaker and smashed it to pieces. The only sounds remaining were the strains of Led Zeppelin, blaring from Alex's cassette player.

Day after day, they rolled along, across the Volga to Orsk, down between the Aral and Caspian seas, and finally to the ancient city of Termez on the Amu Darya River, which formed the border with Afghanistan. The countryside near Termez was an agricultural Eden. Orchards, grain crops and vineyards spread out in every direction. But there was also an unusual number of trains loaded with trucks and tanks and artillery, all heading toward Termez. It looked as if military preparations were under way. Within a couple of years, the Russian invasion of Afghanistan would begin.

At the Afghan frontier, the mood became tense when heavily armed soldiers demanded to examine everyone's documents. The most immediate problem was with the British passports; none contained the stamps required to cross the border. The "British spies" were placed under house arrest in a local hotel, and serious discussions began. It was starting to look as though the international exchange was over, before the team had placed even one foot in Afghanistan. The Brits would have to return to Moscow to clear this up, and the PZA would face a serious diplomatic mess back in Warsaw.

A Russian officer, nicknamed Captain Bollocksoff by the climbers, was assigned to the troublesome situation. After the first day of bargaining, and already exasperated by the delay, Voytek decided to try a different approach to the negotiations.

"Look, let's consider some possibilities here," he began. "If you report this indiscretion, you will have days and days of paperwork, and you will probably be severely reprimanded by your superior."

Officer Bollocksoff nodded his head. This was certainly true.

"Why not forget the whole thing," Voytek appealed. "All you have to do is approve their passage; we will go on our way, and you can have a nice day, without any problems."

The good captain weighed the two options for only a few moments. He waved them onto the ferry with a stern reminder to keep their heads down and their cameras safely stowed, and to avoid looking at anything beyond the ferry.

But John's curious mind couldn't resist. Intrigued by the machine-gun turrets stationed every few hundred metres along the Soviet side, he reached for his camera. An armed soldier glimpsed the movement, charged over and seized the camera, shouting at John in a rage. Voytek saw the incident and sped over to the soldier. Speaking Russian, he somehow convinced him that it had been an innocent mistake and that the naive British fellow should be forgiven. After a few minutes, Voytek sauntered back to John with his camera. "Bury it deep in your sack," he mumbled.

The Russian soldier wandered over and continued talking to Voytek in Russian. When he realized Voytek was Polish, he said, "Ahhh, brother country...how do you like it here?" Voytek answered with some vague niceties, not very interested in talking to the soldier now that the camera had been rescued.

"It's hot here, isn't it?" said the soldier.

"Not so much," answered Voytek.

"Really? Do you find it cold?" asked the soldier, intent on continuing the conversation.

"No," replied Voytek.

Frustrated now, the soldier asked, "Then how is it here?"

"Well, you know, my friend, it's funny and frightening, like fucking a tiger." *Но знаешь, друг, смешно и страшно как тигра ебать* was a Russian saying that only Voytek would think appropriate for this moment on the ferry between the Soviet Union and Afghanistan, having just rescued his British teammate from a well-armed Russian soldier. The soldier shook his head in bewilderment and moved off.

A scene from another planet awaited them on the other side of the river: women in full burka, men in brightly coloured turbans, caravans of camels, and hash merchants everywhere. The climbers piled into the waiting trucks, giddy with excitement. They stopped in Mazar-i-Sharif for nearly a week, waiting for the rest of their supplies to arrive and absorbing the oppressive heat. In their spare time, they discussed a clandestine plan that Voytek had floated back on the train – an alpine-style climb of the Northeast Face of 6843-metre Kohe Bandaka in the central Hindu Kush. In fact, Voytek had been scheming for days about breaking away from the larger expedition with a small team. And now he knew who should join him on the adventure: Alex MacIntyre, John Porter and Jan Wolf. The Bandaka face had repelled a Polish team the previous year and was deemed horribly dangerous. This only added to its allure. But before they could seriously consider it, they had to convince their leader, Andrzej Zawada.

Andrzej pointed out the obvious problem – they had no permit for Bandaka. Their permit was for Kohe Mandaras, which was in a completely different valley. As leader, Andrzej was responsible for the entire team, and he would face a mountaineering tribunal if anyone were injured or killed, particularly if they were on a different – and unpermitted – mountain. He had already undergone this horrible experience with two previous climbing fatalities, and he knew that if foreign climbers were involved it would be even more serious. Voytek and the others kept arguing their case until Andrzej finally relented. But despite some delicate negotiating and several offers of bribes, Andrzej could not secure a permit for Bandaka. Although the others had already given up hope, Voytek persisted. Why not fashion a false permit? With the help of Anwar, their Afghan liaison officer, he took the Kohe Mandaras permit, covered "Mandaras" with a small piece of paper and photographed it. They replaced "Mandaras" with "Bandaka," and it was done. Shameless as it was, their ploy succeeded. Bandaka thus became one in a long line of deliciously "illegal" climbs for Voytek.

When John first saw the Northeast Face of Bandaka, he described it as "massive – ugly, yet compelling." Voytek's reaction was completely different. "When I saw Bandaka it was playing on my imagination so strongly, like good music, that I felt connected. It was something fantastic." Over the next few days, as they watched the forbidding wall – 2500 metres of unstable rock and toppling ice seracs – their enthusiasm cooled. The horrifying rumble of rockfall was so continuous that, as John observed, "it barely deserved comment." The normally laid-back Alex was driven to a near-panic state. It was the arbitrary nature of each rock's trajectory that unsettled him the most: one millimetre to the left, just a whining sound near your ear; one millimetre to the right, your head explodes.

To acclimatize, they climbed up to a col left of the main face at around 6100 metres. They left a cache of food and gas for their intended descent before going down the other side of the mountain and returning to base camp. A week had now passed and Jan Wolf was sick with a racking cough. Voytek could see he was unfit for the Bandaka climb, so he insisted that Jan leave and join the rest of the team on Mandaras, though it meant a long solo trek to catch up to them. The remaining three climbers paced back and forth, watching the wall. It bore down on them as they struggled to come to terms with the complexity of the terrain, the steepness of the middle section, the constant rockfall, and the threatening cornices near the top.

Voytek left his tent and sauntered off to be alone. His gaze lingered on the immense wall he had come to climb: 2500 metres of sheer terror, a scale and complexity beyond his experience. Along with crushing waves of fear, he had a powerful sensation that the landscape around him was alive. The mountain was alive. He yearned to communicate with it, but he couldn't. "I was so close, but it wasn't responding to me," he said. Was it him? Was he incapable of hearing? Had it already spoken to him and he had somehow missed it? In his essay "The Wall and the Books," Jorge Luis Borges wrote that certain places "try to tell us something, or have said something we should not have missed, or are about to say something." For Voytek, this intense, spiritual communion with nature, frustrating though it was, transformed his Bandaka climb into one of the most important of his life.

As he grappled with the feeling that some unique, never-before-experienced, direct communication with this mountain was almost within reach, his solitary ramble changed. When he finally wandered back to camp, he was filled with a feeling of profound connection to this wild landscape – a feeling so deep that it was impossible to share.

At the same time, Alex was experiencing something equally intense – fear. And it was contagious. As Voytek retreated into his tent, he considered leaving the mountain. "I was never, before or after, so scared before entering the wall," he said. "Of course, entering a wall is always difficult, and once you're moving, your emotions settle down. But going into Bandaka was the hardest of my life." He was reminded of his childhood nightmares of an unknown, evil ghost. Once again, he felt a deep primal fear: fear of falling, of dying. Finally, after hours of quiet discussion, dark-haired, calm and serious John reassured him: it might be possible to climb the face and survive. The decision was made, and Alex accepted it.

At 2 p.m. on August 9, they entered the face of Bandaka. John described the opening couloir as a "gateway to a hellish world, one of darkness, fear and continuous threat."[9] Voytek described it as "a Mordor beauty." It was the sinister nature of this Middle Earth scene that attracted him. "The ambition was the impossible: to make the Mordor my ally," he said. They soloed up a snow gully, fully aware that stone avalanches were bombarding the snowfields to their immediate left. Safety came with speed; standing in one place only compounded the risks. Protected at first by an overhanging wall, they reached the top of the couloir at dusk. At this point, the couloir narrowed into a gorge; if they continued they would be completely exposed to any airborne stones. They hesitated. As darkness encroached, the barrage ended, so they entered the narrow gap and, with the help of the nervous, wavering lights of their headlamps, sped up to a broad, snowy ledge. Having climbed almost continuously for eight hours, they stopped at 10 p.m. for their first bivouac.

After two pitches of steep ice the following morning, they were confronted with the biggest disappointment on the face: an expanse of crumbling rock. Precariously perched, gigantic blocks. Completely irreversible terrain. From Voytek's journal: "Incredibly loose and practically no belay. Some Grade III. Kind of missing a sense of climbing, yet alerting all senses." What followed was even stranger – a yellowish, sponge-like section of rock that Voytek christened "halvah." They could only climb it with ice tools and crampons, cutting holds and steps as they ascended. When Voytek reached the end of the rope, he carved a small pinnacle out of the halvah and set up the belay on top. It was surprisingly strong and safe. The monster of Mordor was proving to be tameable.

By late afternoon they had reached the steepest section of the wall, where rocks were accelerating down as if electrically charged. They named it the Cyclotron. When the sun slid out of sight on its westerly journey, the air began to cool and the Northeast Wall grew quiet. No more rockfall. While Alex cleared debris for a bivouac, Voytek and John climbed the first two pitches of the Cyclotron, up through narrow chimneys splitting the overhanging wall. They left two fixed ropes for a quick start the following day and rappelled down to the gravel-strewn ledge. That night, in addition to the discomfort of the sloping ledge, they shuddered at the occasional sounds of small stones hurtling off the face. Luckily, nothing big struck them.

On the third day, August 11, they awoke to a menacing sound. It was as if the mountain had morphed into a hungry, angry monster, roused by the daylight, searching for its prey. Starting with a scattering of stones, the deluge increased to an onslaught of flying debris as the sun worked its black magic on the frozen wall. Voytek and John discussed a strategy for the day. John wanted to start climbing and get it over with. Voytek preferred to wait. He later admitted his tactic was unusual: "In the high mountains you never start climbing in the afternoon. But Bandaka faced east. You could say it was partly intuition, but intuition is the reception of a variety of signals which you don't notice but which cause you to make the right decisions." Voytek knew the Polish team had been defeated by rockfall one year before because they had entered the wall early in the morning. He insisted they should sit tight and wait for the sun to move around to the other side of the mountain.

They waited. But it was oh, so hard. Listening to the missiles firing around them became a kind of torture. There is no sound on Earth that compares to that of the sky exploding with stones. At noon the volley abated, and by 1 p.m. an eerie silence descended on them. It was time to start up the fixed ropes. When they looked up, however, the trap became clear: their two fixed ropes had been in the direct line of fire the entire morning. Hundreds – no, thousands – of rocks had ripped down the Cyclotron, and who knows how many had glanced off their ropes? Who would go first?

John suggested they draw straws. They didn't have straws, but they did have a few small sticks. Voytek arranged three sticks in his hand, their lengths carefully hidden. John drew the shortest. Without a word of protest, he began jumaring up while Voytek watched with his heart in his mouth. The ropes held. Voytek sped up toward him on the fixed lines, and Alex was left with the task of hauling loads. When Voytek reached the top of the fixed lines, he took off his pack and led up through the chimney, bridging across the widest part of the gap in spectacular fashion as John inched out the belay.

About 40 metres up, a formidable obstacle reared above Voytek. John described what happened next: "He stops below a large overhang, which is really a massive chock stone the size of a car, wedged in the chimney. After a short pause and a warning to take care, he pirouettes up over the hanging block far above our heads. There is a sudden shout of panic and then half the block is sailing into space and comes crashing down, barely missing us. Miraculously, Voytek has somehow managed to jump onto the solid other half of the block. Alex and I look at each other with sparks in our eyes and the smell of cordite in our noses."[10]

Although this turned out to be the hardest pitch on the wall, the climbing continued to be difficult, even as the light was fading. John carried on up a narrow, ice-filled chimney, then up a rock step and finally onto an exit ramp leading to a bivouac ledge. Voytek noted in his journal, "Only five pitches this day. V, AO,[11] VI+, VI, III, III." They made tea, cooked some soup and noodles and burrowed into their sleeping bags, confident that they had cracked the greatest difficulties on the face. Voytek was particularly pleased with their decision to delay the climbing that day. "If we had started earlier, we would for sure have been killed. Not 50 per cent, 99 per cent."

That night the good weather held. As Voytek stared up at the star-studded sky, he glimpsed a lightning storm in the distance. Blinking, flashing, strange lights flickering on and off, a faint, distant rumble of thunder. How far away was it? A hundred kilometres? More? In the breathless night, he wondered if some monsoon activity might be approaching them. "I enjoyed it," he later said of that night. But he sent a silent warning to those fluttering lights: "Stay away. Don't come near us!"

They climbed fifteen pitches on their fourth day on the face, making swift progress up slabs, steep rock steps and small icefields, sometimes simul-climbing to save time. After gaining 500 more metres, they stopped early on a comfortable ledge and set up their bivy for another perfect night. Cold but clear. The next day the wall steepened again, but Voytek and

John forged ahead while Alex pulled up the rear with the packs. Seventeen pitches later, they reached the summit icefield, where they stopped to hack out a narrow and chilly ledge. High above the nearest peaks now, they gazed at the Pamirs shimmering in the distance. The only thing marring the night was a mysterious ice feature looming above them, staring down. They called it the Frog's Eyes.

On August 14, their sixth day on the face, they woke to a splendid dawn as the sun gilded the surrounding peaks. Voytek was worried. "What happens if the frog blinks?" he wondered. Eight pitches higher, they climbed directly up the nose between its eyes without incident. But there was one more obstacle: an enormous overhanging cornice. While Voytek and John were discussing their options, Alex arrived with the packs. Voytek remembered the moment. "Alex was behaving totally unreasonably. He was smiling, he was happy. 'Hey guys, I will do this,' he said." Voytek and John looked up at the cornice and back at Alex. They were surprised. Up to this point Alex had been the haul guy on the climb, rather than out front, forging the way. But Alex's offer was sincere. Still smiling, he picked up his ice tools, arranged a few ice screws on his harness and, with utter confidence, headed off.

He front-pointed up the first pitch, using only one ice screw for protection, and then belayed John and Voytek up to him. Moving off again, he reached the overhanging cornice, the source of their angst. Then he disappeared.

Voytek called up, "How is it, Alex?"

"It's good. It's good. Don't worry, guys. I'm over," Alex yelled down.

Unbelievably, he had discovered a diagonal passageway – a narrow slot – up *through* the cornice. Completely hidden from below, it led directly up to the lip of the ice. His enthusiasm and confidence and intuition had saved the day. As he pulled over the top he let out a yelp of joy. "We were all so happy," Voytek exclaimed. "Another hour and we were on the summit."

The summit plateau was broad and flat, so they lingered, brewing tea, relaxed and content. A short way down the other side, they decided to set up a bivy before the tiring descent through the forest of penitentes – thin blades of frozen snow and ice – leading to the col where they had left their cache. They bivouacked one last night, and, the following morning, they headed down the south side of the mountain and finally to base camp on the ninth day.

Bandaka had been a true "ogre," a "man-eating monster." They had experienced extreme fear – even before setting foot on the face. But the mountain had offered an unusual variety of climbing: the first snowfield, the "halvah" section, the chimneys and overhangs and compact rock in the Cyclotron, the summit icefield with its alpine ice, and finally the mysterious ice seracs glaring down from the top. Each climber had contributed something special at the right moment. Apart from the actual climbing, John had calmed their fears in base camp the day before their launch onto the face. Voytek had calculated correctly that entering the Cyclotron was best done in the afternoon. And Alex had appeared like a vision near the top to solve the riddle of the overhanging cornice. They had climbed the 2500 metres of unknown ground in superb alpine style.

The team separated briefly when John and Alex camped at the pass leading down to the main valley and Voytek remained in base camp. He remembered the day as mellow, with a warm afternoon sun. There were just a few rumblings of rockfall in the distance, now of absolutely no consequence to him. "My happy memory is of that afternoon alone," he said. Another moment of precious solitary communion with the mountain.

A day later, they arrived at the summer-grazing settlement of Bandikhan. Camped together now, Voytek and Alex cooked up a pot of hash-enhanced tomato soup and were soon relaxed, sprawled out on their sleeping bags. John refrained. A group of Afghans hovered nearby. One sauntered up to Voytek and suggested they might do some business with lapis lazuli. His price was outrageously high, so naturally Voytek said no.

Unbeknownst to John and Alex, Voytek had negotiated a deal with some porters, weeks before on the way to the mountain, for a magnificent lump of startlingly blue lapis lazuli. He had tucked the semi-precious gem away in his pocket. When the man persisted in trying to sell him some lapis, Voytek laughed and said he had done much better than that, showing off his impressive gem. Another Afghan standing nearby, who appeared to be an authority figure, announced to Voytek that it was illegal to buy lapis. Voytek was nonplussed. "I knew it had been an honest trade, and this guy was bluffing me." Instead of giving up his gem, Voytek tossed it in the air directly in front of the Afghan's face, then caught it and fired it into the glacial river. Before it hit the rushing water, it glanced off a boulder and shattered into a thousand pieces.

The Afghan trader stared in shock. Voytek returned to his sleeping bag, reclined and closed his eyes. Alex dozed, blissfully unaware of the drama. John paced, gripped with fear at the possible outcome of this altercation. A crowd had assembled, including a group of elders; John was sure they were deliberating the fate of the infidels. After a few hours, however, they finally dispersed, and John joined his catatonic teammates, who were now snoozing noisily.

Voytek could irritate people with his confidence, which sometimes seemed to border on arrogance. He could pull it off because of his searing good looks, his athleticism and his firm belief that he knew the local culture better than anyone. He dismissed the entire incident with a wave of his hand. But his casual attitude could be unsettling; certainly, John was disconcerted by Voytek's response to the traders on that hazy afternoon in Bandikhan.

Years later, while in England, Voytek was seated in a restaurant along with Wanda Rutkiewicz and two British climbers. Both Voytek and Wanda were guests of the Buxton Climbers' Festival. As a waitress arrived with plates of food for the customers, Voytek turned toward her to thank her. Ed Douglas, one of the Brits, described the scene: "In those days Voytek looked like Nureyev cast as a gunslinger." When the waitress caught sight of him, her jaw dropped, and so did a plate, which broke on the floor. Shortly after, the restaurant staff came over en masse, presumably believing there was safety in numbers. Ed continued the story. "'What do you do?' one girl said, thinking they must be movie stars. Voytek looked at her with all the wild danger his blue eyes could manage. 'I am Russian-roulette expert,' he said. The waitresses laughed nervously. They didn't understand that he wasn't joking."

It was the same wild and dangerous stare that had defeated the Afghan trader. The next day in Bandikhan, Voytek used it again.

A tense situation began to emerge when the porters demanded double pay to haul their equipment down the valley. Voytek refused, declaring they would rather carry their own gear than submit to this extortion. He directed John and Alex to shoulder loads and head off while he guarded the rest of their gear. Neither John nor Alex was pleased with this development, but Voytek refused to give in to the threat. Off they lumbered, glum and grumpy. The porters stared in disbelief. Voytek glared back. He was worried the gamble might backfire and they would be forced to make multiple trips with their heavy loads, but he didn't let on. John and Alex had walked no more than 200 metres before the porters approached Voytek and agreed to the original price. "It was a dangerous game in terms of logistics," Voytek later admitted.

When they arrived at Zebak, the expedition trucks were waiting. They learned that the rest of the team had made the first ascent of the North Face of Mandaras, as well as several good climbs on nearby peaks. Even Jan Wolf had managed to salvage his trip, despite becoming ill at Bandaka. After a challenging solo trek to Mandaras base camp, he arrived too late to join the climbs already under way, so he soloed Afghanistan's highest peak, Noshaq, instead.

Upon Voytek's return to Poland, Ewa was waiting for him. While he was away she had been pondering their life together, and she now proposed a plan for their future – a move to West Germany. Voytek was dubious. He was only hungry for climbing. All kinds of climbing. The Tatras, the Alps, the Hindu Kush. He finally agreed to give it a try, but it didn't take long for him to realize that he wasn't suited for a life in Germany. "They were slaves to their jobs," he said. "Slaves of money. This extreme precision – working from 8 to 4. It was impossible for me. I knew if I stayed in Germany I would be working six days a week. No chance for climbing." Making a living and making a life were two different matters for Voytek, and after a couple of days he told Ewa he couldn't stay; he needed his freedom. They would have to return to Poland. Ewa protested, but as usual, Voytek won the day.

They packed up their Volkswagen and drove home the long way: through Bulgaria, Romania and on to Afghanistan, where Voytek knew he could do some business. He was familiar with the fantastic goods available in Afghanistan, since he had already been successfully smuggling them into Poland. Poland's official economy was based on the złoty, but the much more robust, unofficial economy revolved around the dollar. Because they travelled outside the country, climbers were ideally positioned to take advantage of smuggling opportunities, bringing in both products and foreign currency. As they developed lucrative illegal trade routes, they were soon able to finance their freedom-loving, climbing lifestyle. Voytek was a master at the game.

On this trip to Afghanistan he focused on sheepskin coats. "These coats were very much in fashion, beautiful garments with embroidery and a lovely body shape. You would be surprised how well they pack in the barrels," he explained. He bought them for around $30 and sold them for a whopping profit at $150. "Can you imagine, with $450 I could buy fifteen sheepskin coats, and in Poland I could live for $25 a month," he exclaimed. "I was a businessman. Doing business two times a year. Strange." Fur coats and *thangkas* and rugs and lapis ... this is how he would finance their lives and his expeditions, not with a six-day-a-week job in Germany.

Voytek's success at smuggling clinched his commitment to climbing, and the Bandaka ascent confirmed his belief that climbing alpine-style in the high mountains was what interested him the most. It provided everything: adventure, the unknown, friendship and creative challenge. He was determined to devote himself to these objectives exclusively in the future, despite the invitations to join large Polish Himalayan expeditions. His biggest problem? What to climb next.

Later that year he proposed a bold new objective to John and Alex. This time it would take them to India.

SIX

Hungry for Hunger

I came so far for beauty.
—Leonard Cohen, "Came So Far for Beauty"

Located on the rim of the Nanda Devi Sanctuary in India's Garhwal Himalaya region, Changabang had been climbed before, but not by the South Face. An Indo–British expedition had made the first ascent of the 6864-metre peak in 1974, and two years later, it was climbed on two sides: the Southwest Ridge by a Japanese team and the West Face by British climbers Joe Tasker and Pete Boardman. And now, in 1978, Voytek wanted to lead a Polish–British team up the South Face of this stunning beauty.

He couldn't have anticipated all the obstacles he would face even before getting the project off the ground. He had given up his job in April of that year. "No more career for me," he declared. But Polish authorities kept a careful record of citizens at that time, and government policy required everyone to be employed. "Completely artificial employment," Voytek scoffed. "There were hordes of people who were employed by companies but who did nothing. But if somebody was without a job, he was branded a social parasite. Of course, you were discriminated against." It wasn't only discrimination, however. An unemployed person could not access his passport – a major hurdle for climbers who wished to travel abroad. "I *had* to be employed," Voytek said. "So some friends hired me for an imaginary job, but I didn't actually work." He also had to supply proof of having enough foreign currency to travel outside the country.

This he did quite handily with his hard-currency bank accounts, topped up on a regular basis by his black-market importing business.

Before leaving for India, Voytek approached the Polish Mountaineering Association for some financial assistance for the Changabang climb. But they were preoccupied, possibly because of other expeditions they were already supporting. A twenty-five-member team was going to attempt the south and central peaks of Kangchenjunga, and Wanda Rutkiewicz was looking for support for her Everest climb. Still, Voytek was one of Poland's leading alpinists and had several notable new routes in Afghanistan in his repertoire. The PZA had seemed impressed in the past, but it was now reluctant to help him. "It was a dream objective and yet they refused me," he fumed. He described the encounter at PZA headquarters in Warsaw: "The vice-president, with his smiley face, said, 'Oh, we distributed all our money already. So sorry.'

'But Mr. Vice-President, what am I to do? I need your support for this climb and it's an international expedition. Joint Polish and British. This is good for Poland.'

'I'm sorry. But I have some advice for you. Ask the Zakopane club.'

'Okay, but why Zakopane?'

'They have money. And besides, they have a good climber in the club. Krzysztof Żurek. You should invite him.'"

Krzysztof had a fine reputation as an alpinist, and although they hadn't climbed together, Voytek felt comfortable about including him. Small and powerful, Krzysztof provided balance to Voytek's wiry frame. The Zakopane club agreed. Now he had enough money for travel from Warsaw to Delhi for two Polish climbers; a Polish doctor and base camp manager, Lech Korniszewski; and the two British climbers, John Porter and Alex MacIntyre. The team was complete.

Once in India, they scratched their way up the chain of command, struggling to navigate the complicated web of the British-style bureaucracy so enthusiastically embraced by the Indian authorities in Delhi. Voytek merely wanted to pick up his permit – the one he had been promised by the Indian Mountaineering Federation. But there seemed to be a problem.

John Porter and Terry King joined Voytek in Mr. Mushiram's claustrophobic little office crammed with furniture and piles of important-looking papers. Terry was there to pick up his Nanda Devi permit, and Voytek and John theirs, for nearby Changabang. Both peaks required travelling into the famed Nanda Devi Sanctuary; this seemed to be the issue. The Indian authorities were still seething about a nuclear-powered "listening device" that had gone missing in action somewhere on Nanda Devi. Placed there by a CIA covert operation posing as a climbing expedition, the device had been swept off the mountain by avalanches and was likely irradiating the Sanctuary, the origin of the sacred Ganges, at that precise moment. The Nanda Devi Sanctuary was closed. Until further notice.

Voytek was becoming irate. He had travelled to India, confident he could collect the permit he had paid for, and now they were being turned away by this timid little man. It was inexcusable.

Mr. Mushiram was polite but firm. "I'm very sorry. But there are other mountains. Beautiful mountains. Why not try Devistan? I can offer you Devistan with no problem."

Voytek scowled. John fidgeted. Terry, no longer able to hold himself back, grabbed Mr. Mushiram, shook him, swore at him and stormed out of the office. Voytek's heart sank.

John leapt into action. "I'm terribly story, Mr. Mushiram," he offered the shaken man. Then, scrambling for an excuse, he continued. "You see, Mr. King is a famous Shakespearian actor, which is why he is so high-strung and short-tempered. It's quite common with actors."

Mr. Mushiram nodded. Voytek glowered. John waited. While Mr. Mushiram sat expressionless, the others held their breath. Finally, he suggested they pay a visit to a certain Mr. Singh at the Ministry of Interior and ask for his assistance.

It turned out that Mr. Singh was a fan of Shakespeare.

And so began a week-long marathon of ardent performances with increasingly important bureaucrats in increasingly impressive offices until, one day, they were seated outside the prime minister's office. This was it! Their last chance. They had finally reached someone for whom this waste of time was too tiresome. He handed them their permits, and the climbers marched out, triumphant.

When they finally arrived at the Nanda Devi Sanctuary, it was blanketed with wildflowers and succulent grass. Granite boulders dotted the meadows, and Nanda Devi's Northeast Face lorded over the entire scene.

They relaxed at their base camp, sorting equipment and gorging on food. Less to carry up the climb.

On the way to Changabang, Voytek, who was a vegetarian, had undertaken his traditional (and unusual) habit of "hunger days" (fasting). Why? He was hungry for hunger. He longed to be empty. He was in love with Kafka's story "A Hunger Artist" and was determined to conquer his own basic urges. Even though he knew he couldn't win this battle, he needed to approach his limits to know the taste of it. "I think this was a matter of dignity," he tried to explain. "To go to your limit. To be free from this base necessity."

But there was more than just dignity behind his motivation. In part, he wanted his body to be light. Voytek was one of the best rock climbers in Poland; rock climbers, like dancers, have a vivid and uncompromising view of their bodies. You can't climb at a top level with unnecessary flab. He carried that lean and mean discipline into the mountains. He didn't subscribe to the Don Whillans school of high-altitude climbing, where you arrive in the mountains fat and leave thin. Voytek arrived thin and left thinner. The biggest challenge emerged after the three days of fasting. He would begin eating carefully – only some fruit and vegetables and a bit of bread. "Oh, it was so good. It was fantastic," he remembered. But eventually, it would end in gluttony. Or at least *his* version of gluttony. "I would have this shameful sequence of hunger days, gluttony, hunger days, gluttony." Although he knew this wasn't the way to stay strong before a big climb, he struggled with the self-destructive pattern. To take his mind off all this while at base camp, Voytek wandered up to the Changabang Glacier and stared at the mountain that had occupied his mind for so long. A crystal mountain of geometric symmetry. Mysterious. Inaccessible. A perfect objective.

Finally, it was time to get a feeling for the wall – to touch it. Voytek led up the first wet, overhanging pitches. The granite wasn't as solid as it looked. They rappelled back down and returned to base, where they sat out a few days of bad weather. But they had made their initial, tentative connection with the mountain.

Taking only thirty-five pitons, three ice screws and a small rock-climbing rack, as well as food for eight days, the team began the climb in earnest. They climbed in pairs, one pair leading all day and the other hauling loads on their backs as they jumared up the ropes. Early in the climb there was so much hauling to be done that the lead climbers had to rappel back down at the end of the day and help with the job. Every second day they switched roles. Hauling was a grim, physical chore. Leading the route, being out front, discovering the secrets of the wall and being fully absorbed was where they all wanted to be. But this was a team approach, and every effort counted. The first pairings were Voytek and John, and Alex and Krzysztof.

Voytek and John were out front on the second day when John accidentally dislodged a block of granite that careened down, slamming Krzysztof's shoulder on the way. Krzysztof screamed out in pain, clutching his injured shoulder. It was now impossible for him to do the heavy load hauling, so the pairing shifted. Krzysztof would climb with Voytek. Pitch after pitch, they crept up the wall. Ten pitches on one day. Only six the next. The hours passed by in a flash for the leader and felt torturously slow for the belayer. The compact granite offered few opportunities for gear, and when it did the cracks were sometimes shallow. Tap tap tap. In went the pitons. Tap tap. Out they came. Far too easily. They would never hold a fall. The cracks led up through a labyrinth of granite flakes resting on more granite flakes. At times, there seemed to be no actual connection between them. Cracks flared into chimneys choked with ice. The wall was a giant geometric mosaic of rock and ice.

The Jumars slipped alarmingly on the frozen ropes for the pair hauling loads. At the same time, they had no idea what was going on up front. Were the lead climbers making steady progress? Were their decisions the right decisions? Were the cracks connecting? Were there dead ends? They had to rely on trust as they continued with their hard, cold labour.

Voytek recorded the grades in his journal: "IV, A2, V, IV, III, A1, Easy, V, II and VI, A0 – not aid but using pitons for aid. Scottish IV, VI, A3." Flipping through the pages of his journal years later, he commented, "Yes, it was pretty serious."

Each night they huddled close together on narrow ledges or hung from their hammocks, stuffed into sleeping bags, waiting for the dawn. Every piece of equipment and clothing was handled with the greatest care. Pots, stoves, mitts. Nothing could be dropped.

By the fifth day on the wall, John could feel stomach pains and Krzysztof was seriously ill. John took three falls on a technical pitch. On the second fall, most of his protection popped out; luckily, one tied-off piton held. He continued, but the strenuous climbing and the repeated falls combined to create a dangerous situation. Mincing up a smooth scoop of granite while Alex concentrated all his attention on the belay, John lost strength in his arms and took a spectacular pendulum fall.

The following day it was Voytek and Krzysztof's turn out front. Krzysztof was leading but had been growing weaker each day. He had climbed about 20 metres when he ground to a halt and called down.

"Hey, Voytek, I'm having some problems. It's really hard aid climbing here."

"Yeah, I can see."

"I'm going to set up the belay. It's too hard for me to continue."

"No, Krzysztof, it's too soon. You should keep going. It's too soon."

"No, this is a good place. I have a lot of pitons in. It's good."

"Okay, fine then."

Voytek was confused. He had a lot of pitons in? What did that mean? He knew Krzysztof was expecting him to collect his equipment, leave the belay and start jumaring up. But, seized by an irrational fear, Voytek couldn't move.

"Krzysztof, are you sure the belay is okay?"

"Yes, yes, a lot of pitons, no problem."

Still, Voytek couldn't move. He felt stuck to his belay, as if his life depended on it. Krzysztof waited for him to move up, but Voytek stayed below, paralyzed. He called up.

"Listen, Krzysztof, the pitch is too short. Can you try to go a bit further? Otherwise we will waste a lot of time with these short pitches."

"Okay, fine. I'll try to continue."

Still shackled to his belay, Voytek paid the rope out to Krzysztof. He was puzzled by this talk about "a lot of pitons." Why so many? It didn't make sense. Krzysztof crept upward. Half a metre. Then a full metre. Two or three metres more.

"Be careful, Krzysztof."

Only silence from Krzysztof. He was concentrating. Suddenly, boing boing boing. He was falling! All five so-called good belay pitons pulled out. Without hesitation, Krzysztof started up again. He moved about 10 metres beyond his falling point and placed a proper belay.

"Okay, Voytek. You can come up."

"Are you sure?"

"Yes, yes. The belay is good. Come up."

As Voytek started up, he replayed the strange experience over and over. How had he known that the first belay was bad? What intuition had chained him to his belay, refusing to let him move? Was it Krzysztof mentioning "a lot" of pitons? Was it the melodic pitch of pitons being pounded in but not securely enough? Could it have been that the pitch of the sound hadn't changed as it should have, modulating from a poing to a ping as the piton moved deeper into the crack? Voytek couldn't pin down what had held him back, but it had surely saved both of their lives. Had he chosen to jumar up the rope to the faulty belay, they would both have been flung from the face as soon as he had weighted the rope. Voytek reached Krzysztof and said nothing. He took over the lead for two more pitches.

While this drama was playing out above them, John and Alex were busy hauling loads. It was near the end of the day when Alex prepared to rappel down to retrieve the last load. The wind blew sideways, whipping the ropes and slings around. Alex gathered up the coiled rope and clipped in, intending to pay out the rope as he descended rather than throw the entire coil down and risk the wind catching it and tangling it. A good strategy, and a safe strategy. One that can save a lot of frustration, fighting with the rope and the wind. But Alex made a mistake. He threaded his rappel device from the bottom of the coil rather than the top. He stepped back from the ledge onto the wall and in a split second was gone. Long moments passed as Alex fell the full length of the rope. The piton anchoring the rope held. By the time John rappelled down to find out what had happened, Alex was gathering the load, white as a sheet.

"Christ! Alex? Are you all right?"

"I don't want to play this game just to have a rucksack named after me," he said, attempting a feeble joke.[12]

The single piton that had held Alex's fall, as well as the weights of both Alex and John as they jumared back up the rope, was wedged behind a small flake. When John began to remove it, the piton came out easily in his fingers.

The next day they climbed up to the Cyclop's Eye, a snowfield in the middle of the face. When John reached Voytek he reported that Krzysztof was acting delirious. Concerned for his partner, Voytek rappelled down to help him. After taking his pack, he jumared beside him back up to the Cyclop's Eye bivouac – Krzysztof on the fixed rope and Voytek on his rappel rope. As they arrived, Voytek confided to John, "We have a problem. Krzysztof thinks he's in Poland."

Voytek was afraid Krzysztof was near death. His hollow shell of a face was twisted with exhaustion. Voytek hardly slept that night for worry. His thoughts darkened. What would they do with his body, should he expire? Would they bring it down? Was it physically possible? Would they leave him on the mountain? These questions racked his mind as he coaxed the collapsing Krzysztof to stay awake. This is the cruellest moral dilemma a climber can face: what to do with a hopelessly injured or ill partner. Abandon him alive, or stay to die with him?

Krzysztof's condition remained the same during the night. On the eighth day on the wall, Voytek led up the final six pitches of demanding mixed ground to the summit ridge and then another 250 metres along the ridge to the top. Suddenly, they could see. Forever, it seemed. No longer focused on the immediate face, their eyes adjusted to the majestic vista around them.

There was little time to linger, given Krzysztof's condition, so they began the airy descent. The first two pitches were down a 60° ridge leading to the col between Changabang and Kalanka. Krzysztof screamed, "Glissade! Faster, faster!" It was a dangerous concept on such a sheer slope and revealed his incoherent state. Swearing in Polish, Voytek brought matters to a halt, and they set up a bivouac on a sheltered part of the ridge. The following morning, they watched Krzysztof closely, worried that his erratic behaviour could bring them all down. Ahead of them were two more days of descent.

After reaching the col, they traversed the South Face of Kalanka and finally entered a maze of gaping crevasses and teetering seracs. John stopped, bewildered by the confusing scene. Voytek yelled down from the back to wait. He would go first. John recounted their progress: "The route goes right, then left, then back again beneath the seracs and around crevasses. Voytek is using some intuitive magic to bring us through these horrors. I am too tired to appreciate the danger of the situation until much later."[13]

Krzysztof improved as they descended, but both he and John were exhausted and weakened by the climb, by the altitude and by their mysterious illnesses. They eventually reached the meadows and safety, yet it was a bittersweet victory because of Krzysztof's brush with death. Voytek later admitted that it was the closest he had ever come to losing a partner on a climb.

Despite their efforts on the wall, Voytek felt strong. So did Alex. After a couple of rest days, they headed over to Nanda Devi. They didn't have a permit, but that didn't bother Voytek, and it didn't seem to worry Alex, the secretary of the British Mountaineering Council, either. "He was a good soul for illegal affairs," Voytek remembered with a smile. They climbed to about 6500 metres on the Northwest Face before hurricane winds forced them down to base camp.

Finally, they agreed it was time to leave the Sanctuary. Voytek recalled an incident with Alex, whom he described as being "lazy" in camp. "He neither cooked nor cleaned," Voytek declared. After returning from their attempt on Nanda Devi, Alex headed off without helping to clean up camp, leaving some of his personal belongings behind. When Voytek found Alex's pants lying abandoned on a rock, he searched for a place to put them for the march out of the Sanctuary. The packs were crammed. Then he spied the empty pressure cooker, wiped it clean and stuffed it with Alex's pants. When they reunited at the next camp, Alex was wandering around, looking a bit confused.

"I've lost my pants. Has anyone seen my pants?"

"Hah! Yes, I found them," retorted Voytek. "Do you want to know where they are?"

"Yes, where are my pants?"

"In the pressure cooker. You should take better care of your gear."

"Why the hell did you put them there?"

"You should say thank you," Voytek scolded Alex. "The pressure cooker is clean. Stop yelling and say thanks."

Two months later, Voytek received a conciliatory message from Alex: "I applied to cooking school. I want to be a better cook in camp."

Upon reflection, Voytek felt immense satisfaction from the Changabang ascent. They had climbed the imposing 1500-metre wall in one continuous eight-day push, sleeping at night in their dangling hammocks or on narrow ledges hacked out of the icy slopes. The elegantly arching, technical lines on those steep, geometric blocks of rock and ice had inspired him every day he was on the wall. Both the free climbing and the aid climbing had been difficult and challenging. But his greatest satisfaction was the feeling of partnership on Changabang. He valued the flexibility, the commitment, the creativity and the independence of their small team. There had been moments of terror, moments of indecision, moments of impatience. But overall, they had pulled together. "Yes, yes, a good team," he said. "I would say a fantastic team."

Thirty-six years later, the strength of their friendship was revealed when Voytek received a call from Krzysztof.

"Voytek, I would love to see you again. Would you like to get together?"

"Krzysztof, what a surprise. Of course. Why don't you come to my place the next time you are in Krakow?"

"No, I don't have a car. And I live about a hundred kilometres from Krakow. Will you come here?"

"Okay, okay, I will come to you. No problem. It will be my pleasure."

A few days later, Voytek drove to Krzysztof's place, a horse farm he was sharing with his partner. The house was ramshackle, almost in ruins. No inside toilet. Plaster falling off the walls. But so warm and cozy. Welcoming. They greeted Voytek and suggested a walk around the farm. A light rain fell as they strolled among the towering beech trees and grassy meadows smooth as polo fields. A dozen horses grazed lazily, sheltering under the trees. After a couple of hours, they moved inside, sipped some herbal tea and continued talking. Finally, it was time for Voytek to begin his drive back to Krakow. Krzysztof seemed agitated. He stopped Voytek at the door.

"Voytek, we spent many pleasant hours together this afternoon, but you know, I wanted to talk to you about something."

"No problem, Krzysztof. We can do it another time."

A few weeks later, Voytek received an email from Krzysztof, explaining the topic he had wanted to broach but hadn't found the perfect opportunity to do so. He wrote: "Do you remember the incident with the water [on the descent from Changabang]? When I was just crawling out of that hole in the glacier where the water was bubbling? The freeze-dried bag with water was in my hand. Then you arrived and asked, 'Krzysiu, would you give me some water, please?' I said, 'Get it yourself' and continued crawling out. When I stepped out of the hole, I saw your figure disappearing down the slope. I relive this episode over and over…This is what I wanted to talk with you about…"

Voytek sat at his desk, stunned. He scanned his memory for the moment. Yes, now he remembered. He *had* felt irritated with Krzysztof for not having passed him up some water. Of course, they were all thirsty. But Krzysztof was exhausted at that point. He had almost died. One small refusal of water surely couldn't be held against him. Voytek read it again. How many years had Krzysztof suffered with that painful scenario? From 1978 until 2014. Thirty-five years. Voytek sent Krzysztof an email explaining that he had completely forgotten the water incident, imploring him to stop suffering over it. He was convinced that Krzysztof's confession was proof of the solid bond they had formed on the mountain. He stored it away in a virtual box reserved for his most precious memories.

SEVEN

Dancing in the Moment

All men dream, but not equally.
—T.E. Lawrence, *Seven Pillars of Wisdom*

Alex MacIntyre shuffled through the teetering pile of paper in his three-tiered green wire tray. As national officer of the British Mountaineering Council, it seemed everyone needed to talk to him about one thing or another.

"This object of despair [the wire tray] had assumed the characteristics of a fast breeder reactor and despite a liberal dumping policy in the waste basket, or on the floor, its appetite was insatiable," Alex later wrote.[14] He refrained from dumping the tray on this day, which was fortunate because buried deep in the pile was a postcard with an alluring photograph of a steep pyramid of ice and snow. On the reverse side was the name of the wall – East Face of Dhaulagiri – and a short note.

> Dear Alex,
> Great chance for great days on the face you see on the card. See you
> in Kathmandu, March 10.
> Love, Voytek
> P.S. Bring a partner.

The seventh-highest mountain in the world, at 8167 metres, Dhaulagiri rises 7000 dramatic metres above Nepal's Kali Gandaki river. A stunning peak, its name means "dazzling, white and beautiful." Back in 1954, an

Argentine military expedition to Dhaulagiri adopted the unusual tactic of blasting inconvenient rock with explosives to create comfortable tent placements. They reached 8000 metres before a storm turned them back. It was a European team that in 1960 made the first ascent of Dhaulagiri via the Northeast Ridge. But the East Face was still unclimbed when Voytek turned his attention to the mountain.

In 1979, one year before sending his invite to Alex, Voytek had been to Dhaulagiri's North Face with a group of climbers from Gdańsk, birthplace of the Solidarity movement in Eastern Poland. He and Walenty Fiut planned to climb independently from the team, with the East Face as their goal. "The idea of a direct line, almost an insolent line, was incredibly attractive to me," he said. "Its alluring smooth icefield looked promising, almost as if it ran directly to heaven."

But the face was devoid of snow in 1979; it was just an endless expanse of loose rock and terrifyingly featureless slabs. They could see it was hopeless, so they returned to the north side of the mountain, where they joined the rest of the team. They reached almost 8000 metres before bad weather and one climber's illness turned them back. The unclimbed East Face remained in Voytek's mind, however, and he vowed to return.

Ice was the key. "I looked at this beautiful East Face of Dhaulagiri and I thought if it was iced up and in good shape, we should be able to climb it quickly." Voytek had already acquired considerable ice-climbing experience in the Alps on climbs such as the north faces of the Triolet, Les Courtes and Les Droites, so he simply projected his experiences in the Alps onto a larger canvas. "It would just be more and more ice," he said.

And who better to climb it with than his favourite partner, Alex MacIntyre? Alex the ice wizard. Alex with his dark, round-faced appearance, which contrasted so sharply with Voytek's pale and angular look. Their characters differed, too. Alex, apart from his fear of rockfall, was calm and relaxed. Voytek was twitchy, nervous and intense. After two expeditions with Alex, Voytek knew he loved being in the mountains with him. He enjoyed his sense of humour, his laid-back style, his eclectic collection of British music and, of course, his climbing ethos. "He was always the unseen member of the team until required, and then he would pull out something exceptional," Voytek said, recalling Alex's intuitive navigation through the overhanging cornice near the summit of Bandaka. "He was like a power card, like the joker in the pack."[15]

Most important, Voytek valued Alex's playfulness. "I appreciate people who have the ability to play," he said. "If somebody can enjoy life and have fun, then there is a better chance for a smaller ego." No doubt Voytek also enjoyed Alex's willingness to be drawn into illegal ways, something Voytek relished. Their ascent of Bandaka was illegal, their attempt on Nanda Devi was illegal, and there would certainly be more illegal opportunities in the future. It was only a matter of choosing.

Voytek planned a British–Polish venture for the Dhaulagiri East Face climb, which is why he suggested that Alex bring a partner. Foreign climbers were essential for the hard currency they brought. For his Polish partner, Voytek invited Ludwik Wilczyński. Ludwik was not only an impressive alpinist but also a talented writer and a musician. Although the two had not climbed together before, Ludwik was a familiar face in the Tatras. But instead of choosing a fellow Brit for his partner on Dhaulagiri, Alex invited the self-assured French mountain guide René Ghilini, with whom he had climbed in Chamonix. Voytek later said that René had a "calming" effect on him, something like what Jurek Kukuczka would eventually achieve. When René and Voytek met again in France more than thirty years after the expedition, René smiled at the comment and admitted that he had found Voytek to be the most highly strung climber he had ever encountered.

On arrival in Kathmandu, they faced the usual hurdle: no permit. It was then that René learned a little about problem solving, Polish-style. Negotiations for the permit were stalled. René sat back and watched as Voytek interacted with the Ministry of Tourism official. Voytek began the conversation with a conciliatory smile, extolling the virtues of the great collaboration between Nepali and foreign climbers with as many flattering platitudes as possible. Then, with a grand gesture, to celebrate their great co-operative spirit, Voytek offered a gift. René was shocked when he saw it: a battered and rusty transistor radio. It looked worthless. What could Voytek be thinking by offering this insulting gift? Surprisingly, the official accepted it with grace and a sly smile. He thanked Voytek and deftly slid open a small latch on the back of the radio to reveal a thick wad of dollars. He thrust the radio and its contents into his desk drawer and, without a pause, continued the conversation about collaboration and partnership and international relations. The permit appeared soon after. When René later questioned Voytek, he replied with a shrug, "That's the way we do things in Poland."

Permit in hand, they hired porters in Tukuche, an important staging village in the Kali Gandaki valley, and began the march to Dhaulagiri. The weather was atrocious. They were still several hours below the 5200-metre Dhampus Pass when events began to unravel. A thick bank of angry dark clouds roiled in around them, obscuring the snowfields leading up toward the pass. The porters grew increasingly fearful for their lives, and finally they abandoned their loads and fled to the valley below. Voytek felt helpless. "I knew that without them, we could never ferry all of our food and equipment over the pass, into the Hidden Valley, and over the even higher French Col to base camp," he said. His dreams and his plans and the expensive permit – all wasted.

The team hunkered down in the storm for three days, devouring bowls of hash-laced tomato soup and listening to the mournful sounds of Marianne Faithfull. "What are you dying for? It's not my reality," she sang. Despite his fretting, Voytek was intrigued by this strange woman. "I asked Alex what kind of person she was, since her lyrics were so troubled, so sad and tired," he said. "Alex told me, 'She is like the history of Poland: everyone has been there, and everyone has done great damage.'"

When the weather broke, Voytek returned to Tukuche to hire more porters while the rest of the team lay almost catatonic in camp. Eight days later they limped into base camp, exhausted and drenched after plowing through the newly fallen snow. But at least they were there, as was their gear. René brought much of the technical equipment from France: the crampons, the Simond ice axes and the Kastinger boots. Voytek brought all the down clothing and sleeping bags from Poland. René was impressed with the quality of the down, the skilful sewing and the design of the garments. "But there were no zippers," he laughed. "Only buttons. Our jackets, vests, sleeping bags – all done up with buttons."

Now at their mountain, they needed to acclimatize. Playful Alex had a strategy for acclimatization that he shared with his teammates. "This is a process which…involves the consumption of vast quantities of garlic, making love for hours on end in a series of two knuckle press-ups and hopping up big hills on one toe, to the strains of Wagner from your free, portable lead-weighted Japanese micro-cassette. This conditions the body."[16] But all joking aside, they *did* need to acclimatize, so they hatched a plan that relied on the good graces of some climbers from another expedition.

Near them in base camp was a Swiss team planning to climb the Northeast Ridge. Voytek approached them about using their route to acclimatize. Reluctantly, they agreed. Up and down they went, getting fitter and stronger with each lap on the moderate route: 6500 metres; 7000 metres; 7500 metres. On one of their acclimatization climbs, Voytek and Ludwik left a cache high on the ridge at the point where they would likely exit the East Face. "We were only two hours or so from the summit," Voytek said. "It looked so easy. But I didn't want to spoil the anticipated pleasure of going to the top directly from the face ... I wanted to remain faithful to the face. Once the summit was climbed, who knows how we would behave in extreme conditions on the face?"

Years later, Voytek explained that climbing a mountain by any route was not a challenge for him at that time. "I had no motivation for those regular routes," he said. "They were missing the most essential heart of the game with the unknown. Besides, they were mostly technically easy and gentle, so they were missing the aesthetic of the vertical. And it was the beauty of the vertical that made my wings rise. What was the sense of climbing without wings? What remained? Just hard work! No, thank you!" He laughed at his youthful attitude. "It could be I had a wrong perception in those days. Now I don't need that huge drama. My relationship with the mountain turned into a much more meditative attitude. Just to be close to its beauty! To be a part of it is what matters now."

Having fully acclimatized, the climbers were ready for the East Face. They began at 2:45 a.m. on May 6. Alex remembered it as "a night of rare beauty, awash in moonlight and clear to the ends of the earth."[17] The snow was crisp and firm under their crampons. They marched up from the col to the foot of the face in little more than an hour. Alex described the scene: "The East Face, dressed for the occasion, beckoned cold and blue."[18] The first obstacle was a compact rock band, which took them more than three hours to climb. They used the rope only once on the first, Grade v pitch, which was perfectly frosted with a thin layer of ice. Dispensing with the rope and soloing now, they moved above the rock band, weaving a route through runnels of ice and snow, searching for weaknesses, hunting for threads of ice leading upward. They tried to avoid the rock, which lay in strange, roof-tile formations. Instead, they gravitated toward whiteness. But it was all disappointingly thin. Glassy, fragile ice; crystal shards of ice; feathery fronds of snow. Little protected them on the loose, downsloping rock.

At noon on the first day, they found a little rocky knoll that provided an ideal spot for a tea break. Sitting there, they noticed a few wispy, skeletal fingers of cloud scudding along in the distance. With no access to weather forecasts, they had to rely on their mountain instincts. This was probably just an afternoon buildup. A little troubling, to be sure, but a daily occurrence on this mountain.

They carried on.

Soon thunder began to rumble, and a threatening cloud bank engulfed them, low and heavy and dark. As the gentle tea-time breeze stiffened, it began to snow. They continued up, still climbing solo. "We didn't consider roping up," Voytek said. "It wasn't terribly steep: 50–55° or sometimes a bit of 60°. A few mixed pitches a bit higher." Each climber found his own way, moving at his own speed, finding his own rhythm, spaced out on the face as much as 20 or 30 metres apart. Each climber alone in a shrinking sphere of swirling snow and hissing spindrift.

At mid-afternoon, they tucked in under a rock wall where they were sheltered from the snowfall and spindrift. By now it was obvious that the face wasn't going to provide any comfortable ledges, so at around 6450 metres they began to hack out some narrow platforms on which to perch, the first of three exceptionally uncomfortable bivouacs. There was little talking, as Voytek recalled. Just chopping and more chopping, arranging the bivouac sacks, hours of preparation before finally beginning the awkward and precarious job of cooking. Voytek remained optimistic. "Somehow, after the first day, we became assured that there was less chance of huge avalanches," he recalled. Then he added a realistic caveat: "Still, we had 1000 metres above us, and if you have a big avalanche, you are in trouble." Although uncomfortable, their first bivouac was five-star luxury compared to what awaited them the next night.

They continued tracing independent lines up the icy face, avoiding areas of deep, soft snow or black ice. Each member of the team was highly skilled on snow and ice, which meant they could move quickly and steadily, in silence and alone. As they climbed higher, the ice grew increasingly hard, polished black and shiny by the wind. The thunder persisted and spindrift pulsed down around them. At one point Ludwik and Alex found themselves stranded on their front points in an all-engulfing stream of hissing snow, unable to move or reset their gear for fear of being swept off the face.

After a long day of climbing, it was time to construct their second bivouac. Voytek remembered it clearly. "There wasn't enough room for two platforms," he said of the tiny ledge they excavated on the face. "They [Alex, Ludwik and René] somehow managed to squeeze into a two-man bivouac sack. But there was no room for me. I was outside, unable to even get into my sleeping bag. There was no cooking. It wasn't too steep – maybe 60° – but there was no chance to cut a ledge, because only 20 centimetres down we hit rock." Voytek slumped in his slings, half sitting on a tiny, crumbling ice ledge, his bivouac sack draped upside down over his head as protection from the incessant, wind-driven powder snow as he tried to ignore the chaos around him. There was neither food nor liquid on the second night. Only an unsettled doze. In the Polish hierarchy of bivouacs, this one ranked at the highest level.

They fled at the first hint of dawn. Climbing upward, they couldn't help but notice fresh banks of black clouds churning toward them. They found shelter in the lee of a large rock buttress and fired up the stove for a pot of tea. Alex described the scene: "Here we had a brew, standing like early morning commuters in a daze sipping lukewarm cups of tea, before shuttling on up, and finally out of the face in the last of the evening light, stumbling over the mixed ground to a bivi site underneath a large boulder on the ridge, and the full fury of the Dhaulagiri's winds."[19] It was on this uppermost part of the wall that they used the rope for the second time, when Voytek climbed up through an exposed rock chimney and threw down a belay to his teammates before escaping the wall. Their third bivouac was on the Northeast Ridge at around 7900 metres. Voytek remembered that, finally, they could crawl into their sleeping bags. That they were bitterly cold. And that they were bone-tired.

But they had unlocked the secrets of the unclimbed East Face. Despite the rumbling thunder, the biting wind and the falling snow, the only thing remaining was to climb to the top. They woke shortly after midnight on the morning of May 10 and began preparing for the summit. First, they needed to rehydrate, so, for several hours, they melted snow and drank. By dawn it was clear that the bad weather wasn't abating. If anything, it had worsened. After moving just 30 metres through the knee-deep snow they realized the avalanche danger between them and the summit was extreme. The snowpack whumphed and settled with each step. Sinister fracture lines ripped across the slope in jagged outlines. The only option was to retreat down the Northeast Ridge to base camp.

Voytek was crushed.

After racing down the ridge, they found the Swiss still hunkered down in camp, aghast at the terrible weather. They rested a few days and discussed what to do. "Guys," said Voytek, "I don't consider we have done it. We're not finished with this mountain." He suggested climbing the East Face again, this time going all the way to the summit.

Alex shook his head in amazement. "Don't be stupid. We've *done* the face. It's enough if we go to the summit via the normal route." Voytek admitted that the idea of going back up the face wasn't too appealing. Yet he insisted, "We have to do something about this summit." He suspected that neither René nor Ludwik cared whether they climbed it at all, but they eventually agreed to go back up the mountain via the Northeast Ridge. On May 18, shortly after noon, they reached the summit of Dhaulagiri after four days on the ridge. By May 20 they were all back in base camp. Mission accomplished. But it was still a niggling little failure for Voytek, the perfectionist, whose vision had been to reach the summit via the East Face direct. Voytek later recounted the nature of the climb with typical understatement.

> The climbing was simple – just moving continuously on 50° or 55° ice. Some sections had harder ice, and they were a bit tiring. Other sections were hard, frosty snow. We rested our calves by cutting a step with our axe and then standing on it. We didn't eat during the day. While climbing, never. It would take too much time. Sometimes we took a sweet, possibly a chocolate. We didn't place ice screws to secure ourselves, because it wasn't necessary. If you are

continuously climbing, it somehow seems safe. Of course, if you fall, it's 2000 metres. There was a simple solution for changing your jacket or taking off your pack – put in an ice axe quite firmly and hang on it. At this elevation, we had to stop every couple of metres anyway. The ice wasn't fragile, so we didn't worry about dropping ice. Our movements weren't violent, because we were just using our crampons and placing our ice axes. It was repetitive. The challenge of this type of climbing is a kind of boredom and a kind of psychological stamina.

When asked if it was interesting, Voytek answered, "What was interesting was sensing the distance to the summit and stubbornly overcoming my own weakness and moving, moving up, only occasionally discovering with great satisfaction that I'm stronger than my weaknesses." The Dhaulagiri East Face was the first time that he punctured the 8000-metre ceiling, and it was here that he encountered the ultimate game of pushing himself to his own limit. Upon reviewing the facts, Voytek admitted that climbing any 8000-metre peak was mostly about suffering. "This is the essence of high altitude," he claimed. "Every step is overcoming your weakness. Since it's totally deprived of vertical pleasures, this kind of high-altitude creativity is simply about overcoming your pain. And overcoming your pain results in an exhilarating sense of liberation."

He considered Jurek Kukuczka to be the grand master of this game. "The ambition of Kukuczka was directed exclusively this way – he was a fighter of his own weakness," Voytek said. "He didn't enjoy the game with the rock – the game with your body. For Kukuczka, the game was about winning against weakness. Progressing, progressing, further every day, weaker every day, but huge determination, trying to pursue the final objective – the summit. This was his game, his version of creativity."

Every aspect of Voytek's life demanded a creative approach, including his financial survival. He had garnered a bit of support from the PZA for the Dhaulagiri trip but not nearly enough to cover the costs. And he hadn't held a job since April 1978. "I was making money from trade," he explained. "It was illegal of course," he laughed. "Whenever I was on a trip I sent parcels back to Poland. Hundreds of boxes of Nescafé: it was a luxury in Poland. Also, jewellery. And garments. On one trip I sent fifty parcels!" Voytek called it the Golden Decade of Polish Domination, not only in Himalayan alpinism but in the smuggling scene as well. "Everybody made a killing," he said.

But smuggling wasn't as easy or as glamorous as it sounded. It was forbidden to send more than two or three parcels from Indian post offices, and repeat visits were met with suspicion. To deal with this problem, Voytek soon became familiar with every post office in Delhi. And that was just on the shipping end. At the other end of the transaction was the receiver. Again, too many parcels arriving at one address in Poland was a problem. "I sent them to different people back in Poland – family members and friends," Voytek explained. Everyone assumed a certain amount of risk and everyone realized some profit. His friends and family were delighted at the chance to earn extra money in Communist Poland. And everything – every transaction, each step of the entire process – was illegal.

Voytek's business expanded in many directions. He shipped Afghan sheepskin coats to France, where they were particularly popular. He shipped chewing gum from Poland to Russia because the Russians were crazy about gum. "Can you believe it? The Communist idiots couldn't supply chewing gum to Russians!" He imported colourful postcards from Poland and sold them in Nepal. In Afghanistan he bought scarves embroidered in bright red flowers, later selling them by the dozens to the Kazakhs in Termez, despite the Russian officials who watched every move with suspicion. The profits were huge. "For ten boxes of chewing gum sold in Russia I could buy diamonds. Really. I could sell them in Poland or in West Germany." Illegal trade was so common for Polish climbers that many shops in Delhi and in Kathmandu's Thamel district eventually displayed signs saying "Polish spoken here."

After the Dhaulagiri climb, Alex and René returned to Europe and Voytek and Ludwik to Poland, where they met little fanfare. Voytek wrote a short report for the PZA, but there was no media interest in the ascent, even though their commitment level, once they had started up the massive ice face without fixed ropes, was enormous. It was an impressive example of alpine-style climbing on a big, unscaled face at 8000 metres – the future of climbing in the Himalaya. The only big face of an

8000er that had been climbed alpine-style up to this point was Gasher-brum I, by Reinhold Messner and Peter Habeler in 1975.

It's not too surprising that Poland ignored their climb; the country was preoccupied with much more serious issues. In fact, it was teetering on the brink of chaos. When the Communist Party raised food prices, a rash of strikes broke out in factories across the nation. Strikes were illegal, so the party tried to subdue them with the usual combination of bribes and threats. Although this strategy had worked in the past, it didn't this time, thanks in part to the persistence of an electrician from the Gdańsk ship-yards, Lech Wałęsa. He had already been jailed dozens of times for his underground activities, but when a strike erupted at the Lenin Shipyard, Wałęsa took over. Twenty thousand workers were barricaded inside the walls, and thousands more were outside the gates, cheering them on. The eyes of the entire world turned to the Lenin Shipyard, where, over the next few days, Wałęsa's team negotiated an agreement that applied to the entire country. From it came the name *Solidarność* (Solidarity) and the slogan that electrified the country: "Workers of all enterprises – unite." The birth of the free trade union was Poland's first major step on the long road to democracy.

Despite all the excitement, daily life still had its familiar austere rhythm. Women stood in line for hours to buy food, and men did the same for gas. Alongside this mix of familiar hardship and revolutionary change, Voytek's life was complicated by problems in his personal life.

"We came back from Changabang, and I wasn't sure if my wife would be waiting at the airport," he laughed. Ewa was tiring of Voytek's extended and repeated absences. While on an expedition in this pre-cellphone era, he would disappear into a fathomless void as silently as if he had flown to the moon. Ewa was a passionate woman, and she wanted a man *in* her life, not on the periphery. Their marriage had become strained. Voytek wasn't even sure if there was a need to return to Poland between expeditions. His time spent in Nepal lengthened after each trip as he stayed on to arrange permits for future climbs. He saved money by not flying home and in-creased his net worth by shipping those all-important packages.

It wasn't only the prolonged absences that widened the chasm between Voytek and Ewa. When he returned from the mountains he was a different person, a more private person, completely at peace with himself. "There is this level of inner calm that is not reachable in everyday life," he explained. "When you are in a very calm state, when you are really at peace with yourself, your surroundings are completely different. You are serene. You can accept that you will die one day." He couldn't share this with Ewa. "It's difficult to be an alpinist and have a stable home life," Voytek commented. "If you are waking up with climbing dreams in the middle of the night, it is not acceptable to your partner." He noticed that when he fantasized about specific climbs, tiny drops of perspiration appeared on his hands. He called the effect the "magic pump" and added that Ewa was growing increasingly intolerant of it.

Voytek simultaneously craved domesticity and ran from it, but his fascination with climbing had replaced his fascination with his marriage. As Russian dancer Mikhail Baryshnikov once observed, the artist's life is a comparatively easy one. It's those around him who suffer the most. The same could be said for an alpinist.

Over the next two years, Voytek spent little time at home. There was a 1981 spring expedition to Makalu's unclimbed West Face with Alex and two others. A fall expedition to Makalu's still-unclimbed West Face with Alex and Jurek Kukuczka. A summer 1982 expedition to K2 on Wanda Rutkiewicz's permit, and a winter expedition the same year to the South Face of Cho Oyu with Reinhold Messner.

The Makalu expeditions were forward-thinking in the extreme, since they planned to tackle the formidable West Face in alpine style with no concessions to traditional techniques. Bad weather on the pre-monsoon trip turned Voytek and Alex back at around 7000 metres, so they returned in the fall with Jurek. Jurek and his barrels of delicacies: mouth-watering sausages and sweet, fatty hams and cans of savoury sauerkraut. Everyone knew that Jurek's favourite vegetable was ham. Even vegetarian Voytek couldn't resist these treats from home.

From September 4 to October 2, they acclimatized on the normal route and left a cache of food and a tent at the Makalu La. It was while traversing a snow slope from the Makalu La that Voytek could hear a distinct whoomph with each of Jurek's steps as he broke trail in the deep snow. He didn't like the sound of it and called out, "Jurek, it's too dangerous. It's not steep, but there is avalanche danger."

"Don't worry. There is nothing wrong," Jurek called back.

"Please, Jurek, stop."

"Look, nothing is happening," an impatient Jurek yelled back down.

Voytek began to doubt himself. Had he lost his edge? "My fear was animalistic," he said of that moment. "I felt this horrible sense of despair, and I couldn't reconcile myself to this fear." Just then, the invisible threat became real. With a deafening crack the entire slope below Jurek's track broke into a million small slabs and began sliding down. The fracture line grew to a kilometre as the snowpack calved off below him. They stared in disbelief as the avalanche swept down the mountain and off into the void. Then they looked up. The gigantic snow slope above Jurek was still hanging, now completely unsupported.

"Hey guys, everything is okay now," Jurek yelled down.

Voytek shook his head in disbelief. How could he think this? Jurek likely didn't, since Alex and Voytek had little trouble convincing him to turn back.

October 4 was their first day on the West Face proper. Every single bivouac was an ordeal – sitting on narrow ledges hacked out of the consistently steep ice. But they continued fighting their way up the demanding face until around 7800 metres, where they came to a bulging 500-metre rock barrier. It was a critical juncture. "There comes a specific moment on a climb when no one talks to anybody else, but we all observe one another, watching the will to win gradually die," Jurek later wrote.[20] "The pace drops; everything goes slower, with greater resistance."[21] Voytek broke the tension. "I see no chance. We won't do this." They needed more food and more equipment to finish the face, and they didn't have either. They descended to base camp, where the discussion continued.

Both Alex and Voytek were completely focused on the West Face, and only the West Face. Alpine-style, and only alpine-style. One year later, Alex had the occasion to discuss the climb with Andrzej Zawada when they were both speaking at a mountaineering conference in Buxton, Northern England. Zawada was unequivocal in his comments to Alex: to be sure of success on a climb such as the West Face of Makalu, a large team was essential. Small teams with ambitious objectives on 8000-metre peaks were doomed to failure. "Why waste so many resources and risk failure?" he asked. "Success is paramount."[22] But Alex, like Voytek, was committed to a different vision, where the "summit was the ambition, but the style was the obsession."[23] Their obsession may have contributed to their ultimate defeat on Makalu's West Face that year, yet for Voytek, it was another step on the long road to self-respect and dignity.

Jurek, however, was interested in success above all. And success meant the summit. Surely this splendid peak was worth climbing, regardless of the route? Since neither Voytek nor Alex was interested, Jurek announced he would try it alone. Alex left for Kathmandu, but Voytek, even though he was done with the mountain, waited for Jurek at base camp.

Jurek started up at around noon, merely to take a look. Conditions were good, and as afternoon turned to evening, he still felt fine. In the falling darkness, he was blessed with the light from a full moon bathing the mountain, so he continued. At 11 p.m. he found a partially buried tent from a previous expedition; he dug it out and crawled in. He slept late the next morning, with the full intention of going down. It had been an interesting experiment. He made some tea and crept out of the tent. Despite a strong wind, the sky was clear, cobalt blue. What to do? Up or down? He strapped on his crampons and headed up.

He stopped at the Makalu La at 7410 metres, where he, Voytek and Alex had stashed a tent. The following morning, he continued up the unclimbed Northwest Ridge. At 8000 metres he dug a platform in the snow and pitched his little tent; almost immediately, he started hallucinating, chatting with an unannounced guest. He carried on the next morning, now at the utmost limits of risk and commitment, completely on his own up there. At 4:30 p.m. he was on the summit. He left a plastic ladybug toy belonging to his son, snapped a couple of pictures and raced down. He made it to his tent late that night and to base camp the following afternoon. As he walked in, tired, grey and hollow-cheeked, Voytek approached him and asked, "So, how was it?"

"I got to the summit," Jurek replied.

It was a moment dense with meaning. A moment that presaged their future relationship as alpinists. A moment that gave Jurek and Voytek an inkling that, despite their apparent synchronicity on the highest mountains on Earth, their values and their approach to those mountains were not perfectly matched. Jurek was focused on summits, and Voytek was obsessed with style. Their actions and decisions on Makalu had demonstrated some fundamental differences; these differences had potential for conflict but would not stop them from climbing together.

Jurek and Voytek tagged on to Wanda's K2 permit in the summer of 1982. It was a miracle that she had managed to organize the expedition at all, since Poland was paralyzed by martial law. The troops had moved into Polish city streets on the night of December 12, 1981, and by early morning the next day, the streets were filled with tanks. Chaos all over again. The shops and offices were closed, operational phones and buses became a thing of the past, and expedition funding was impossible to find. But Wanda was a star in the Polish climbing community and was determined to show the government that she, along with the other alpinists, wasn't intimidated. Yielding to the authorities would have killed their spirits. By challenging martial law, they defended their values. If Wanda wanted to go abroad to climb, she would do whatever was required to make it happen.

Newly married, Wanda used contacts that her Austrian physician husband and her new friend, superstar Reinhold Messner, provided her, putting together an all-women K2 team. Wanda didn't want the boys (Jurek and Voytek) on her route, even for acclimatization purposes, so they wandered over to nearby Broad Peak to acclimatize. Voytek and Jurek had no intention of going to the summit, but they weren't excluding the possibility. Their official reason for being on the mountain was to "take photos" for the women's team; they had no permit for Broad Peak.

The acclimatization was successful, and on their way down from their deliciously sweet, illegal summit, they ran into Reinhold Messner, on his way up. Reinhold struck up a conversation with Voytek.

"Hi, guys. Where have you been?"

"Hello, Reinhold. How are you? We are just acclimatizing. We're here for K2."

"Super. How high did you go?"

"Ah, Reinhold, somewhere near the summit. Quite high, actually." Voytek was intentionally vague.

But Reinhold was too smart to be fooled. "To the top?"

Voytek squirmed and Jurek remained silent. Reinhold laughed. "No problem, boys. I'll keep your climb quiet." He walked off.

By the time Voytek and Jurek were ready to attempt a new route on the South Face of K2, the weather had deteriorated, the mountain was out of shape, and one of Wanda's teammates, Halina Krüger-Syrokomska, had died suddenly at Camp II. The expedition was over.

Messner's Cho Oyu trip was slated for December 1982. When invited to join it, Voytek said yes immediately; he assumed that the climb would be alpine-style. After all, it was a Messner expedition, a dream opportunity. All expenses paid. Messner level of comfort (high). No planning required. Well-organized. In fact, it was even more interesting: Reinhold had envisioned an expedition combining not only alpine objectives but also cultural aspects. He had invited a poet and a painter and several wives and girlfriends to round out the roster. As Austrian climber Oswald Ölz summarized in his official report of the climb, "We were accompanied to Base Camp by four women, a writer and a painter."[24] Base camp featured a roomy octagonal tent with extended porches at strategic positions, where climbers could enjoy privacy to sit, think, create or sleep. "You could 'retire' to your porch," Voytek recounted with a smile.

To Voytek's great surprise, he discovered that the team would not be climbing alpine-style but in siege style. The base camp was run by Sherpas, the camps on the mountain were set up by Sherpas, and the fixed lines were placed by Sherpas. They reached around 7000 metres on the steep ice festooned with giant, leaning snow mushrooms, before they retreated. For Voytek, by far the most memorable aspect of the expedition was the interaction between artists and climbers. Siege style didn't feel remotely creative; climbing for Voytek was more than an upward ascent. "It is essentially the difficult attempt to ascend above oneself," he wrote with typical earnestness. "It is grasping toward freedom."[25]

It was this yearning for complete freedom that made him climb "unleashed." "I prefer to use 'unleashed' because 'alpine style' sounds a bit like an accountant's report," he laughed. "And besides, it doesn't say anything about the state of mind of a climber who runs away from the leash." His definition of "leash"? Fixed ropes, fixed camps, all the accoutrements that create a tangle or web on the mountain. "It kills the sense of climbing," he insisted. He admitted that the tangle could provide a sense of security, but it eliminated the sense of freedom and any real connection a climber might have with the mountain. He equated it to climbing a free route on rock by pulling on slings.

"It is worth pointing out that many existing routes on 8000-metre peaks don't have a real ascent," he insisted. "Even the first ascent of the Abruzzi Ridge on K2 changed the ridge into a monstrous pyramid of ropes that, until today, has created a completely artificial construction. The Abruzzi Ridge remains virgin." He cited other mountains and their often-climbed routes: Everest, for example, where climbers use ropes and ladders in the Icefall as a matter of course. Taking his argument to the next level, he declared, "I won't even mention the rapes by the Russians of the west faces of K2 and Makalu!"

Voytek needed to be free of the tangle to feel close to the mountain. "Only breaking the leash allows you to dance with the moment." Understandably, he was indifferent to the climbing experience on Cho Oyu with Reinhold's team. Instead, he cherished those days high on the East Face of Dhaulagiri, and the weeks of searching for the solution to the puzzle of the West Face of Makalu with Alex and Jurek. On Dhaulagiri and Makalu, he was dancing. He, Alex and Jurek were already planning another expedition for 1983, this time to the Karakoram.

Voytek was at the Polish Embassy in Delhi when a group of Polish climbers arrived. He was wandering down the hallway, his headphones pulsating with the magical sounds of Jimi Hendrix:

Hello my friends,
So happy to see you again,
I was so alone,
All by myself, I just couldn't make it …

Ryszard Warecki stopped Voytek in the hall. "Voytek, did you hear about Alex?" he asked.

"No. What about him?" Voytek answered, removing his headphones. There was a moment of silence. "What about Alex?" he repeated.

"Alex is dead," Ryszard finally replied. "On Annapurna."

Voytek had last seen Alex at the end of their Makalu trip, when Alex left for Kathmandu after their final attempt and Voytek stayed on to wait for Jurek. This news must be wrong, he thought. Alex was special, the ideal climbing partner. He couldn't possibly be dead. No way. He looked at Ryszard with doubt in his eyes, but Ryszard held his gaze. Reeling, Voytek turned away. He had to keep moving. He continued down the hallway, jacking up the volume as he left.

Forget about the past, baby,
Things ain't what they used to be,
Keep on straight ahead,
Keep on straight ahead.

EIGHT

Enfant Terrible

Everybody rolls with their fingers crossed.
—Leonard Cohen, "Everybody Knows"

Voytek's plan for the Gasherbrums wasn't turning out as he had intended. The 1983 trip was meant to be with both Alex and Jurek, to create a remarkable trio of complementary characters. Voytek had always marvelled at Alex's imagination in the mountains, as well as his pre-climb strategy: drink heavily the night before. Alex seemed to approach all the great events in his life with a hangover, reasoning that the mass destruction of brain cells prior to climbing at altitude left fewer of them to be destroyed by the absence of oxygen during the climb. Voytek took such delight in Alex and his crazy ideas.

They had shared a lot in the mountains. "For Alex and me, alpine style meant a way of life and a state of consciousness that allowed us to fall in love with the mountain and, in consequence, to trust our destiny to it – unconditionally."[26] Voytek had even written about Alex's unique qualities in *Mountain* magazine: "Will I ever see you again? Oh yes, in a week I'll see Alex with all his dominating tranquility and confidence, which, when I look back through my mountains and even more through my anxious returns to the plains, I was always so lacking and longing for. I'll see him again and he'll make me believe for a while that I can seize this tranquility again."[27]

When Alex was killed on Annapurna, struck by a falling stone, the expedition dwindled to two: Jurek and Voytek. But this unlikely pair was a formidable team. They had already proven themselves on Makalu and Broad Peak. They managed to coexist for weeks in the Himalaya, like an "old, comfortable couple," as other climbers observed. They shared small tents on their airy bivouacs, cooked and ate together, and managed the stress of altitude and risk. Voytek was the "idea guy," whereas Jurek brought confidence and strength. They never seemed to talk but always seemed to be in touch.

Voytek laughed as he reflected on their differences. "When I was in pain all over, I would notice Jurek showing some small signs of suffering. When I was already deeply afraid, Jurek still did not feel any fear for a long time. When I experienced *dreadful* fear, Jurek was only slightly worried." Voytek's meticulous planning and strategy balanced Jurek's more spontaneous and aggressive approach. Voytek's slender frame and his technical climbing skills complemented Jurek's remarkable strength and endurance. "Jurek was the greatest psychological rhinoceros I've ever met among alpinists, unequalled in his ability to suffer and his lack of responsiveness to danger," Voytek said. "At the same time, he possessed that quality most characteristic to anyone born under Aries – a blind inner compulsion to press ahead. Characters like that, when they meet an obstacle, strike against it until they either crush it or break their own necks."[28] Those who observed them in the mountains called their partnership "magical."

The Gasherbrum group comprises six peaks encircling the South Gasherbrum Glacier in Pakistan's Karakoram Mountains. Gasherbrum I, sometimes known as Hidden Peak, is the highest of the six peaks, at 8080 metres. It was first climbed in 1958 when Nick Clinch led an American team to the summit. Afterwards, border disputes between India and Pakistan closed the area to expeditions for many years. Then, in 1975, Reinhold Messner and Peter Habeler made an alpine-style ascent of Gasherbrum I, without supplemental oxygen, and established a new standard in Himalayan climbing. The same year, Wanda Rutkiewicz led a team up 7946-metre Gasherbrum III, making a first ascent of the highest unclimbed peak in the world at that time.

Gasherbrum II, the second highest in the Gasherbrum group, at 8034 metres, is an even more angular piece of geometric perfection than

Gasherbrum I and was first climbed in 1956 by an Austrian team. Voytek and Jurek were going to the Karakoram for both Gasherbrum I and Gasherbrum II. And they intended to climb them both by new routes.

They arrived at the India–Pakistan border, their truck fully loaded with barrels of food and climbing equipment. Hidden among all this was an illicit cargo of thirty-six bottles of whisky, which they planned to sell. They knew the routine: roll up to the border, breeze through Indian customs, drive through a 200-metre no man's land, unload the trucks, reload the barrels into a Pakistani truck and, finally, pass through Pakistan customs.

Voytek had spent long, tedious hours packing the hidden contraband in the barrels. "We were in a cheap hotel and the temperatures were high," he said. "There was no air conditioning, only a fan. We were sweating like wild dogs. Really horrible. So it wasn't easy to pack them. I painstakingly put every bottle either in a sleeping bag or in a bag stuffed with socks and soft clothing. Then I placed them at the bottom of the barrels." Most of the barrels were "clean," but three contained twelve bottles each. Jurek had watched in amusement (and with some impatience) while Voytek swaddled the precious bottles and distributed them among the three barrels, all carefully marked for easy identification and placed at the back of the load, should there be any problems at the border. They weren't concerned about getting out of India; it was entering Pakistan that might be tricky.

Their truck crawled up to the Indian border crossing. It was a sultry day; the sun hung heavy in the muted sky. The Indian customs agent was suspicious and surly. They were stunned when he ordered them to unload the truck for inspection. Voytek protested. "Come on. We are leaving your country, not entering it." The agent mumbled something about just following orders. After a somewhat cursory glance into the top of each barrel, he ambled over to his commanding officer and reported that all seemed okay. The officer snapped at him, accused him of shoddy work and insisted he do it all over again.

Voytek and Jurek had already reloaded the barrels but now realized that the inspection was not over. Voytek's hands were sweating, and Jurek felt queasy. Whisky was not considered "necessary food provisions," and it certainly didn't qualify as climbing equipment. Jurek walked around the front of the truck, sat down on the ground and lit a cigarette. Travelling with them to base camp was a trekker; the man walked off in terror, convinced he would spend the rest of his life in an Indian jail. To calm himself, he had some tea.

Voytek refused to help the border agent. "I was thinking, no, I will not help them. 'Sorry, sir, it is very hot. It is too much for us. Open them yourself.'" The forty-something, balding agent opened each barrel in the first row and inspected the contents piece by piece. "He was ruining my packing job," Voytek remembered. "I thought he would give up after a couple of barrels. It was more than 40°C and he was sweating like crazy." When the inspector finished the first row, Voytek began to repack the entire mess, confident that the ordeal was done.

"Next row, please," announced the inspector.

Trying to hide his impatience, Voytek remained calm and answered, "Of course. Please, enjoy." He described the scene: "I noticed that Jurek was now on cigarette number three. The trekker was on his third cup of tea. I was sweating and the customs guy was dripping."

"Next row," demanded the agent.

"Really? If you want it, go ahead," Voytek gasped, throwing up his hands in frustration. Piece by piece, the customs agent examined the barrels in row three. Then he demanded row four.

Directly behind row four was guilty row five. "I knew what was in it," Voytek recounted. "What to do?" He came up with a risky scheme to surreptitiously exchange the row-five barrels with the already-inspected barrels sitting outside the truck. He became helpful again, hoping to confuse the agent with his eager co-operation and to bury him in senseless details. "I began explaining things to him. These are shoes, this is a stove, a sleeping bag, these heavy tins are meat." During all this, Voytek managed to slip one of the "dirty" barrels to Jurek to place outside. Incredibly nervous, Jurek returned to the front of the truck to smoke. He knew there were only two barrels left in the truck and they were both dirty. Puff. Puff. Puff.

Voytek turned back to help the customs agent. "I was taking out the sleeping bag wrapped around the whisky. I carefully placed it down on the truck so it didn't clink like glass. I explained to him that this was my clothing; this was my equipment." The agent nodded in approval and moved on to the last barrel. Voytek was so tense he felt ready to explode. The veins on his forehead bulged as he lifted each sleeping bag packed with whisky as if it were a newborn child wrapped in swaddling clothes. Gently, almost tenderly, he removed the sacks of heavy socks and climbing pants, all hiding whisky. Miraculously, the bundles remained intact.

He glanced around at Jurek and saw that his package of cigarettes was finished and his face looked slightly green. The trekker, his face flushed, was completely out of tea. The weary customs agent declared the inspection over and staggered off.

After repacking the barrels into the truck, the three extricated themselves from the Indians and approached Pakistan customs.

"Do you have any alcohol?"

"No, sir, we do not."

The wily trio retrieved their stamped documents and sped off, visions of dank Asian prisons fading as the mountains shone in their place.

Now that they had managed to get all their supplies and whisky into Pakistan, their next major problem was eggs. They arrived in Skardu, the jumping-off point for expeditions to the Karakoram, and began buying fresh food with the help of their liaison officer, Pir Sadiq Shah. A dignified Pathan and extremely religious, Pir Sadiq took the needs of his climbers seriously. Voytek calculated that they needed two eggs per person per day. The expedition was planned for sixty days. There were two of them, so that amounted to 240 eggs. Then again, to be safe, better take 300. Jurek shook his head in disbelief. Why so many eggs? They had dozens of cans of delicious Polish ham. Why eat eggs when there was ham? Voytek prowled the bustling market, inspecting eggs, touching them, lifting them, shaking them. Even breaking them. Their quality was appalling, he felt. Many were old and rotten. Jurek couldn't understand why he was obsessing about these eggs. Eggs were eggs.

After a couple of days of egg hunting, Voytek was distraught. "Pir Sadiq, what are we going to do about the eggs? They are terrible. Not all, but most. How can I be sure our eggs will be good? It's essential that we have good eggs."

"It's true, Mr. Voytek. I too am surprised at the poor quality. I think we will have to do the egg tests to be sure."

"What egg tests?"

"Oh, you don't know the egg tests? There are three. I will show you."

First, they needed to shake the eggs close to their ears and listen for any unusual sounds. Clunking or thudding eggs would be discarded. Next, they had to hold each egg up to a strong light. Eggs showing rot or blackness or large blood clots could also be rejected. The final test, and the best one, was the water test.

"Mr. Voytek, you must get a bucket of water and take each egg and place it in the bucket."

"But why? I want to eat the eggs, not float them."

"Yes, that is the point. If they float they are rotten. Don't buy them. If they sink a bit and then float in the middle, they are old eggs. Don't buy them. If they sink, they are good. These are your eggs. These eggs you must buy."

Voytek was concerned about how much time all this testing would take, but he was a perfectionist, particularly about eggs. And he knew that Jurek would have nothing to do with the egg testing; he was on his own. So he shook them, he held them up to the sun, and he placed them in water. He finally accumulated 300 sinkers but then realized they were all rather small. Better buy more: 100 additional small, sinking eggs, and the task was complete.

Now he needed a strong, sure-footed porter to carry the eggs to base camp. Again, he enlisted the help of Pir Sadiq. "We made a bad choice," Voytek later admitted. "He was a real stumbler. Every day he lost more eggs. One day it was ten eggs. The following day, twenty. One day he actually lost thirty of our eggs." Nonetheless, thanks to the overbuying, they still had plenty of eggs when they reached base camp.

Relieved, Voytek took the precious box of eggs and placed it in a safe position atop a large flat rock a little above camp. He gloated a bit, congratulating himself on the egg victory. They were busy constructing the kitchen with rocks and canvas when they heard a distant noise. It grew louder. Voytek and Jurek both looked up in horror as a boulder, dislodged high up the mountain, came bouncing down toward them, leaping and lurching as if chased by the devil. It gathered terrific speed and then landed, with uncanny precision, on the box of eggs. Jurek looked at Voytek, offering a feeble smile and a slight shrug of his shoulders. But he didn't say a word. "That was a unique quality of Jurek," Voytek remembered with a smile. "He could be really tolerant."

They still had one critical issue: they wanted to climb two mountains, but they only had a permit for one. Back in Islamabad, Jurek had watched his partner wriggle like an eel while he negotiated with the Ministry of Tourism official, Mr. Muniuddin, knowing full well they had two mountains in their sights. But even after selling the whisky, they couldn't afford two permits, so, for the time being, their permit for Gasherbrum I would have to suffice.

As they studied the mountain from base camp, it soon became clear that Gasherbrum I was too dangerous to climb at the moment. Enveloped in a deep blanket of snow, it rumbled with avalanches. Besides, Voytek had always planned to climb Gasherbrum II first, so he set in motion the next part of his strategy.

"Pir Sadiq, what do you think about Gasherbrum I? It seems there are a lot of avalanches."

"Yes, sir, that is the case. Very dangerous."

"I have never seen anything like this. We are very afraid. We have a permit for this mountain, but it seems too dangerous. I think we might die up there. It is such a shame we hadn't chosen Gasherbrum II instead. What do you think?"

"Mr. Voytek, it is too bad about your permit, but you shouldn't worry. I am your liaison officer, and I am also an officer in the Pakistan Army. I forbid you to climb Gasherbrum I," Pir Sadiq declared, with some authority. "I cannot allow you to die on this mountain. I order you to climb Gasherbrum II. It is much safer."

"We simply can't. We don't have a permit."

"I will write a letter today and send it to the authorities. Your permit will be waiting for you when you return. I insist. I order you as an officer in the Pakistan Army."

What to do? They had been ordered by an officer in the Pakistan Army to climb Gasherbrum II. They had to obey. Voytek thanked him for his sincere concerns and moved camp over to the base of Gasherbrum II.

On June 12 they began three days of acclimatization, climbing up through the Gasherbrum icefall to the Gasherbrum La at 6500 metres and then to 7000 metres at the summit of the Pyramid. A first ascent. By June 15 they were back at base camp. For the next five days, they rested. On June 21 they climbed all the way to the Gasherbrum La in one push – almost 1500 metres. Better acclimatized now, they were moving faster. They climbed to the Pyramid the following day. And on June 23 they continued up to just below the summit of Gasherbrum II East, where they bivouacked in a snowstorm. Voytek's journal describes the unpleasant situation: "Jurek is feeling bad. Cooking is not possible because of snowfall. Tent is full of snow. Only one pot of fluid." Despite the bad night, they made the first ascent of 7758-metre Gasherbrum II East the next morning and descended to the Pyramid. The following day, they moved all the way down to base camp.

The weather was now good, and they felt strong. Voytek's resting pulse rate dropped to between forty-five and forty-eight beats per minute, proof that his acclimatization efforts were paying off. They rested in base camp for three days, eating and drinking, at first with a Swiss team that soon departed for Broad Peak, but later alone, just the two of them, with plenty of extra food left by the Swiss. Delighted, they rummaged through it, together with the ravens, scavenging for exotic Swiss goodies.

On June 29 they raced up to the Gasherbrum La, with a short stop at the traditionally used Camp I to ransack more abandoned Swiss supplies. The ravens accompanied them. The next day, they climbed to 7400 metres, and on July 1, they stashed their packs at 7700 metres at the base of the summit ridge of Gasherbrum II, stopping to rest there and enjoy a pot of tea. By 4 p.m. they had reached the short summit ridge, where the wind increased dramatically. Clinging to the bullet-hard ice and buffeted by the hurricane-force wind, they crawled the last 400 metres to the summit, reaching it shortly after 5 p.m.

The unpleasant descent lasted two days. After returning to their packs on the col, they bivouacked for the night. Then, venturing onto the normal route, which was unknown to them, they began downclimbing through a blizzard. The wind lashed their faces and coated their goggles with a film of ice, partially blinding them. The day ground on. They traversed the first 200 to 300 metres of dangerous snow slopes below the rocky summit pyramid in poor visibility, then they continued down, staying close to the crest of the ridge. As they rappelled the steeper sections, they came across some old fixed ropes; although none of them inspired confidence, they reluctantly used them. At 6 p.m. they arrived at the Swiss team's Camp I. Exhausted from the traverse, they slept soundly.

The following day, July 3, they continued to base camp, spending almost eight hours navigating a nightmarish icefall choked with traps: teetering seracs, soft snow, drooping snow bridges. They reached base camp at 4 p.m., having completed the first traverse of Gasherbrum II, and the first traverse of multiple peaks at that altitude – all done in alpine style. Voytek explained why it had been so appealing: "A high-altitude traverse is the essence of adventure. You can hardly invent a more unpredictable kind of venture in alpinism." They felt in top form to tackle Gasherbrum I.

Voytek and Jurek settled in to wait for good weather. They waited some more. Twenty days of snow and cloud. Their only entertainment was the purple-black ravens circling overhead and begging for food. Voytek was eager to maintain good relations with the ravens, and they were swimming in extra food, thanks to the Swiss. So he fed them. The ravens seemed particularly fond of noodles and ham, but they waddled away in disgust from any offerings of porridge or cornflakes. As the good news spread, ravens arrived in flocks, hopping around camp with their ungainly stagger, squawking to each other and waiting for their daily treats. Voytek would take out a 3-kilogram tin of Polish ham, cut it into pieces and toss them out to the ravens, who would swoop in and grab them. The birds were so greedy for the ham that they almost choked on it. It was a great diversion and helped pass the time. Voytek felt a strong connection to those beautiful and intelligent birds.

But Jurek wasn't happy. "Voytek, I know you are not listening to me, but I can't watch what you are doing," he complained. "I know we don't need this ham, but to treat the food like this, to throw it to the birds, this is not the proper way. This is wasting food."

"But Jurek, we have so much food. There is no better way," Voytek responded. "Do you want to leave it here to rot? The Pakistanis won't take this ham. You know they won't. It's against their religion."

Jurek understood the logic, but he was troubled by Voytek's lack of respect for the food. Particularly the ham. Voytek relented and stopped throwing ham. The ravens waited, staring at him. The boredom grew. Eventually the two climbers retreated into their respective tents. Voytek read. Jurek slept. They emerged for meals together and waited for the weather to turn.

One day British climbers Doug Scott and Roger Baxter-Jones arrived for a visit. They were climbing over on K2 and needed some company while they waited out the storms. Voytek and Jurek were happy to accommodate them, whipping up fine meals of odd combinations from the Swiss and Polish food supplies: sardines with cheese sauce, chocolate fondue, bacon with potatoes. When the British guests left, Voytek and Jurek were left to themselves again. They took turns preparing meals, and the increasingly complex and bizarre menus became the focal point of each day. Despite all the good food, Jurek was losing weight. In contrast, Voytek was gaining weight, losing his edge. He felt as heavy as a sack. He would need a few hunger days once the climb was over to regain his desired strength-to-weight ratio. "Spending a lot of hours in the kitchen," Voytek wrote in his journal.

The snow and rain continued.

When Voytek first wrote about those long weeks in camp, his words sometimes expressed deep despair. "Totally alone and isolated on our moraine we suffered twenty days...empty and dreary days."[29] But there is a flip side to bad weather that most climbers, including Voytek, will acknowledge: meditative days spent relaxing with little stress. "Learning a language, reading, trying to think about writing, literature, but not a single beautiful sentence comes to my head...thinking about home..." he wrote.

When they could no longer tolerate the inaction, Voytek and Jurek carried supplies over to the base of the face of Gasherbrum I. They had just dropped their loads and were about to turn back to base camp when a horrifying, muffled sound emerged from the mountain. They watched as two enormous ice avalanches swept down the entire length of the face and across the cwm to the foot of their intended route. Clouds of snow billowed up like an atomic explosion. Then the mountain lay silent, dusted in white. Shaken, they trundled back to camp, where the memory of the avalanches conjured up alarming visions of suffocation, falling, burial, death. Voytek's journal revealed his dark thoughts: "Air pressure falling. Today I'm thinking more about descending than climbing. Fearing the wall. I'm afraid of the lower cwm. Giving up."

On July 17 the air pressure soared, the temperature dropped and the sky cleared. Their optimism soared, too, but despite the good weather, they were on high alert, psychologically and physically. Voytek and Jurek spent the next day fretting. There was so much to consider: the deadly cwm, the treacherous snow conditions, the avalanche hazard and the summit rock barrier. On July 19 they woke at 2 a.m. The stars were obscured by cloud, and it was warm (−3°C) and a bit windy. They gave up and returned to their tents. When they woke up later that morning, the sky was bright and clear, with perfect visibility. The temperature had cooled and the air pressure had risen. In other words, the conditions for climbing were perfect. To ease their guilt at not having started earlier that morning, they broke trail through the snow to the foot of the wall, saving time for the next day.

Excited and anxious, they considered their options. In only two days the porters would arrive to break camp and carry their equipment down. Could they climb Gasherbrum 1 by a new route and descend to base in two days? Definitely not. Leaving their camp unattended was risky; they both knew that. And if the porters arrived at an empty camp, they would likely assume the climbers had been killed on the mountain. They would leave, and Jurek and Voytek would be stuck with all their gear, or worse, without any gear at all, depending on the porters' moral compasses.

Voytek hustled over to his tent and hunted among his books and papers. He grabbed the largest piece of blank paper he could find, marched away from the tent and studied the face. He sketched a rough drawing of the mountain and then placed two stick climbers on the face with arrows pointing to the summit. Surely the porters would understand this. No, he shook his head in frustration; it wasn't clear enough. He added five more stick figures at base camp with arrows pointing to the kitchen tent. Now they would understand that they were supposed to stay and wait, using the kitchen tent for shelter. Confident that the message would be clear, Jurek and Voytek placed a large rock on the drawing, carefully buried their passports and money, and loaded their packs.

They set out at 3:15 a.m. on July 20. At 5:30 they arrived at the base of the cwm. No ice avalanches, no snow avalanches, not a breath of wind. The silence felt ominous. They stared up at the ice cliffs and towering seracs leaning above the cwm that they needed to traverse. Voytek later described their decision: "We switched off our brains and moved steadily into danger. Ten minutes later we emerged."[30]

Starting up on steep snow and ice, they soon encountered a rock barrier that blocked access to the upper mixed ground of the summit wall. They called it the Fork. Up until now they had made good progress, but this pitch of Grade v slowed them down. The next morning they emerged into a dazzling scene of snowfields and towering ice seracs. The sun hammered down. The silence deafened. They tested the snowpack with one foot, then another. It was inconsistent, collapsing in places, holding firm in others. To avoid the huge, unstable wall of snow, they moved closer to the left-hand pillar, where their crampons scratched against the rock. It was impossible to develop a rhythm on this awkward terrain. Still, their spirits were high, and Voytek felt as free as the ravens playing in the thermals overhead. He felt encouraged by the ravens – almost protected. Voytek and Jurek tunnelled and navigated a route up through the serac barrier until they reached around 7200 metres, where they found a reasonable spot for a bivouac. Tomorrow would be summit day.

They arose at 2 a.m. on July 22, cooked two pots of tea and crawled out of the tent at 5:30. The miraculously calm weather was holding. A pastel dawn crept across the upper slopes of the mountain while the valleys below remained cloaked in darkness. After crossing the upper snowfield, they reached the greatest unknown of the entire climb: the highest rock barrier. They opted for a line slightly right of centre but neither felt confident it would go. After just one pitch of climbing, they knew they wouldn't finish before nightfall. Frustrated, they stopped and set up a rappel to return to their last bivouac. Jurek went first. When he was down and off the first rappel, Voytek began. Suddenly he heard Jurek cursing loudly. Voytek glanced down and, out of the corner of his eye, spied one of his own crampons tumbling down the slope. Disaster! They limped back to the bivouac, Jurek belaying Voytek most of the time and Voytek relying on a single crampon for security.

Once at the bivouac, the severity of their situation set in. They were high on the Southwest Face of an 8000-metre peak. Steep, complex terrain lay between them and the base of the mountain, and downclimbing it with one crampon was a terrifying prospect. The summit was within reach, but that would require even more finesse. And to add to the stress, they knew the porters were probably already in base camp, waiting for them. Unexpectedly, Jurek offered a solution that seemed to completely ignore their precarious situation but that appeared reasonable enough to him. "We can get to the top tomorrow by traversing to the right to the South Ridge," he assured Voytek.

"With one crampon? I don't think so."

"Hmmm, that's a problem, all right. Well, I'll go to the summit alone. You can stay here and wait for me. No problem. I'll take the rope with me to the summit and then tomorrow we can go down. I'll help you with the descent."

Voytek couldn't believe what he was hearing. Jurek was going to leave him at 7200 metres on the Southwest Face of Gasherbrum 1 with one crampon and no rope. What if Jurek fell? He would be abandoned on the mountain with no way of escaping. As the hours passed in their little tent, Voytek's emotions vacillated from annoyance to bitterness to a sense of total abandonment. Finally, feelings of anger emerged to help him make the final decision. If he was going to be abandoned here, he would rather die in an even more dangerous situation, but at least together with his partner. He calmed himself and announced, "No way, Jurek. I'm not staying here alone. Okay, if you want the summit so badly, I'm coming with you." Jurek shrugged his agreement.

They rose early the next morning and began traversing much lower than their previous line. Jurek was out front. Suddenly Voytek heard an alarming scream. He yelled up. "What?! What happened, Jurek?"

"I found it. Your crampon. It's here." Jubilant cursing followed as Voytek caught up to him and reattached the precious crampon. It had fallen around 500 metres but had miraculously caught in the snow. Fully cramponed now, they angled over to the South Ridge and continued up the steep, rocky and confusing terrain, which was partially covered with loose, unconsolidated snow. They reached the summit at 2:30 p.m.

The majestic Karakoram spread out below them. Like Gothic cathedrals, countless rock spires emerged from rivers of ice to reach upward toward the heavens. "I sensed a vague but familiar affinity to something great and enormously calm...I felt this affinity intensely," Voytek later wrote.[31] It was as if he could touch Eternity. But as their eyes adjusted to the distant view, Voytek noticed something else: clouds swirling upward from the valley below. They had to start down.

By the time they reached their bivouac tent, it was snowing steadily. They ate their last remnants of food and burned their last few ounces of gas for tea. Then they slept, deeply. The following day's descent was long and tedious, even with two sets of crampons. They mostly downclimbed the precipitous terrain, but a few rappels were required. Although they searched for good piton placements for their rappel anchors, they were sometimes forced to rappel from single blades only partly hammered into shallow cracks. Each one held. They stumbled into base camp on July 24.

The porters were waiting.

When Jurek and Voytek reached the Ministry of Tourism office a few days later, Pir Sadiq's letter was sitting on the official's desk. Voytek smiled and began the usual dance with Mr. Muniuddin: thanking him so much for all his help, praising the good advice of Pir Sadiq, expressing their thanks that he had seen the solution to the problem of Gasherbrum I's dangerous condition, relaying their unquestionable obedience to Pir Sadiq's order to move over to Gasherbrum II, and promising to speak with the Polish Mountaineering Association the minute they arrived back in Warsaw, since it was the PZA that would pay for the extra permit. "There will be no problem with this payment," Voytek assured Mr. Muniuddin. "They will be happy to pay, because they will be extremely pleased and proud that we have managed two new routes on two 8000-metre peaks in one expedition. This is good for Poland." He silently congratulated himself that the whole thing had been done for the equivalent of around $4,000. "Pretty cheap routes," he laughed, years later.

Nonetheless, his confidence in the PZA was misplaced. It's true, they were extremely pleased that their two star climbers had managed two new routes on two 8000ers – the first time in history that it had been accomplished. Well done, boys! But what about this unexpected additional cost? That wasn't the agreement. The managing committee huddled around the table in the association's office, debating the pros and cons of paying for the second permit. Most agreed it was a small price to pay for this fine Polish mountaineering achievement. Yet not all. One dissenter was piqued that the two were flaunting their success in front of the association, showing alarming signs of arrogance and disrespect. Voytek and Jurek feared they might be grounded in Poland. The authorities eventually relented and paid the invoice for the second permit, while Voytek and Jurek were merely reprimanded. Voytek, however, gained a new nickname in the process, coined by association secretary Hanna Wiktorowska: he was now known as the "enfant terrible."

Twenty-five years after Jurek and Voytek's Gasherbrum ascents, Russian alpinists Valery Babanov and Viktor Afanasiev climbed two new routes on 8000ers in one season: Broad Peak West Face and Gasherbrum I. Theirs was an impressive achievement. However, Valery, reflecting on their climbs, couldn't help but give due respect to Voytek and Jurek, who had been so ahead of their time. "Already 25 years have passed since their ascents, but no one has done anything similar in these mountains. So where is the progress in world alpinism? Or did this pair, with their creative thinking, outstrip their time by many years?"[32]

When Voytek looked back on the Gasherbrum climbs, there were many vivid memories: the difficult climbing, the confusing route finding, the dropped crampon. But one of the most resonant was of those long weeks in camp when he felt a sense of perfect freedom and a deep physical and mental well-being. "I wasn't lonely at all," he said. "You know, staying in base camp in the bad weather was always such a pleasure. Of course, it was kind of a waste of time, but still, it was like holidays for me. There was reading, music; every day we were changing the cooking duty, so one day I was cooking, then one day I was served. We invented such incredible dishes."

His recollection of those long days of idleness echoed words penned by young Japanese climber Kei Taniguchi. Shortly before her untimely death in the Japanese Alps, she wrote: "I don't like rushing to a destination, reaching the base of a peak in the shortest possible time and starting to climb right away. To me, that approach would be like walking into someone's house with dirty shoes. Instead, I'd prefer to knock on the door of the mountain and say hello, to speak with it until we understand each other better, and only then to enter more deeply into its heart."[33]

Voytek's handwritten journals from that time tell a different story. A story of frustration and boredom. But memory is malleable and selective. Time changes its perspective. And with time, Voytek's perception of his experience in the Gasherbrums changed. Ultimately, it was the time in camp, playing with the ravens, being alone with his thoughts, slowly getting to know the Gasherbrums, that mattered most.

Voytek Kurtyka and Ewa Waldeck-Kurtyka. *Ewa Waldeck-Kurtyka collection.*

The Changabang team from 1978: John Porter, Krzysztof Żurek, Voytek Kurtyka and Alex MacIntyre. *John Porter collection.*

Voytek Kurtyka on the last day of climbing on Changabang. *Voytek Kurtyka collection.*

Descending the original route from the summit of Changabang. *John Porter.*

The long and complicated descent route off the summit of Changabang. *Voytek Kurtyka.*

Alex MacIntyre and John Porter taking a break on the tedious glacier descent from Changabang. *Voytek Kurtyka collection.*

A slightly thinner Changabang team, after having climbed the South Face. From l. to r.: Voytek Kurtyka, John Porter, Alex MacIntyre, Krzysztof Żurek and base camp manager and doctor Lech Korniszewski. *Voytek Kurtyka collection.*

The Changabang team enjoying a warm reception upon their return to Warsaw. From l. to r.: Voytek Kurtyka, Krzysztof Żurek, John Porter and Alex MacIntyre. *Voytek Kurtyka collection.*

Changabang, 6864 metres, Nanda Devi group, Garhwal Himalaya, India. New route on the South Buttress, by Voytek Kurtyka, Alex MacIntyre, John Porter and Krzysztof Żurek in 1978. *Voytek Kurtyka collection; route outline by Piotr Drożdż.*

Portrait of Voytek Kurtyka.
Ewa Waldeck-Kurtyka.

Alex MacIntyre soloing on the East Face of
Dhaulagiri in 1980. *Voytek Kurtyka.*

Dhaulagiri, 8167 metres, Nepal. New route on the East Face (to 7500 metres),
alpine-style, by Voytek Kurtyka, René Ghilini, Alex MacIntyre and Ludwik
Wilczyński in 1980. They later summited via the Northeast Ridge.
Voytek Kurtyka collection; route outline by Piotr Drożdż.

Voytek Kurtyka in Kathmandu after climbing the East Face of Dhaulagiri.
Voytek Kurtyka collection.

The 1980 East Face of Dhaulagiri team after the climb. From l. to r.: René Ghilini, Voytek Kurtyka, Alex MacIntyre and Ludwik Wilczyński. *Voytek Kurtyka collection.*

Voytek Kurtyka, Jerzy Kukuczka and Alex MacIntyre on the Makalu West Face expedition, 1981. *Jerzy Kukuczka collection.*

Voytek
Kurtyka
and Alex
MacIntyre
on Makalu,
1981. *Jerzy
Kukuczka.*

Climbing on the Makalu West Face.
Voytek Kurtyka collection.

Alex Mac-
Intyre
starting up
through
the rock
barrier on
the Makalu
West Face,
1981. *Voytek
Kurtyka.*

Voytek Kurtyka at Makalu base camp. *Jerzy Kukuczka.*

Wanda Rutkiewicz on crutches at K2 in 1982. Voytek Kurtyka and Jerzy Kukuczka helped carry her the last couple of hours to base camp. *Wanda Rutkiewicz collection.*

Voytek Kurtyka and Jerzy Kukuczka in K2 base camp, 1982. *Janusz Kurczab.*

Voytek Kurtyka on the 1982 Messner winter expedition to Cho Oyu.
Voytek Kurtyka collection.

Porters on the way to the Gasherbrums in the Baltoro, 1983.
Voytek Kurtyka.

Voytek Kurtyka
on the summit of
Gasherbrum II
East, 1983.
Jerzy Kukuczka.

Gasherbrum II,
8034 metres,
Karakoram,
Pakistan. New
route on the
Southeast Ridge,
alpine-style, by
Voytek Kurtyka
and Jerzy
Kukuczka in 1983.
*Voytek Kurtyka
collection;
route outline by
Piotr Drożdż.*

ok. 7300

▲ ● 6400 na Gasherbrum La

Voytek Kurtyka approaching the rock barrier on Gasherbrum I on the first day of the climb. *Jerzy Kukuczka, Voytek Kurtyka collection.*

Voytek Kurtyka and Jerzy Kukuczka arrive in base camp after having completed a new route on Gasherbrum I in 1983. *Voytek Kurtyka collection.*

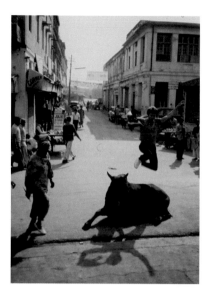

Jerzy Kukuczka at the high bivouac after having summited Gasherbrum I in 1983. *Voytek Kurtyka.*

Voytek Kurtyka burning off some excess energy in Kathmandu. *Voytek Kurtyka collection.*

Gasherbrum I, 8080 metres, Karakoram, Pakistan. New route on the Southeast Face, alpine-style, by Voytek Kurtyka and Jerzy Kukuczka in 1983. *Voytek Kurtyka collection; route outline by Piotr Drożdż.*

NINE

Line against the Sky

I know that this transcendence will be fleeting, but while it lasts, I spring along the path as if set free.
—Peter Matthiessen, *The Snow Leopard*

Voytek sat perched on a sticky, vinyl-covered stool in a sweltering Islamabad hotel room. He was signing postcards. Hundreds of postcards. In those days, it was the custom (now considered quaint) for Himalayan expeditions to mail autographed postcards to friends and supporters. He was in a splendid mood, signing each card with a flourish and stacking them in neat little piles on the wooden table. Everything was going so well. It was June 2, 1984, and his pre-arranged permit for Gasherbrum IV was in order. Not only that: he had recently secured a permit for Broad Peak. His truckload of supplies was in transit from Poland, rumbling southward through the Balkans, Turkey and Iraq, all the way to Pakistan – a route unofficially known as the Polish Silk Road. All he had to do was meet up with his partner, Jurek. Smiling to himself, he continued signing and stacking the cards.

There was a knock at the door. Voytek leapt up from his stool and bounded over.

"Yes?" he said, opening it.

"Mr. Voytek, you have a call at reception. Please come now. You have an urgent message."

He ran down to reception and picked up the phone. It was Jurek.

"Voytek, I have some bad news. There has been an accident with the truck."

"What do you mean? What happened?"

"It went off the road. It's down a very steep bank. A long way down."

"Is there any damage?"

"The front axle is broken. One wheel is completely detached."

"What about the guys? Our equipment? Our supplies?" Voytek could see the entire expedition disappearing before his eyes.

"The equipment has been saved. And everybody is fine. No injuries."

Voytek swore under his breath in frustration. Now he had two permits and a truck in the ditch. It seemed to him that stretches of abnormally good luck always ended in disaster. He spent the next hour pacing his stuffy room, his mind racing about what to do with this dreadful situation. First, the facts: the truck didn't belong to him and it was probably worth about $7,000. Then, the possibilities: there might be a market for it in Pakistan; it was easy to sell products in Pakistan, especially Western items. Surely someone would want this truck. But not for the full price. Or maybe they could repair the truck? Pakistan had brilliant vehicle repairmen. They could turn a tired wreck into a fully functioning vehicle, complete with decorative tassels and a blaring horn.

He clutched his head in frustration: what a nightmare. Still, the sun was shining, he was healthy, and the beautiful Karakoram peaks were still there, waiting for them. He finally arranged for the truck to be hauled away to a repair shop, promising to check in after he had returned from the mountains.

Voytek and Jurek arrived at base camp on June 19 and joined the rest of the Polish team: Janusz Majer, Ryszard Pawłowski, Walenty Fiut and Krzysztof Wielicki. Thankfully, the supplies that had been transported by the broken truck were all there, including some special food items that Jurek had arranged. He had somehow cultivated an underground network back in Poland that provided him with first-class, perfectly cured ham and sauerkraut – delicacies that normal Polish citizens craved but couldn't buy, due to the austerity measures imposed by martial law. Jurek was so well-connected that, despite martial law, he could arrange for vast quantities of the stuff: enough for the expedition members plus his family and friends.

Many continued to regard Voytek and Jurek as an odd pair. Their personalities were completely different. They didn't socialize together in Poland. They never climbed together in the Tatras. It was only in the Himalaya and the Karakoram that they came together, where nobody could match them. They were the Polish dream team, and they had a bold objective, a traverse of all three summits of Broad Peak. It was called Broad Peak for a reason: over 10 kilometres of airy ridge linked the three summits – the 8051-metre Main Summit, the 8011-metre Central Summit and the 7490-metre North Summit. Voytek and Jurek's plan was only possible for a small, nimble team. Attempting the traverse in siege style, with its web of fixed ropes stretched across kilometres of high-altitude ridges, would have been absurd.

The pair began acclimatizing on the South Ridge to better understand what they would face on their descent from the traverse. After reaching only 6400 metres, Voytek knew the plan was flawed. They could both see that the next 400 metres were glazed with bullet-hard, glistening water ice. To reach 7000 metres on the South Ridge, they would need to make four trips up and down the steep water ice and mixed ground, fixing ropes for a safe descent. It would take weeks of effort in perfect weather – much too long. Plus, all that fixing of lines would spoil their plan of doing the traverse alpine-style.

They moved over to the normal route to acclimatize, with the understanding that they would start the traverse on the north side. But Jurek was reluctant to give up on the South Ridge. "Why don't we go back to the south side and begin the traverse there," he suggested.

"No, Jurek. That doesn't make sense. You know our priority is to traverse all three summits of Broad Peak. It's never been done. If we go back to the South Ridge, we will waste way too much time and effort."

Jurek wasn't easily dissuaded. "But the South Ridge is more interesting."

Voytek stuck to his guns. "Look, Jurek. If we start from the south side and spend five days getting to the summit…we will need a lot of pitons – as many as sixty. We will need ten days of food. Our packs will be so heavy that we won't be able to move quickly." He knew that speed was critical for this project.

Jurek disagreed. He wanted this new route. By 1984 Jurek had already climbed six 8000-metre peaks. He was starting to consider a grand plan – climbing all fourteen of them. Jurek's plan was like Reinhold Messner's, but different in that Jurek wanted to climb them all by new routes or in winter. Climbing the south side of Broad Peak would add another new route to his collection.

They continued to argue. Voytek insisted his plan was best. Besides, the whole idea of the traverse had been his. Jurek finally acquiesced, and in the first few days of July, they and the rest of the team acclimatized on the normal route of Broad Peak, climbing as high as 7400 metres. Up and down they went, building strength and increasing red blood cells in their systems. Good acclimatization was fundamental to their plan, since they would be spending several nights at extremely high altitudes.

On July 8 the weather turned bad. Snow and rain confined them to their tents. Voytek's journal entries reveal his musings, not about the route or the mountain or acclimatization, but about beauty: "Beautiful man. Beautiful game of chess. Beautiful talk. Beautiful music. Everything is beautiful, but what does beautiful actually mean?" More than thirty years later, Voytek wrote a poem based on his earlier reflections.

How can it be that we can speak
Of beautiful love and beautiful death?

What is that beautiful link between
The beauty of the desert and the beauty of motherhood?

Can there be a
Common measure
For the beauty of the cosmos and a beautiful dance?

And is the triumph of a beautiful life
A beautiful death?

Or is this all but a beautiful illusion?

Because they had agreed to launch their traverse of Broad Peak from the north side, which was closer to K2, Voytek and Jurek moved to the K2 base camp on July 11. And there they found a pleasant diversion: Wanda and the girls. Yes, Wanda Rutkiewicz was back with another women's team to try K2. Sadly, Voytek and Jurek couldn't linger because they had taken only enough food for the traverse and they needed to get started.

They tore themselves away and moved to the base of Broad Peak North in preparation for the climb.

The wind howled all night. By morning it was almost a hurricane. They delayed and delayed, hoping for some improvement. But by mid-afternoon it was clear they had lost an entire day. One day's food allotment consumed before starting. It wasn't a good sign.

Friday, July 13, dawned clear and cold. (Voytek often claimed that Friday the 13th was his lucky day.) They solo climbed up a "dirty gorge of a gully," threatened the entire way by a chain of ice pinnacles overhead. Breathing a little more easily upon reaching the ridge, they then wove a line through a forest of towering black gendarmes until they discovered the perfect bivouac site, a comfortable concave dip on the shoulder, close to a tiny frozen tarn. The good weather held.

On July 14 they continued solo climbing up mixed ground. "We do not touch the rope; the rope misguides you," Voytek wrote. Sometimes Voytek climbed ahead, other times Jurek. "Hooked on our own distress, we climb slowly, lonely, as though we are wandering two different ways."[34] Voytek later expressed disappointment that, when Jurek was ahead, he seemed not to care about how his partner was doing. "He rarely looked back at me. Perhaps it was only my feeling, but he seemed uninterested in me." Then he remembered his own behaviour two years earlier, when Jurek had been slower on the descent from their illegal Broad Peak climb. "It's true, I went ahead. I only waited for him down in camp," Voytek admitted. He added, "Sometimes Jurek acclimatized a bit slower, but his physical and mental stamina and motivation were unmatched. Maybe in all history."

Voytek's mood changed when he reached a strenuous chimney that required the rope – and his full attention. "What beautiful climbing," he wrote in his journal. Up and up they went. "Gorgeous, with two kilometres beneath my feet," he gushed. Only after 1000 metres of climbing did they find a suitable bivouac. He later described the scene in full poetic colour: "The sun is touching the Hispar ridge, and frost is crawling in the long shadows. But as the blue gloom thickens in the valleys, we reach a tiny snow crest. Here we dig out our nest."[35] In his diary, Voytek wrote in simpler words: "Evening time – the miracle continues. The weather is still beautiful."

With that beautiful weather came good visibility, and from their nest they could clearly see the ridge of Broad Peak Central. It looked scary. Hopeless. Unclimbable. Much worse than the pictures they had studied back in Poland. Voytek drifted off into a restless sleep, wondering where he would find the strength to face this monster, hoping that the mountain was just testing them with its frightening appearance.

On July 15, their third day on the mountain, they reached the summit of Broad Peak North at 3 p.m. It took less than an hour to descend to the col between Broad Peak North and Central at around 7278 metres. "Now we are right in the heart of the trap! There is no retreat from here. We are together, oh Mountain."[36] Even though it was early for a bivouac, the col seemed a logical place to stop. "Fantastic mountains around. On all sides, endless mountains with distant little clouds." He continued in his journal, "I do not doubt that the little clouds will be growing."

There, on the high col between two of Broad Peak's summits, Voytek had one of the most ethereal experiences of his entire career as an alpinist. He felt total confidence, trust and a sense of unity with space and light. "I remember it like a delirium – walking and walking around – I was simply unable to go into the tent. It was a fantastic experience with a rare quality. It was deeply spiritual. Of course, mountains are always beautiful, but this was different."

Voytek did not share the intensity of his experience with Jurek. By now they were so accustomed to each other that they felt no need to talk. Jurek remained in the tent, preparing water and food, while Voytek wandered around in an aesthetic trance. (To be fair, it was Jurek's turn to cook.) With each shift in the light, the mountain's features revealed deeper, more hidden shades of beauty. Stunned by its power, Voytek struggled to explain: "Beauty is some kind of laser connection to higher worlds. That is what I learned, in the middle of our traverse, between the lower and middle summits." And the best view of all was of the Broad Peak Central ridge. The pair could now see that horribly scary blade of a ridge from a different angle, and it looked – barely – possible. Enormous, but not quite as intimidating as before.

All the next day they climbed and climbed: ice, seracs, vertical rock steps, chimneys, and more steep, hard ice. Finally, they reached a long, gentle ridge. Extremely long, and all of it above 8000 metres. Each step sounded hollow in the wind-affected snow slope. Nervous about the ominous echoing sounds, they took out the rope. Up and down the ridge meandered, torturing them with its length, testing their patience. "Shame, shame gnaws for the lack of patience. The white, soulless belly rises in front of us again."[37] Suddenly Voytek could see Jurek waving his arms madly above his head as if doing battle with the wind. But no, he was on the summit of Broad Peak Central. It was 3 p.m.

By now the weather had turned. A sharp wind was depleting their bodies, penetrating deeper and deeper into their cores. As a towering bank of gloomy black clouds rolled in, they began searching for places from which to rappel down to the col. They were surrounded by a confusing maze of swirling clouds, impenetrable murk and steep, shadowy walls leaning in and leading nowhere. They searched the friable rock for any hint of solid ground for their pitons. "With cold arms I embrace a loose rock spire, then a furious gust snatches it and throws it into hell."[38] Each one of their five rappels felt insecure and shaky, as if it could be the last one. Voytek later wrote about the raw terror of the moment. "The east side opens into hell. It's wriggled into convulsive snow lines, stripped to purple ice. The icy devil is howling, carving painful and hating shapes with frost and wind."[39]

Three hours later, at 6 p.m., they reached the col, and 100 metres further, on Broad Peak Main, they found a snow platform large enough for a comfortable bivouac. Wisps of snow carried by the gusting wind filtered into their tiny Salewa inner tent. It was Voytek's turn to cook. He struggled with the stove, willing it to light. Only after hours of coaxing did it begin to hum its soothing sound and produce three victorious pots of liquid.

At 4 a.m. the following morning – their fifth on the mountain – they began cooking breakfast. Even after two pots of tea, their mouths still felt like sandpaper. Their lips cracked from the cold, and their thirst was impossible to sate. Jurek and Voytek crammed their meagre possessions into their packs, strapped on their crampons with stiff, aching hands and crawled out of the tent. They started plodding up the ridge at 7 a.m., and by 9:30 they were on the top, surprised that after five days of high-altitude climbing, the approach to the Main Summit seemed pretty easy. It was their third summit in five days. "Oh, Mountain!" Voytek sighed, savouring this instant of total fulfillment, when every expectation had been met and the world was perfect.

Moving slowly now, but over familiar terrain, they began descending the normal route. They stopped after an hour and made more tea, then continued ever downward to Camp II on the normal route. Shortly before reaching their destination, Voytek almost lost his life. While traversing above the camp, he came across an old fixed line, which he grasped for balance. It broke. He flew into the air and accelerated down. After only a few metres one of his crampons caught, allowing him to ram his ice axe into the bullet-hard ice before he catapulted off the cliff below. He righted himself and carried on.

Jurek and Voytek walked into base camp on July 18 like champions. Though weary, their young bodies were firm, and their steps had spring. The scene in camp was jubilant. Three members of the team had done the normal route on Broad Peak, and Krzysztof Wielicki, with his deceptively soft voice, his world-weary face, his large unruly moustache and his tiny energetic frame, had made a speed ascent of the mountain – up 3000 metres and down 3000 metres in 21 hours and 30 minutes. It was the fastest climb in the history of 8000-metre peaks, and the first one-day ascent. And now Voytek and Jurek had done the impossible: the complete Broad Peak Traverse, an unprecedented achievement in the history of Himalayan climbing.

The team congratulated the pair and assumed they would want to rest. But Jurek was hungry. He marched over to the cook tent and whipped up a gigantic pot of spaghetti, enough for the entire camp. Later that night, instead of retreating to the comfort of his tent, Jurek joined a post-dinner card game that lasted well into the early-morning hours. Some alcohol was consumed. Krzysztof shook his head in admiration: "Physically, he was unbreakable." Voytek could only nod in agreement.

Jurek and Voytek had both attained a level of calmness on their airy traverse, during which they were willing to embrace whatever the elements and the mountain required of them. The sediment of their lives had drifted away, leaving only clarity. They treasured the precious quality of those five and a half days of climbing the 10-kilometre-long ridge, despite Voytek's low-key retelling of their climb in a 1986 *Climbing* article. "The story of the first ascent of Broad Peak's North Ridge is simple and devoid of dramatic adventures ... after all, one can hardly acknowledge as an event the monotonous and patient plodding toward the summit over thousands of meters of rough and beloved rocks and ominous streaks of blue ice."[40] This strange account was devoid of emotion, and it did not acknowledge his luminous experience at the col.

It was eleven years before the traverse was repeated, this time by a Japanese team. The second repeat came in 2010, by a strong Basque team: 1984, 1995 and 2010 – the Broad Peak Traverse is clearly not a popular objective.

His transformative experience at the col between the North and Central summits of Broad Peak confirmed Voytek's belief that mountaineering provided him with a different state of consciousness where the world took on new colours and qualities. He carried this heightened state of awareness with him when, after days of waiting for better weather, he and Jurek moved to nearby Gasherbrum IV for their next objective – the unclimbed West Face. Many believed that the enormous, steep and technical face was impossible for a two-man team, but Voytek had convinced Jurek there was a plausible route.

Once they reached the glacier in front of Gasherbrum IV, Voytek's enthusiasm vanished. They could see nothing on the face above a 6000-metre cloud ceiling. The weather had recently been warm, with daily afternoon snow showers, so he knew the wall was plastered with snow, even though they could see very little of it. They stopped to discuss what to do. Considering the conditions, Voytek declared that it was too dangerous to enter the face. But Jurek still wanted to go, and once Jurek was convinced of something, he wouldn't give up. After all, they had the permit in their hands. Voytek smelled danger; Jurek smelled a new route. They finally agreed to abandon the idea. When it was time to leave the area, the two climbers left separately, each on his own solitary trek.

Voytek tried to provide a gentle perspective on what seemed to be a painful split: "By 1984 Jurek and I were a bit tired of each other, although we still had good relations." They had spent many days together on Broad Peak. Voytek insisted their only common interests were climbing and eating, but surely they had spoken about their dreams for the future. And by now it was clear that Jurek's ambition was to climb all fourteen of the 8000-metre peaks. Voytek didn't respect his goal. "Peak bagging is a form of emotional consumption, a sign of a mountaineer overwhelmed by a desire to collect," he wrote. "If there is such a thing as spiritual materialism, it is displayed in the urge to possess the mountains rather than to unravel and accept their mysteries."[41]

Voytek was also sure that Jurek's dream was in direct competition with Messner's plan. Years later, Voytek even challenged Reinhold on the topic. "I like the things you are doing, but I don't understand the things you are saying…You say, 'I was never in competition with others…others are in competition with me…' But also you are saying 'I, Messner, did it first!'"[42]

Voytek maintained that competition was totally distasteful to him, at least within the mountaineering context. If you had to prove you were the best, you were already lost as a human being, he insisted. The competitive aspect inherent in a "sporting" approach worried him because it seemed the inevitable precursor to suffering. Not physical suffering; he was no stranger to that. Rather, he was referring to emotional and intellectual suffering. For Voytek, submitting to ambition and ego usually led to suffering. Climbing helped free him from his self-acknowledged strong ego. But not if he was climbing to compete. "As an activity, it [mountaineering] expresses the classical opposition of the urge for self-preservation and the need to test mortality. To feel in control of one's fate spontaneously frees the spirit from mortal skin. While sensing these frontiers, a mountaineer experiences his greatest joy."[43]

Voytek was beginning to sense an unacceptable aura of danger with Jurek, who seemed willing to ignore all the warning signs and push on to force a successful outcome. "I smelled danger," Voytek said. "I smelled corpses!"

The two climbers eventually agreed to disagree: Jurek would climb 8000-metre peaks (in fact, he made two first winter ascents later that same year), and Voytek would search for interesting lines. The dream team was finished. They never climbed as a twosome again. Voytek summed it up with slashing accuracy: "Our climbing partnership was like a broken marriage; we no longer found each other attractive."

Despite his practical explanation of the reasons for the split, there was a trace of sadness in Voytek's article about the traverse in *Climbing* that may have signalled the end of their magical partnership.

In summer of 1984
I wandered with a friend

Over the desert wasteland
Which was barred by three great mountains
Here, we have just crossed them
The landscape changed
But the horizon remains equally distant.[44]

When Voytek arrived back in Islamabad, an unpleasant task awaited him. At first, he was relieved to learn that the truck was repaired. But when the owners of the truck arrived to inspect it, they doubted it would survive the journey back to Poland. Voytek would have to sell it. While it was easy to sell whisky in Pakistan, selling a truck was much harder. Particularly if not done on the black market. The formalities were endless. He finally managed a sale but with a shortfall of $2,000.

Still, together with Jurek, he had accomplished the first traverse of Broad Peak's three summits in one push. In retrospect, he realized he hadn't applied for permits for all three of them. "I never thought too seriously about the lack of permits for the other two peaks – I thought I would say it was the 'route' to the main peak. Luckily, they didn't ask us." Another couple of "illegal" summits for his collection.

Eleven years later, Voytek received a postcard from Japanese climber Toru Hattori, who had just completed the first repeat of the Broad Peak Traverse. "A Happy New Year! We had a wonderful time at Mount Broad Peak. We could feel friendship with Broad Peak. Simple climbing is wonderful because I can feel a lot of voice from God. Thank you very much for your advice again." Voytek read the card with pleasure, certain that Toru had felt a similar connection with the mountain to the one that he had experienced high on the col between the North and Central summits. Another tiny treasure to place in his virtual box of memories.

Thirty years after the Broad Peak Traverse, Kei Taniguchi expressed similar sentiments about the pleasure of days spent up high, traversing airy ridges, exploring new ground, sleeping high, eating high, relaxing into a kind of high-altitude wandering sensibility. "While fast can be important in alpinism, it's not so bad to be able to spend a little more time with a mountain you love."[45]

Climbs like the Broad Peak Traverse were fundamentally life-changing for Voytek. The psychic experiences he felt high up on those peaks distinguished themselves by their intensity. Fear and anxiety, extreme psychophysical exhaustion, despair, hunger and thirst – all these were part of the Broad Peak Traverse. Albeit mostly negative, each of those feelings opened the possibility of an opposite response. Elation. Confidence. Calmness and peace. It was as if the doors of perception were flung wide. All of this was the privilege of the high-altitude climber.

TEN

The Shining Wall

Heaven is the place where you think of nowhere else.
—Pico Iyer, *The Art of Stillness*

If there is one mountain that will forever be associated with Voytek Kurtyka, it is Gasherbrum IV. More specifically, the 2500-metre West Face. Sometimes called the Shining Wall, the West Face is split by a band of marble-like rock that shimmers in the evening light. American alpinist Michael Kennedy described it as "at once a glimpse of perfection and a daunting call to action."[46] Voytek first saw Gasherbrum IV in 1976 when he was part of the Polish K2 expedition led by Janusz Kurczab. He was enchanted by its geometrically perfect, triangular shape. Stark and elegant, it induced an insatiable desire to be high on the West Face, to explore its secrets, to touch its elusive summit.

Fourth-highest of the six-mountain Gasherbrum group, 7932-metre Gasherbrum IV is the most challenging to climb. It is a "climbers' mountain," revered more for its difficulty and beauty than its height. Just shy of the magical 8000 metres, it is sometimes overshadowed by its loftier neighbours: Gasherbrums I and II, Broad Peak and K2. But the sustained difficulties found on every side of the peak have created an aura around it; only a handful of teams have been high on the mountain, and only three teams have reached the summit. Located at the northeastern end of the Baltoro Glacier, it was ascended first in 1958 by Riccardo Cassin's Italian expedition via the Northeast Ridge. Walter Bonatti, a member of the team, described the peak as "slender, rocky and aerial."[47] He and Carlo Mauri made the final, successful summit push, and their long, complex and dangerous route remains unrepeated.

During the late 1970s and early '80s, several teams from Britain, the US and Japan attempted the mountain, some by the West Face and others by the Southwest Ridge. An American team led by Steve Swenson reached slightly higher than 7000 metres on the Northwest Ridge in 1983 – during the second of four attempts – before being stopped by deep, unstable snow. They were joined by Michael Kennedy and Mugs Stump, who attempted the West Face, alpine-style. The pair reached 6900 metres before being turned away by storms, avalanches and dwindling supplies. The following year, Werner Landry led another American team on the Northwest Ridge but turned back at a rock band on the upper ridge at around 7350 metres.

Voytek and Jurek had the unclimbed West Face firmly in their sight-lines when they wandered over to take a look in 1984. But the plan fell apart as the two discussed the climb. Some observers thought Voytek seemed overly anxious about the proposed route. Others felt Jurek was bullheaded about plowing ahead despite the marginal weather. Voytek's recollection is clear: the daily snowstorms had made the West Face un-acceptably dangerous, and his desire to climb it was outweighed by the threat of avalanches. It wasn't the right moment to attempt the West Face of Gasherbrum IV.

His caution that year did not mean he was giving up on the West Face. Not at all. He had memorized the wall, analyzed its architecture, and con-cluded that at least some of the problems could be avoided by ascending a long couloir, right of centre on the face. It provided direct and swift access to the heart of the wall. Since the couloir was an obvious funnel for ava-lanches, the conditions had to be perfect to climb it safely; 1984 was not the right year. But he could wait.

Voytek returned in 1985 with Robert Schauer, a tall, strapping man with a broad, open face and an even broader smile. Born in Graz, Austria, in 1953, the slightly younger alpinist already had an impressive climbing resumé: Pumari Chhish, Gasherbrum I, a new route on Nanga Parbat, and ascents of Everest, Makalu and Broad Peak. They initially planned to be a party of three, but due to some differences of opinion with Robert, the second Austrian, Georg Bachler, backed out at the last minute. When questioned about his choice of partner on this important climb, Voytek was clinical in his response: "I didn't know Robert, except for a fleeting meeting at Broad Peak base camp the year before. He showed a positive fascination with Gasherbrum IV, which was a convincing asset not to be ignored and the most important factor in inviting him. Besides, I needed someone who had climbed to 8000 metres, and he had excellent references. I also needed him for currency. In a way, he was a partner of convenience."

The pair reached base camp on June 9, 1985, with thirty-one loads of equipment and food, significantly more than on expeditions with Jurek. As Voytek pointed out, Robert brought a bigger budget, which meant a more comfortable camp. Robert and Voytek studied the face; it was almost free of snow because of the long dry spells earlier that season. Perhaps 1985 would be the year.

They began acclimatizing on June 14 by moving up to the cwm located left of the West Face and directly below the col on the Northwest Ridge. The following day they climbed up toward the col, the line the American team had tried the previous year. They were stopped by bad weather about one rope length below the col, so they returned to base camp, where they were pinned down for several days. But on June 28 they tried again, this time establishing a camp in the cwm. "It was hotter than India," Voytek said. They stripped down and hid under a tarp stretched across ski poles to escape the burning sun. The next day they ascended to the col at 6400 metres.

On June 30 the weather switched from oppressive sun to driving snow. They huddled at the col for two nights and then continued up on July 1, following some old fixed ropes left by the American team. As they felt their way up in the fog and snow, the wind increased to a gale. From a high point of 6700 metres, they retreated to the col and the next day (July 2) continued down the dangerous gully to their advanced base camp in the cwm and then all the way to base camp. Voytek wrote in his journal: "Descent is dangerous."

For the next four foggy days, they remained in base camp. Single-word entries from Voytek's journal indicate his frame of mind: "Uncertainty. Tiredness. Loneliness." Part of this loneliness had to do with his memories of Alex. Some of Robert's expressions, particularly his smile, reminded him of Alex, and Voytek missed him.

On July 6 the weather improved enough to leave base camp and climb the full 1600 metres to the col. The next day they pushed higher, to around 7000 metres. On June 8 they moved another 100 metres higher and deposited a small food cache, which they planned to use on their descent from the summit. But the weather broke down again, and they made a difficult retreat to the col. On July 9 their world turned sideways from the hurricane winds, so they fled to base camp. Voytek's bleak mood continued.

The weather eventually began to look promising, and since they had no access to a weather forecast, they trusted their instincts – their "nose," as Voytek described it. On July 12, at 3 p.m., they marched over to the base of the great West Face. Although their packs felt leaden with weight, they contained only their clothing, a double rope, a few pieces of climbing equipment, their sleeping bags, a bivouac sack, some food, fuel and a stove. The afternoon approach to the face took much longer than expected: four hours of trudging through deep snow. After setting up a bivouac close to the wall, they cooked until 10 p.m., and then, after only two hours of sleeping, they fired up the stove again at midnight. Deep in their own thoughts, they said little. The good weather held. In the silver, pre-dawn hours of July 13, they crossed the bergschrund at the base of the wall and entered the couloir. "It looks like hell, deeply carved with black unknown ice canyons," Voytek wrote. As dawn crept over them, they began to recognize the features of the gully that they had previously studied. They raced up, climbing unroped, each with 17 kilograms on his back.

Their first bivouac at the top of the couloir was, in retrospect, relatively restful. The following day offered them mixed terrain, as noted in Voytek's journal: "50 degrees, Grade IV, some mixed rock and ice, IV, IV, V." On the night of June 14, they reached their second bivouac site, at around 7000 metres. Because of the protruding rocks on the tiny ledge, they were unable to use the bivouac sack, so they simply spread out their sleeping bags and tried to rest in sitting positions. Although uncomfortable, it was the only possible arrangement.

Voytek took over the next day, leading five of the six pitches. They were now on the luminous Shining Wall, where the difficulties fluctuated between Grades v and vi. The undulating waves of rock reflected the light in subdued milky hues, but the wall offered few cracks into which he could place protection. Their belays were often "psychological," since both Robert and Voytek knew the pitons would never hold a fall. A distance of 40 metres between points of protection – almost a full rope length – was common. Every movement had to be calculated and precise. Up and up.

Each climber's memories of a tense situation are often starkly different, depending on the individual's perspective. Robert later wrote that he was concerned that Voytek was wasting time, obsessed with creating safe belay anchors and placing protection. Voytek remembered it differently. Although he was a careful and meticulous climber, Voytek was fully aware of the alarming yet necessary, runouts: "How beautiful, the horrifying long rope, swinging away!"[48] While he feared each successive movement up into the unknown, Voytek refused to accept retreat. He climbed higher and higher, against all reason. Each time he overcame his fear there was a momentary feeling of exhilaration and gratitude. But then another obstacle appeared. Another demon. The climb had become a kind of psychological terrorism. His journal entry at the end of the day: "Bivouac 3 at 7200…Grade vi. Horrible bivy, again on spiky rocks that require levelling their unacceptable pointed beaks with a hammer." But at least it was calm. No Karakoram wind tormented Voytek and Robert.

After an uncomfortable night on their jagged bed, the situation intensified on July 16. They climbed only five pitches on compact marble that day, advancing a mere 100 metres up the face. Robert's lead up a delicate 30-metre AO slab took three excruciating hours. The long, cold belays were as mind-numbing as the climbing was all-engrossing. Their bivouac at 7300 metres was simply a half-sitting perch on a snowy ledge. Voytek's journal entry described the worsening situation: "Disaster. Hurricane. Notorious shortage of sleep. Blowing snow. Food is finishing. Chronic shortage of sun."

The following day they managed ten pitches of climbing through mixed ground to around 7600 metres; again, the level of risk was extreme. The soft snow didn't support their weight. Under the snow was rock, but they could neither see it nor place protection in it. The climbing felt awkward and unstable, and the belays were unreliable at best. Voytek described the terrain as the "trick of high mountains. Risky and bad belays. Almost no protection. Not enough food. Not much to drink." They had been on the face for five days at this point and were running out of both supplies and strength. But the most exhausting part was the constant inner doubt they suffered as they second-guessed each decision, finding solutions to each problem and feeling momentary relief even as they sensed that another obstacle would surely soon confront them. The unknown – which had attracted them in the first place – now had to be managed by breaking it down into pieces, one step at a time, one pitch after the other.

On July 18 Robert and Voytek reached 7800 metres. They had arrived at the final slabs and snowfields leading to the summit, but by afternoon it began to snow in earnest. The snow continued throughout the night, building up around their bivouac sack and threatening to push them off their airy perch. They no longer had food, and they were out of gas. That meant they couldn't make more water. They could barely poke their heads out of the bivouac sack because of the blowing snow. They waited all the next day for the storm to break, but it persisted. The snow piled up around them at an alarming rate. Voytek wrote: "Snowstorm. Jail at 7800 metres. No food and no liquid." Retreat was out of the question, since they only had ten remaining pitons, not nearly enough to rappel down the face they had climbed. Their only option was to outlast the storm.

Sleep-deprived, hungry, thirsty, hypoxic and stressed, they drifted into a delirious state. It was at this point, in extremity, that both Robert and Voytek sensed something – an independent spirit on the mountain that, for Robert, grew more ominous and real with each snowflake. So real that they waited expectantly for some signal or action from their invisible "third man." Robert began to blame their imaginary companion for having slowed them down on the face. As avalanches surged over them, nudging them, almost burying them, Robert became convinced that the third man was trying to push him off the ledge into oblivion.

It's not unusual for an invisible person to appear in dire circumstances such as these, but in most cases the presence is helpful, giving suggestions and support and companionship. When Stephen Venables was descending Everest after having climbed the Kangshung Face, he was forced to bivouac not far below the summit. He wasn't alone, however. An imaginary old man kept him company throughout the night and on his exhausting descent the next day. Once Stephen and the old man reached the South Summit, they were met by an imaginary (and long-dead) Eric Shipton, who helped by warming Stephen's hands. There are countless high-altitude examples of these wonderfully kind, unexplainable creatures, yet Robert's third man was strangely malevolent.

Voytek, while acutely aware of their new partner, was preoccupied with carrying out odd experiments, such as pinching his thigh and wondering if the pain would disappear when he neared death. He relished the pain, for it confirmed that he was still alive. He was already imagining the distinct possibility of turning into a lifeless block of ice on the narrowing ledge slowly disappearing under drifts of snow.

Occasionally they would burrow out from one end of their bivouac sack to remove enough snow to avoid suffocation. As they shivered on their ledge, they considered their options. Again, thoughts of retreat were discussed then quickly abandoned. Going up was also out of the question in this storm. Waiting – the most agonizing option of all – remained the only feasible choice. Cold and hungry and so dreadfully thirsty, they waited. From time to time they reassured each other with little niceties.

"Are you feeling okay, Robert?"

"Oh, yes, I'm feeling fine."

Robert described it as a "fragile mood of hope."[49] Voytek recalled that he had never had so much "free time" on a climb. "We had two nights and a day up there. We just sat. We had a stove, but the gas was finished, so we had nothing to do but think." Time became warped, stretching and contracting at will. One hour was the same as one day. The darkness pushed down on them, coating their heaving lungs. It felt aggressive, as if it would swallow them.

Voytek's thoughts drifted into dangerous territory. Death was something he had often mused about in the past, and now it seemed inevitable and barely worth worrying about. What was most important to him was to be fully aware of the experience. Being completely conscious of the process of dying, particularly in this remote and savage place, would be interesting.

As he pondered his own demise, Voytek became concerned about Robert. Was he also aware of how close they were to death in this terrible place, this wonderful place? It became incredibly important to him that Robert understand what was happening – that they share this almost sacred experience. But it was a delicate topic, and Voytek struggled with his decision to speak with Robert. Finally, he could no longer hold back. He began, his voice raspy with cold and fatigue, "Robert, I...I...I'd like to..."

Robert interrupted quietly but firmly in a painful whisper, "I know what you're thinking. I'm ready. I'm prepared for this. Don't worry."

That night the sky cleared and the temperature plummeted. They shivered uncontrollably, since their wet sleeping bags offered little protection from the cold. But the shivering felt wonderful, like coming back to life. When the morning of July 20 dawned, Voytek and Robert were still alive. They bent their stiff legs, stretched out their hunched shoulders and flexed their frozen fingers and toes. "My voice was gone, my throat painful and absolutely dry," Robert explained. "I was no longer hungry, and felt nothing in my stomach but the cold."[50]

Slowly they emerged from their snowy coffin. It took their frozen fingers thirty minutes to attach their crampons. This was their eighth day on the wall, and they had brought food and fuel for five. With leaden legs and empty stomachs, they climbed up an ice runnel swept free of snow by avalanches. Voytek recalled that it was a pleasant surprise because, although he had to stop periodically, he felt almost rested and eager to move after their extended bivouac. After two pitches of climbing, they entered a concave depression containing knee-deep snow, whose upper wall reared above them like a fortress. They kept moving up.

Hours passed. Eventually they realized that their bivouac platform was disappearing far below. When they could no longer see it, they knew they were making progress.

Early in the afternoon they approached the main ridge. The slow, rhythmic punching motion through the deep snow was gratifying. Voytek described the moment. "We had a lot of time left in the day. In fact, we had infinity before us. I understood this with alarming clarity. But each step drained the scarce resources of our life force. We didn't want infinity! I was never so sure that every step upward was a step into infinity." They glanced across at what appeared to be an easy traverse to the summit. There was no need to talk. As it had been so often on this climb, and despite tremendous fatigue and mind-boggling stress, their judgment was sound. Instead of moving straight up to the summit col, which seemed so near, they turned left. They would go down, not up. Thirty years later, Voytek remembered the moment clearly. "Surprisingly, we were doing quite well at altitude. But I knew – I was positive – that we would not come back from the summit."

As soon as they began descending the Northwest Ridge, the ominous feeling that had weighed on them for days slipped away, only to be replaced by phantom creatures and brilliant mirages. Still, each downward step took enormous effort. The deep wall of snow resisted their awkward, lurching movements as they lifted their legs at impossibly odd angles, searching for some weakness in the snowpack, some little bit of softness beneath the wind-hardened drifts. Plunge-stepping down the ridge, they felt that every metre forward was a small victory.

Robert stopped and bent over his ice axe, gasping for air. When he straightened his back, his eyes refocused from the snow in front of him to the sky above. A raven hovered, effortlessly. Robert stared spellbound, willing himself to soar, imagining himself as that raven gazing down at this pitiful wreck of a man clinging to the Northwest Ridge of Gasherbrum IV. Like a miracle, Robert became the raven. "In a most intense fashion I felt every sense of flying – the wind in my face, the biting cold, the weightlessness."[51]

Voytek's brain split into two channels. On Channel One, images and sounds raced out of control. Casual acquaintances popped up, talking gibberish. Rocks and clouds resembled people and faces. Channel Two, while observing and reflecting on the activities on Channel One, was also focused on belaying, the rope, the ice axe, the descent. He knew he was on the verge of hallucination, and this condition interested him. Later, when the shapes and voices disappeared, he missed them.

Voytek was a little ahead of Robert when he sensed the return of the "third man," his presence even more real than Robert's. Voytek slumped down in the snow and looked back, calling, "Robert, I would like to tell you something, but it's very strange." Robert stopped gazing at the raven and, once again, collapsed over his axe.

"I know what you mean," he gasped. "He's here again."

"Yes."

No longer threatening, the third man filled them with confidence. They would survive this ordeal with the help of their friend. Robert's thoughts turned to food: succulent sausages and crusty dinner rolls smothered in butter. His stomach now ached with hunger, and his eyelids drooped with fatigue, but he was filled with a sense of well-being. Voytek was racked with thirst, his mouth furry and pinched and foul-tasting. He dreamed only of tea. When they reached 7600 metres on the Northwest Ridge, they stopped and bivouacked.

The following day, July 21, they continued down, intent on finding their food cache. They had not eaten one morsel or drunk one drop of liquid since July 18. Three days. Seventy-two hours. Voytek moved ahead into a slightly concave couloir. He descended about 40 metres, post-holing in the knee-deep snow, belayed by Robert from above. The snow was unstable. He felt anxious. At any moment, he would run out of rope and the belay would be finished. At that point they would need to move together down the questionable slope. Fighting exhaustion, he reversed his steps, plodding all the way back up to Robert, where he explained that this seemingly easy slope was a death trap and that a steeper but safer line among some exposed rocks lay further to the right. It's hard to imagine the self-discipline Voytek mustered to go back up at that moment, when every fibre of his body must have been screaming down, down, down.

After traversing to the right, he set up a rappel, and they safely descended the ridge. "I doubt many would do this," Voytek said laughingly, thirty years later. "For sure, not Kukuczka. He would have continued down. He believed in Jesus Christ. Not me. I decided, 'Jesus, you proved millions of times you don't care for us. I don't trust you.'" Instead, Voytek believed in his own mountain judgment.

At 6900 metres, they found their meagre, yet incredibly precious, food cache: a gas cartridge, tea, a small piece of cheese and thirty candies. Throughout the entire climb, Voytek had worried about birds attacking their simple nylon food bag and stealing its paltry contents. Relieved to find it intact, but not happy with the steep terrain, they moved down another couple of hundred metres before they stopped to light the stove and make some tea. It was now midnight. After four days without sustenance, their stomachs were incapable of handling much of anything. A few sips and a couple of candies. Their sleeping bags were wet and their packs were frozen. Voytek retained little memory of this bivouac, other than its brevity.

When they reached the col, they stopped for an hour and a half for another pot of tea and a bit more food. "Oh, how wet was the tea, how sweet were 30 candies!" Voytek wrote in his report of the climb.[52] They continued into the night, front-pointing down the couloir, half-asleep. Voytek described the night: "I remember these movements – like sleeping and moving, sleeping and moving. Half conscious." They hadn't worried about a night descent from the col, because they knew the terrain was straightforward. But after ten days of snow and sun, freezing and melting and avalanches, the slope had changed dramatically. In fact, it was no longer a "slope." It had been transformed into a series of funnels, each one deeper than the height of a person. Now using headlamps on this, their tenth day on the mountain, they struggled down. "The more tired I was, the more careful I became," Voytek remembered of the endless night. "Obsessively. Somehow I combined the calculation of exhaustion into the calculation of danger."

Manoeuvring between the funnels was complicated. At one point, they decided to pull out the rope. Now tied together, they front-pointed down through the funnels, crossing back and forth from ridge to funnel, from funnel to ridge, with no possibility of a belay. "I was afraid," Voytek recalled. "Extremely tired. And if one of us had fallen we both would have fallen. We would have been beefsteaks at the base. No, more like hamburger." When moving from funnel to funnel became too precarious, they descended into the mouth of one particularly large funnel. But that too presented additional risk, because if anything came trundling down off the mountain, the bottom of this conduit would be its path.

It finally became obvious that they should dispense with the rope. At this point it was a hazard. But who would carry it? "I didn't want to carry the whole rope, because I was exhausted," Voytek explained. "But I didn't want to give it to Robert, because he was also exhausted. So I untied. But still, I didn't want to lose my connection with the rope. If the funnel became too demanding I might need the rope, so I put it into my mouth and downclimbed with the rope in my teeth." He laughed as he described the technique as "bizarre but perfect." It eliminated the danger of pulling his partner off in case of a fall, but the rope was still loosely attached should they need to use it for an emergency rappel, which they did, several times. Robert was blissfully unaware that he was only attached to Voytek's teeth.

In this way, they moved down the slope a couple of hundred metres. But by now their fatigue was bottomless. Time after time, Voytek drifted off while waiting at a belay. He would wake up in terror, grabbing at the belay slings, certain he was falling. But he refused to stop and rest, reminding himself, "Those who sit down sleep sweetly forever." This experience convinced Voytek that dying of exhaustion would be a painless death, even pleasant.

They arrived at the cwm at 2:45 a.m. on July 23. There, they huddled together for an hour and a half for another pot of tea and some candies. Still in darkness at 5 a.m., they forced themselves to stand up and continue down. Voytek's head was swimming with sounds: twittering birds, whispering voices, music. Fascinated, he struggled to trace their origins. In most cases, he could deduce that one was from a bit of wind, another from the rustle of a piece of fabric or the hissing of moving snow. The evocative sounds provided welcome distraction from the fatigue and discomfort.

Later, the sounds became louder, more precise. A woman's voice serenading his descent was so beautiful that he stopped to listen. When he stopped, the voice stopped. Intrigued, he moved forward. It began again. It was definitely Barbra Streisand. He stopped. She stopped. Why was she toying with him? Hers was such a lovely voice and she sang such a comforting melody: "I stumble and fall / But I give you it all." While Channel One enjoyed the music, Channel Two struggled to discover the source. He finally attributed the musical serenade to the sound of the rope sliding over the rough snow surface, punctuated by his steps. That, plus his imagination, was his only explanation for the start-and-stop nature of it. He continued down Gasherbrum IV, awash in the lyrics from "Woman in Love." "Life is a moment in space / When the dream is gone / It's a lonelier place."

They reached base camp at 9 a.m. Robert was alarmed at Voytek's appearance; his face was swollen and red. Voytek brushed aside Robert's concern over what appeared to be edema, more interested in sharing his Streisand experience. What exactly had happened inside his brain up there? He finally described it as "the sounds of the human machine breaking down."[53] He was convinced there were remote corners of the brain that could only be accessed in extremity. Gasherbrum IV had opened the door to one of those secret places, and he accepted this insight as another gift from the mountain.

Voytek was profoundly disappointed that they hadn't reached the summit of Gasherbrum IV. "I really love this face," he said. "But it's not given to me to stand on the top. It's a very important sign, but I'm still too stupid to understand it." The final sentences in his *American Alpine Journal* report were heartbreaking. "Though it was the most beautiful and mysterious climb I have ever done, I feel miserable for having failed to reach the summit. I can't resist the conviction that this Beautiful Mountain and its Shining Wall are too splendid and too perfect to consider any ascent of it without its most essential point – the summit – as really completed."[54] Gasherbrum IV was the ultimate paradox: Voytek's greatest success and his biggest disappointment.

Robert, on the other hand, was strangely content. From the moment they arrived back in base camp, he was proud of their accomplishment. He was an early adopter of a more modern approach to big-wall climbing with a different set of performance indicators, where the summits were not as important as the actual walls. Australian alpinist Greg Child was equally positive about the climb, but for a different reason: "The fact that they called off the real summit after getting to the top of the face makes it a better story because it was the right decision to survive – therefore the climb was not out of control."

As time passed, Voytek's painful splinter of disappointment changed to acceptance, even gratitude. "There are times when these undertakings miss the final point and this signals human weakness, which makes them more beautiful," he said. Like Schubert's "Unfinished Symphony," the climb acquired an aura of mystery and beauty that was greater than a fully completed climb could ever attain. It was a sign to Voytek that alpinism was more an art than a sport. "Only in art does a missing link contribute to the meaning of a piece," he said. Once again, the words of Kei Taniguchi echoed his philosophy: "For a climber, if there is no artistry, no beauty in alpinism, then there is no life," she wrote.[55]

Their effort had been staggering: eleven days on the mountain, seven bivouacs around or above 7000 metres, two bivouacs at 6900 metres, two nights without sleeping, three days without food, two without water and a twenty-four-hour push to reach base camp. They had clawed their way back from the edge of the abyss. Around the world, the ascent was called the "Climb of the Century." Voytek used more-specific labels: "a great joy of creation, a perfect trap, illusory, a thorn." He questioned the overwhelming praise of the climb. "Does it make sense to declare a poem of the century? Can you choose a woman of the century? ... Did anybody repeat GIV to confirm our illusion of it?"[56] Voytek was aware of the trap of fame that this ascent offered, and he wanted, above all, to avoid it. He later articulated it in writing: "But, you know, climbing can help us or hurt us to the same degree psychologically. We can get closer to our 'starry destiny.' Or conversely, bewitched by what we've accomplished, we can slide into a cocky pride that transforms easily into arrogance."[57]

As he ruminated about having failed to reach the elusive summit, he gradually began to accept the benefits of failure and humility, for he realized they could help prepare him for the disappointments life would surely pose: weakness, sickness, loss. In the end, Voytek said that his greatest reward from the Gasherbrum IV climb was the understanding he gained about death. During those hours and days of reflection at the highest bivouac on the West Face, he managed to maintain dignity and calm while facing his mortality. This experience, he felt, prepared him for the rest of his life.

After a few days of rest at the base of Gasherbrum IV, Robert and Voytek walked over to K2. Yes, K2. (The humility part had obviously not yet kicked in.) They started up the mountain, reaching Camp 1 on the Abruzzi Ridge. Voytek explained their plan: "We were hoping this would be some bonus to Gasherbrum IV. Initially, of course, we were planning something harder, something new. But in this shape, we changed to the Abruzzi. Now I realize we were too tired. Moving too slowly." Wind, snow and sheer exhaustion turned them back on K2, a mountain for which they did not have a permit.

Robert and Voytek never climbed together again. Soon after returning home, Robert wrote a report for the climbing magazine *Der Bergsteiger*. Voytek read the piece and was disappointed with Robert's version of the story. A rift developed between the two. Sadly, the bond they had formed while peering deeply into each other's souls, preparing for their imminent death together high on Gasherbrum IV's Shining Wall, appeared too fragile to withstand the pressures of lower elevations. Years later, the estrangement softened into a cordial relationship. It seems the third man continues to watch out for them.

Ten years after Voytek and Robert's Shining Wall ascent, Slovenian alpinist Slavko Svetičič, famous for his impossibly bold solo climbs, tried to solo a route further left of their line on the West Face. He died at around 7100 metres. A couple of years later, in 1997, a Korean team sieged a route on the Central Spur of the West Face. But as mountaineering historian Lindsay Griffin wrote in *Alpinist* online in 2008, "Their [Robert and Voytek's] bold, alpine-style, two-man push remains one of the greatest climbs in the history of Himalayan/Karakoram mountaineering, and the route is unrepeated to this day."

All the mountaineering heavyweights had their say on the Gasherbrum IV climb. Reinhold Messner called it superb. Doug Scott described it as an impeccable alpine-style ascent up the most technically difficult rock and ice ever climbed at that altitude. Greg Child, who climbed Gasherbrum IV's Northwest Ridge to the summit the following year, said, "Voy and Robert's route was, and is, about the most inspirational thing I have ever absorbed about alpinism."

More than twenty-five years later, Lindsay, then president of the Alpine Club in Britain, commented again: "Intuitively, the purest [style] is alpine-style... At really high altitudes this style is perhaps still best exemplified by the 1985 ascent of the West Face of Gasherbrum IV."[58]

Slovenian alpinist Andrej Štremfelj made some interesting observations about the psychological elements of the climb.

> A consistent characteristic of daring alpine-style ascents is an intense psychological pressure that exhausts the climber completely. After such an ascent, climbers are often not capable of performing an ascent of that difficulty again for several years, or perhaps ever. The most beautiful example of such a daring ascent is that of Robert Schauer and Voytek Kurtyka on the west face of Gasherbrum IV in 1985. This jewel among alpine-style ascents was carried out ahead of its time... To contemporary climbers, such a demanding ascent represents an obstacle rather than encouragement, as there is little chance of anybody exceeding it.[59]

Raphael Slawinski, a highly respected Canadian alpinist of the next generation, understood this dilemma when he wrote, "And arguably no alpine-style ascent has surpassed the commitment of Voytek Kurtyka's and Robert Schauer's first ascent of the Shining Wall of Gasherbrum IV... So where do we go after a climber of Kurtyka's calibre has pushed the alpine envelope?"[60] Erhard Loretan simply declared, "When he descended from Gasherbrum IV, Voytek had become a living legend. That is the outcome that mortals reserve for those who have cheated death."[61]

The deep, universal respect for their still-unrepeated climb is based on both the physical and psychological challenges they overcame. One of the boldest achievements ever in the Greater Ranges, it included great technical difficulty, enormous uncertainty, commitment, and formidable length. Voytek eventually understood and accepted this assessment of the climb, but his initial motivation for tackling Gasherbrum IV's West Face was, as usual, rooted in aesthetics. The architecture of the mountain mesmerized him. The mystery of the face lured him. The elegance of the line of ascent pleased him. Every move, every problem, every solution on that long, involved wall was an act of creation. His decision to climb alpine-style was a foregone conclusion because only alpine style could offer him the ultimate creative relationship with the mountain. "When we entrust our faith to an absurdly beautiful mountain, we are being true to our vocation," he wrote. "This is why I find climbing to be one of the most encouraging and exhilarating efforts of my life. This is the drug of mountaineering – the liberation."[62] On the West Face of Gasherbrum IV, his liberation was boundless.

ELEVEN

Fork in the Road

He who is in pursuit of a goal will remain empty once he has attained it. But he who has found the way will always carry the goal within him.

—Nejc Zaplotnik, *Pot (The Path)*

As an alpinist, Voytek was at the top of his game. But his personal life was unravelling. At some level, he understood that his behaviour was unacceptable. "Alpinism necessitates some selfishness and egotistical behaviour... A possessed alpinist is a reprobate, a poor wretch, condemning himself and those around him to loneliness and pain. And yet climbing forms a connection with the mountains that stirs feelings of love in us."[63] Perhaps, but not within his marriage. After thirteen years, Ewa and Voytek agreed that it was over. "I moved out of her apartment without a fuss one cold January morning, taking the bed, a dresser and my library to the upper level of a stand-alone house on the outskirts of the Balice airport."[64] At least he was closer to the airport. That would make it easier to return to the mountains.

Although now officially single, and so a completely focused climber, Voytek found 1986 to be a trying year. Early in the year, he failed on an attempt of the East Face of Trango Tower with three Japanese climbers. But at least they all returned safely. That was not the case for many expeditions. Wanda Rutkiewicz became the first woman to climb K2 that year, but two of her three partners, Liliane and Maurice Barrard, died on the descent. Another Polish climber, Janusz Majer, led a team up a new route on K2 called the *Magic Line*, but one of the climbers, Wojciech Wróż, fell to his death on the descent. Polish alpinist Mrówka Miodowicz-Wolf also died while descending K2, and though Jurek succeeded in putting up an astonishing – and still unrepeated – new route on the South Face of that mountain, his partner, Tadek Piotrowski, fell to his death, also on the descent. It was not a good year for Polish high-altitude climbers.

While Jurek continued to collect 8000-metre peaks, Voytek was sticking to his philosophy of new routes, small teams and, without question, alpine style. But despite their divergent directions, their paths kept leading to the Himalaya. It was inevitable that they would encounter each other again.

When Jurek returned to Poland after his tragic K2 climb, a young Himalayan climber, Artur Hajzer, came to the Warsaw airport to meet him. For years, Voytek had been Jurek's preferred partner. But when the partnership faltered, Jurek, like Voytek, had moved from one climber to another, adapting to whatever situation arose. Jurek sensed a close bond with Artur, despite the fourteen-year age difference. Artur was now as active in the Himalaya as Jurek, undertaking two or three expeditions per year.

Their airport reunion was muted. Artur didn't interrogate Jurek about Tadek's fatal fall, and Jurek offered not one word about the tragedy. Artur recalled that he seemed numb, focused only on the next trip. As Artur nosed the car onto the highway heading south toward Katowice, Jurek broke the silence. "How are the preparations for Manaslu?"

A little taken aback, Artur answered, "Good. Everything's good."

Jurek nodded, staring straight ahead. "Are the barrels packed?"

"Yes," Artur replied – even though they weren't, completely. "We leave in three weeks."

Jurek was quiet for a bit and then nodded. "Good. I'll be ready."

Voytek had been looking for a fall expedition to the Himalaya that year, so when Jurek suggested he join them on Manaslu, he agreed. Despite their differences and their painful separation in 1984, Voytek missed Jurek. "I was attracted to him by my old sentiments. I valued the 'brotherhood in arms' we had shared in the past. I liked his silent perseverance and courage, and I missed his quiet company in the mountains," Voytek said. "I regretted that our ways had diverged. My going to Manaslu with

Jurek was an echo of this regret. His invitation renewed my faith that a true bond still connected us." With them were Artur Hajzer and Carlos Carsolio, a young Mexican alpinist who was gaining an impressive reputation in the Himalaya. Carlos had been invited because of his talent and, at least in part, for the foreign currency he was bringing to the table. Having a foreigner along was like "winning the lottery" for Polish climbers, Artur explained. He and Carlos were the students on this climb, under the tutelage of Voytek and Jurek.

As close as Artur felt to Jurek, he was equally wary of Voytek. The two had never connected, and Artur felt intimidated by Voytek's cool glamour. He recalled their first meeting at the Polish Embassy in Delhi.

> All the stars of Polish Alpinism were there…The meetings with the great ones were very official in character. This was especially true with Voytek Kurtyka, who built around himself a bit of a wall that was impossible to break through…He had a lean face, dark glasses, a Walkman and a whole slew of the beautiful sex who kept him in his own sphere. Visually, acoustically and physically. Whole days without a word, stuck to his beach chair, surrounding the bathing area, listening to his favourite jazz musician, Keith Jarrett, and his Köln concert recording and sunbathing his obviously beautiful body… This is the image of Voytek that I had for the next few years.[65]

Not a particularly reassuring or supportive impression of a partner on a Himalayan climb.

The team set its sights on a new route on the Northeast Face of the main peak of Manaslu, as well as an "unofficial" ascent of Manaslu East. At almost 8000 metres, this slender pinnacle was Nepal's highest untouched summit. For Jurek, Manaslu was the first of two 8000ers planned for that autumn; the second was Annapurna. He was on his twelfth of the fourteen 8000ers, and the clock was ticking because he was only a hair's breadth behind Messner in the race they both denied. Messner had reason to be nervous; as he freely admitted, Polish climbers – and Jurek in particular – were "hungry, and very, very strong." Still, the Italian's lead widened when word arrived in base camp that he had climbed Makalu, his second-last of the 8000ers. Only one to go for Messner.

Rather than discouraging Jurek, this news only spurred him on. He walked out of the mess tent for a few moments of privacy, then strutted back in and announced that it was time to head up. Time to climb this mountain!

Jurek's enthusiasm wasn't shared by Voytek. The preceding weeks of warm, wet weather had loaded the slopes with tons of unstable snow, poised to avalanche at the smallest trigger. The weather had cleared, but the route was obviously still dangerous. Carlos watched the discussions, unable to participate since they were in Polish. "They all sounded like arguments to me," he laughed.

During the approach march to Manaslu, he had begun to get to know Voytek. "We had a lot of time to talk – deep conversations about culture and technique and philosophy," Carlos later said. But despite his growing bond with Voytek, Carlos was closer to Jurek. They had climbed together on Nanga Parbat and had learned to appreciate each other's toughness and determination; they had demonstrated to one another a shared ability to suffer.

Carlos watched them both, closely. "They were idols to me," he said. He was awed by these elders of the Himalaya, and he trusted them implicitly. He could learn so much. "Voytek and Jurek seemed to have a good relationship," he said, years later. "Even though they were very different. Jurek was quiet and had strong opinions, like Šrauf [the famous Slovenian alpinist Stane Belak]. Voytek was more flexible, with a much broader knowledge about life. He was more diplomatic." Carlos noticed other differences too. "Voytek was extremely fit at the time. Jurek was already a bit heavy, but so strong." Carlos thought Voytek had a better sense of humour than Jurek. "He accepted jokes from us young guys. Hajzer was sarcastic, and Voytek accepted this style of humour. Jurek wasn't so happy with Artur's jokes."

When the discussions and joking finally ended, they agreed to start up the mountain. It was clear from the first moment that the avalanche hazard remained high, and at around 6000 metres they watched several avalanches slide down from all sides of the ridge they were on. All except the central slope, rising above the ridge – the one they were about to enter. "It was loaded with millions of tons of ominously sparkling snow, silently waiting in the hot sun," Voytek recalled. "It was like a Russian-roulette gun pointed at the brain, but with a little difference, since it was loaded with not one but three bullets."

"Stop," Voytek yelled. "I'm not going on. It's too dangerous. I'm going back."

"Voytek, we have accepted the risk from the word go," Jurek yelled down with annoyance. "We knew it would be like this."

They huddled to discuss the situation. A heavily laden, 200-metre-high snowfield rose above them; if they could climb this slope without triggering an avalanche, they would reach a potentially safer section of the ridge. But Jurek and Voytek disagreed on the level of risk. Carlos recalled the discussion: "I was only twenty-four years of age. Voytek and Jurek were about fifteen years older. It was a case of old masters and young kittens. And we were treated like that. They made all the decisions." Frustrated with the argument, Jurek suggested a vote.

"I'm going down," Voytek announced. "This is senseless. I'll do you a favour if you want to continue: I'll manage the descent alone. Don't worry. The ridge is marked with our trail and it's safe," he said, his voice flat and final. One vote for down.

Artur chimed in, "I'm the youngest here. It's true the risk is high. Fuck it – if I knew which side of the ridge I was going to fall off, I wouldn't mind going up, but since I don't know which side will be avalanching down, this is fucking hard for me." Artur opted to continue up.

One vote for up, one vote for down.

Everyone knew Jurek would vote for up, so that made two for up, one for down. All eyes turned to Carlos. The air bristled with tension. Carlos agreed with Voytek that the risk was very high, but in a serious and measured voice he said, "As Mexico's economy is deteriorating rapidly, it is my firm belief this is going to be my last expedition to the Himalaya. For that reason, I'm going on and I'll do everything in my power to get to that summit."[66] Despite the gravity of the situation, everyone broke out laughing.

They needed to regroup, so they headed down to base camp. Voytek was sullen, upset with Jurek because he felt he was being unreasonable and reckless, endangering not just himself but his partners as well. But Voytek's emotional turmoil was not only focused on rashness: he could feel his affection for Jurek transforming into something else entirely – disdain.

"I began to visualize Jurek's great 'heroic' climbs, and the images that raced through my mind were littered with death: Skorupa dying just beyond Jurek's outstretched hand, Tadek falling to his death after their insane push to the summit of K2 after three lethal nights above 8000 metres, Czok dying just 100 metres below the camp from which Jurek started for the summit of Kangchenjunga, and his seeming indifference to the death of Piotr Kalmus on Nanga Parbat. These actions were revolting to me," Voytek said. "The danger on the ridge of Manaslu only triggered this mental process." The silence between them was as vast and cold as the Arctic.

"We could feel the tension between the two masters," Carlos said. "We had been there a long time. Our money was gone and our food was almost gone. The ambience was not good. It was snowing. Finally, after a day or two, Voytek left quickly, agile as a cat. There was no fight. He just left."

After a few more attempts, Jurek, Artur and Carlos were back on the East Ridge of Manaslu. The sheer arête was loaded with a dangerous wind slab, identical to the one Voytek had railed against. Carlos, the outsider, sat on his rucksack and listened as Jurek and Artur discussed the situation in Polish. He wondered what they were saying. "I couldn't understand and I couldn't contribute," he said. "It was a long discussion with a lot of arm movements."

Suddenly, Carlos stood up and started speaking. "I had this crazy idea – one of the craziest ideas of my life." His brainwave was beyond crazy; it was almost suicidal. He suggested that one of them move out onto the dangerous snow slope to trigger a slide. The avalanche would be intentional, but the climber who triggered it would be securely belayed from the other side of the ridge, which, in theory, would be safe from sliding. "I thought, we could do that, pitch after pitch." Jurek and Artur agreed that it might work.

"Carlos, you go first," suggested Jurek.

Carlos tiptoed out onto the slope. A wind-hardened slab lay on the surface. Underneath was a metre of soft snow. And under that layer of unconsolidated fluff was rock-hard ice. Carlos minced his way across in complete silence, trembling with fright. "Artur was belaying me. Jurek was silent, looking awfully serious. We knew we were doing something crazy," recalled Carlos, laughing. After 10 metres, there was a sudden crack and the slope broke. "I fell with the avalanche," Carlos said. "It was heavy. But

I was belayed, and I swung away from the falling debris. I was hanging free on the sliding surface, and I was okay. It was a desperate technique, but we were happy as children because we had gotten away with it." With a nervous laugh, he scrambled back to the ridge.

Now that the avalanche hazard had lessened, at least in the immediate area, Jurek continued leading up the ridge. But eventually they reached another section of the route holding tons of undisturbed snow. This time it was Artur's turn. Another tentative foray across the face, more ominous silence, a terrifying crack, another avalanche, a frightening pendulum into space, and a frantic scramble back to the ridge. On the third attempt, an even bigger avalanche let loose, cleaving the entire face. "We finally realized it was now too dangerous, so we retreated," Carlos said. "We had a lot of respect for the mountain, and we felt we had done something disrespectful." This was what Voytek had objected to when he insisted on going down. He couldn't agree to this Russian-roulette approach to avalanche danger. He knew that if you played the game too often, the bullet would eventually find its mark.

Voytek was profoundly disappointed, for even though he found little or no value in Jurek's obsession with collecting 8000-metre summits, he had looked forward to his company. "It seemed strange, but I still wished him success in the game that I considered so poisonous," Voytek said. "I simply believed that as long as we were just two ascending beasts connected by the rope, I could ignore his involvement in the transformation of the climbing art into a vanity fair. I thought that my emotional ties with him were stronger than the ideas that separated us. The heart is not a servant."

But he was wrong. The gap between their approaches to the mountains had widened to an unacceptable chasm. When Voytek left base camp, he sensed this was the final split with Jurek. "We could all feel it," Carlos said. "Artur and I didn't say anything, but we knew it was serious. Jurek was angry, but the way he handled it was to turn to the ridge and say, 'Let's climb it.'" Carlos understood that the two masters' differences had contributed to their previous unmatched success as a team. "Jurek had this strong connection to suffering," he explained. "Voytek was tough, but he was different. He had the toughness of an artist – more rational. Jurek was more animal-like. More instinctive. Voytek was methodical and technical. He was elegant. Even his rucksack was elegantly packed," he laughed.

"Every step was elegant. Jurek, not so much." He added, "Voytek was willing to turn back." Then sadly, "Jurek, not so much."

Voytek's Dhaulagiri partner, Ludwik Wilczyński, termed his willingness to turn back "a quick evacuation," and he analyzed Voytek's ability to withdraw.

> Regrettably, what usually accompanies a mountaineer's life is a gradual dulling of sensitivity to all types of risks, combined with a subjective sense of immortality. "An airy route is no big deal," "a horror is always welcome" are frequent and pride-driven statements. It is somehow comparable to increased tolerance for alcohol on one's way to alcoholism. It helps to break sport-specific barriers, but often results in going beyond the barrier of life and death. The prominent spiritual component of alpinism promoted by Kurtyka is in fact about safeguarding one's natural sensitivity, a part of which is also the fear of losing the most precious gift, life.[67]

Ludwik, one of the few survivors from that generation of Polish climbers, understood and appreciated that Voytek's retreats were what had saved his life – and the lives of his partners – on several occasions. Canadian alpinist Barry Blanchard, who has executed his own fair share of retreats, agreed in full. "I consider going down as succeeding in the covenant with those who created the game."[68]

Many mountaineers, including Voytek, speculated about Jurek's refusal to turn back on a climb. It was common then for expeditions from Western European countries to arrive in the Himalaya with excellent equipment and superb training, but climbers like Jurek were the ones who stayed on and on, often outperforming their Western counterparts. Of course, not without cost. There were the abandoned families back home, the injuries and frostbite, and the ever-increasing death toll.

Some attributed the seemingly unique Polish toughness to a deep sense of inferiority. But Voytek scoffed at this theory. He even dismissed the idea that Polish climbers had inferior equipment, acknowledging that although Polish gear might have been poor in the 1970s and early '80s, he and his fellow climbers had equal access to good equipment by the mid-1980s. "In fact, I consider my lightweight set of equipment better for alpine-style climbing in the Himalaya than anyone's," he said. "Sometimes I was annoyed with Western climbers, who seemed to be missing a sense of lightness." Voytek remembered that, of his partners, only Alex had the same desire for weightlessness on his climbs.

Another theory about Polish persistence in the mountains stems from Poland's history: so many wars, so much occupation, so much poverty. Coming from a disadvantage, Polish climbers tried harder to prove themselves in the international sphere. Voytek doubted this was the case with Jurek, saying that climbers from Poland also carried a tremendous sense of pride, stemming from all those centuries of oppression, of "living between the hammer and the anvil" of Germany and Russia. Polish alpinists, including Jurek, had a heightened sense of persistence, courage and strength, he insisted.

Another possible theory for Jurek's refusal to retreat was his mindset, similar to that of the samurai: if a man is overpowered by another human being or even nature, a force stronger than him must exist, resulting in a tragic loss of dignity and honour. Voytek knew this mindset could lead to bushido ("path of the sword"), an ancient Japanese tradition that grew out of the feudal system and that required unwavering loyalty on the part of the vassal. It borrowed heavily from Zen Buddhism and Confucianism. In its fullest expression, bushido demanded loyalty, self-sacrifice, indifference to pain, even martyrdom. This code of conduct is similar to the Polish tradition of the knight's honour, which Voytek felt matched Jurek's way of being; his code of honour didn't allow retreat. "And that attitude was, I'm 100 per cent sure, responsible for the eventual tragedy of Jurek," Voytek said. "Jurek hardly ever failed, and when he did, it shook him to his core. Deeply religious, he would demand of his God, 'Why did you do this to me? I never did anything wrong in my life. I followed your way. I didn't deserve it. Why? Why?'"

Voytek also believed there was something else at work with Jurek. "It's true that Jurek was exceptionally bold, and some of that was possibly due to a deep sense of duty to the Polish tradition of bravery," Voytek said. "But there was another reason for Jurek to blindly push on; he lacked a certain sensitivity and imagination. This lack of imagination enabled him to go blindly into danger, because he simply didn't perceive that danger. He didn't notice people dying around him. Neither death nor extremely obvious signs of danger evoked in his brain the acknowledgement of that danger or an understanding of what might happen." Voytek struggled to articulate his thoughts about his former partner with both detachment and empathy. Finally, he summed it up with "Jurek was a concoction of superior obligation to bravery and a severe lack of sensitivity."

He remembered the lack of sensitivity shown when Jurek had suggested leaving him alone with just one crampon and no rope at 7200 metres on Gasherbrum I. He recalled Jurek's insistence on entering the West Face of Gasherbrum IV, despite it being completely enveloped in cloud and washed daily with snow showers. There were striking similarities to Manaslu, when he refused to acknowledge the avalanche danger. "In the past, I had managed to curb his insane urges and could forgive his insensitivity," Voytek said. "We never suffered even a minor scratch. Now things had changed. When we stopped climbing together, his unrestrained zeal went wild. In just two years he lost three of his partners, yet he seemed unaffected by this horrible record. He seemed almost unaware of the death of his partners. I was now much less disposed to forgiveness."

But Voytek didn't speak to Jurek about any of this. "Today, I consider it a mistake that before my departure from Manaslu base camp I didn't talk to Jurek about how seriously I connected his actions to this tragic history," Voytek later said. The moment passed and the conversation never took place.

Voytek never climbed with Jurek again. It was a sad but probably inevitable ending to an unprecedented Himalayan partnership. Jurek carried on to finish his 8000-metre collection, primarily with his protege, Artur. And Voytek looked further afield for partners who were equally motivated by beauty, difficulty, style and freedom. "My propensity for falling in love with certain mountains was alien to Jurek, particularly as some of the objects of my love were less than 8000 metres," he explained. "Nor did he share my fascination with technical difficulties – rather he shunned them. His passion was surviving in the death zone, at the highest altitude."[69]

Two of Voytek's new partners were Swiss alpinists Jean Troillet and Erhard Loretan. They were at the cutting edge of lightning-fast ascents of Himalayan peaks, often by the most direct lines. Together, the three planned an incredibly ambitious objective for 1987: the daunting West Face of K2. When Erhard dropped out because of a back injury, Jean and

Voytek decided to try it as a team of two. They devoted fifty-six days to their effort, but bad weather kept them in base camp for all but three days. Greg Child was at K2 that summer, too, equally frustrated with the weeks of screaming winds. He laughingly described Jean and Voytek as the "odd couple" at base camp. Jean with his bear-like shape and Voytek, eternally thin as a reed.

One evening, Greg wandered over to Voytek's tent, which glowed from the light of a single candle. Rather than fuming about the bad weather, Voytek was immersed in a French text, trying to learn the language. He seemed to savour the solitude and inactivity. Good weather, good conditions and good climbing were wonderful, but they left little time to enjoy the peace and contentment of a quiet evening alone in one's tent at the base of a beautiful mountain. By now, after many weeks spent in base camp, listening to the rain pelting down on the roof of the tent, to the snow hissing across the tent poles and to the wind buffeting the tarp, Voytek had learned to appreciate the small, exquisite examples of beauty around him.

Another benefit of bad weather was that idle time offered a chance for friendship and companionship, which, with Jean, often meant laughter. Jean had a face that inspired laughter; it was as if he were always on the verge of telling a joke or enjoying one. His smile split his face in two.

Voytek related the details of one of their fifty-six evenings spent at base camp. It was a peaceful night, the two of them enjoying a pot of tea and chatting about inconsequential topics. At one point, Jean crawled out of the tent, walked a respectable distance away, sighed a contented sigh and began to pee. Lazy snowflakes floated down from the perpetually overcast sky, tickling Jean's eyelids and lips. He continued peeing. Distant avalanches growled, but without threat. Still more peeing. Voytek was watching closely now. "Jean's sighs grew louder and louder as he peed, and finally they seemed to express a pleasure close to bliss." Voytek wondered what might be going on, speculated on a couple of options and concluded, "Well, it's a hard life we have up here, so why not enjoy small pleasures?"

Jean continued peeing. "But, what the devil, something's wrong," Voytek remembered thinking. "He has been peeing for two or three minutes already. Nobody can pee for so long! This is physically impossible!" Jean's sighs grew even louder, drowning out the sounds of the distant avalanches while the fog closed in. As Voytek stared intently at Jean's back, Jean suddenly turned around with a roguish grin on his face. Giggling, he held out a rubber water bottle, which he had hidden under his down jacket. The mystery was solved. "The ability to derive inspiration from failure is a rare gift," Voytek said. "I learned a bit of it in the company of Jean. Now it helps a lot. Thank you, Jean."

After the K2 West Face attempt, Voytek was painfully aware that sticking to his ethos of lightweight style and difficult new routes meant failure was always a distinct possibility. He was also learning that the disquieting choice between a safe defeat and a hazardous victory was a good battle, one worth fighting. The solution to the battle was to stick to his "path" – that place without rules or routines, where the only advice comes from deep inside.

Regardless of success or failure, Voytek returned from each climbing adventure with a new perspective on everyday life. "The mountains worked like some kind of giant broom that swept away all the junk, all the trivialities, all the burdens I took with me from my neurotic daily life. I came back from these mountains an immaculate and clean person." He became more receptive to the beauty of life and of the world surrounding him. He learned to be more accepting of life's realities: growing weaker, older, sick. He was struck by something Slovenian climber Tomaž Humar said: "I carry out a climb for my soul. Every climb is a story in itself. You come back changed from each one. Your consciousness grows; this is the most important thing. And if you enjoy each journey, then all the rest is superfluous."[70]

Voytek also understood that this feeling of enlightenment was ephemeral. Eventually he needed another adventure to cleanse himself and to repair his spiritual delamination. He struggled to find this catharsis in other activities: gardening, love, nature. But ultimately, at least for a time, it was climbing, and the force and power he sensed in the mountains, which created an almost mystical or spiritual experience for him. Through climbing he could discover the most profound truths about himself. Who he was, what he was. What was most important in his life.

Many of his ideas originated in the philosophical and religious traditions of the East. He felt a particularly strong affinity to Japanese culture and often referred to the Japanese "Middle Path" and the "Samurai Way."

Both require extreme discipline and concentration, as well as physical and mental perfection. Both deal with the problem of facing death on a mountain. Both articulate equally vague purposes: goodness over evil; positive ethics. And both stress the importance of physical movement. "The best way to feed your spirit is to feed your body," Voytek claimed. "Physical exertion is the best food for your spirit and your brain."

In his essay "The Path of the Mountain," Voytek explained how "the path" represents a way of living that is determined not only by a code of ethics but also by a system of practical considerations such as diet, meditation and breathing. By observing these guidelines, one could follow the path to a higher state of enlightenment. Mountaineering was the path that led to Voytek's physical and spiritual growth, opening the door to his self-actualization.

TWELVE

Trango Tower

I love to draw beautiful lines as simply and silently as possible…
—Kei Taniguchi, "Being with the Mountain"

Of all his Himalayan climbs, Trango Tower was the one Voytek chose most purely for aesthetic reasons. It wasn't terribly high. It wasn't exceptionally famous. But it was oh, so beautiful. That gleaming shaft of golden rock; those parallel lines of enticing cracks; the mysterious shadows on the face, hiding who knows what? The refreshing splashes of white, suggesting possible bivouac sites. Trango was undeniably beautiful.

The elegant spire is one of a group of granite peaks located on the north side of the Baltoro Glacier in Pakistan's Karakoram region. While not the highest in the group, Trango Tower (sometimes called Nameless Tower) soars to 6239 metres and was first climbed in 1976 by a British team. That was the year Voytek first saw the mountain, on his way to K2. He remembers meeting British alpinist Martin Boysen and legendary rock climber Joe Brown, who were on their way back from making the first ascent of the tower. But it was later, when he was returning from Gasherbrums I and II with Jurek in 1983 and was camped on the Dunge Glacier, that the Trango Tower captured him completely: "Oof, what an impression. When the first sun is catching it like a flame in the sky. You can only approach it and beg that you might just get near it." Voytek was hopelessly drawn to that monolithic pillar piercing the sky like a samurai sword, and he knew he would return.

It takes little more than a casual glance at the tower to grasp the seriousness of climbing it: steep on all sides, guarded by ice, threatened by rockfall and Karakoram storms, and slender as a needle. As Boysen wrote in *Mountain*: "This fabulous and freakish rock tower throws out a challenge so obvious that every expedition travelling up the Baltoro must have been tempted to ditch its snow slog and have a go."[71]

Nine years later, when Voytek and Robert Schauer were at K2 base camp, hoping for a quick trip up the mountain after having climbed the West Face of Gasherbrum IV, they met a Japanese team that included acclaimed alpinists Noboru Yamada and Kenji Yoshida. Voytek and Robert enjoyed frequent visits to the Japanese mess tent, where the cuisine was exotic and the sake flowed freely. Voytek was surprised at their formal manners. "Whenever a climber would enter the tent, he would almost bow to the leader," he explained. "Even here, in this space of ultimate freedom and truth, they preserved the functionality of the powerful structure that ruled their human relations."

One night he and Robert reciprocated the Japanese hospitality by hosting a party at their camp, Polish-style. "It was a huge drinking party," Voytek laughed. "They were crazy about alcohol and Polish ham. Mashed potatoes and *golonka* [pork knuckles], with some onion, salt and a bit of sugar. It was fantastic." When Voytek suggested a Polish–Japanese attempt on Trango Tower for 1986, Noboru and Kenji said yes.

But despite his best efforts, Voytek couldn't find a single Polish climber interested in this bold project, so he appealed to the Japanese to bring one more team member. They suggested Kasuhiro Saito. All were experienced Himalayan climbers with solid reputations. It looked promising.

Voytek should have guessed something was amiss when they first arrived at the mountain. His Japanese partners announced that the best place for their base camp was on a flat, sandy site at the bottom of a large moraine. Voytek protested. "I told them, 'Friends, this is a dangerous place because rocks could come down the gully and kill us.'" They listened politely to Voytek's concerns and then, just as politely, said no. Voytek was confused. There had been no discussion. No consultation. But it was obvious they were about to set up camp in a lethal bowling alley. Freshly broken debris was scattered everywhere. And if an avalanche let loose they were in the direct line of fire.

Voytek understood the Japanese tradition of "saving face," so he didn't push back. They set up the camp. As the evening sun dipped out of sight and their camp slipped into darkness, the sky turned the colour of a fading bruise and the tip of the tower lit up with a soft rosy glow. He forgot all about the location of the camp and basked in the beauty of Trango. But later that evening, after crawling into his tent, he wondered how this dubious decision could have been made by three such experienced alpinists. Perhaps they were more accustomed to large expeditions where decisions were made by the leader – no questions asked. Now they were in a different, more democratic situation where leadership was replaced by partnership. He drifted off into a restless sleep.

The next night brought driving rain and wet, slushy snow. By morning, their flat tent sites were awash in flowing water. Their sleeping pads were soaked, their sleeping bags useless, and their clothing – everything, actually – perfectly saturated. Quietly, and again without any discussion, they relocated the camp to the top of the moraine. Voytek said nothing as he spread his clothing and equipment on rocks and suspended his sleeping bag on slings to dry.

On June 8 they carried 100 kilograms of food and equipment up to 5200 metres at the base of the tower. Over the next two days Voytek led up five pitches, graded VI, A2. He and Yamada reached a ledge where they could set up their first bivouac on the wall. By June 20 they had transported all the food and gear up to their bivouac and were poised for the next part of the tower. The Japanese led for the first two days. Then it was Voytek's turn. He was just finishing a fine pitch and was scanning the terrain above, looking for a possible line, when he heard voices from below.

"Voytek, come down. You must come down now."

"Why? There is no problem. It's good. The rock is good. I can see the way."

"No. This situation is too demanding for us. We are not ready to deal with all of this. We must retreat."

Voytek was stunned. Surely they were joking. Perhaps someone was sick. They were just getting started, and the route looked magnificent. The rock was gorgeous, with splitter cracks. Confused, he slid down the lines to the bivouac site to confront his partners. The tension was palpable as he marched over.

"I don't understand. What is the problem? Am I climbing too slowly? You have to understand; this is difficult climbing so it will be slow. But it's exactly as I envisioned it. It's perfect. This is a perfect pillar."

"No," Noboru said. "You don't understand. We don't believe we can do this climb. It's too hard for us." Voytek shook his head in amazement. Noboru, of all people. He was the best high-altitude climber in Japan. He had already climbed K2 and Everest without supplemental oxygen. What Voytek didn't know was that, while Noboru was a brilliant high-altitude mountaineer, he was not as comfortable on rock. And Trango Tower was primarily a rock climb.

Desperate now, Voytek tried another approach. "Okay, I understand if you don't all want to do this climb. But Kenji, you are a good rock climber. Why don't we continue? I'm sure we can do it."

"No, Voytek," Kenji replied. He took some time to explain to Voytek the concept of a team, and the loyalty of each member. "We are a team. You know our mentality. We came as a team of four, and I can't break the team. These are the rules. I'm sorry."

Voytek realized it was hopeless. By midnight they were back at base camp, where, strangely, the atmosphere cleared and the tension dissipated. They joked with each other and ate a good meal. There was no anger. It was as if nothing had happened and they were merely taking a couple of rest days.

Voytek later began his official report of the climb in the *American Alpine Journal* with a surprising statement: "Still today I don't know what happened on the Trango Towers. The weather was splendid, we had more food than we could eat, and the tower was enthralling." Voytek admitted that he had been eager to get close to these Japanese climbers, to dismantle their formal structure and to transform them into true and spontaneous friends. With time, he understood that his hope had been too ambitious. "I came back to the plains with two loves greater than before…" he wrote. "Trango, and the Japanese. Defeats are good."[72] He felt his defeat on Trango had a lot to do with his failure to function well with the Japanese climbers and to fully understand them. "Believe me, my love of the Japanese is still with me," he said. "If somebody asks me about my greatest failure in the mountains, I would say it was my inability to establish a lasting relationship with those Japanese guys."

But Voytek still wanted to climb the tower. His search for partners in Poland was futile, in part because by the latter half of the 1980s, there were far fewer Polish alpinists to choose from. He later reflected on the sad situation in his essay "The Polish Syndrome."

> Following the recent tragic years, Polish Himalayan climbing has died down. Horrifyingly, the majority of inspired climbers who devoted their lives to the mountains, have been killed. Many of them, like Heinrich, Chrobak, Piotrowski, Rutkiewicz, Wróż, died around the age of fifty, after following for years the voice they could not resist. If only one could be certain it is the voice of truth and not illusion! My head is full of wandering, fearful dreams of mountains and I feel caught in a trap. Almost physically I sense in Poland the subsiding of the great mountain inspiration. I believe it is being replaced by the onerous awareness of a new era and the necessity of meeting its demands.[73]

Two years later he was back at Trango Tower – this time, with a partner from Switzerland.

Born in 1959, Erhard Loretan trained as a cabinetmaker and worked as a mountain guide. By the time Voytek teamed up with him, he was already a legend in the Himalaya: nine 8000-metre peaks, including a lightning-fast ascent (and descent) of Everest with Jean Troillet in forty-three hours. Erhard was a tiny human being, light and lean. He sported an impressive, bushy head of hair, an even more imposing set of eyebrows, a spectacular nose and a completely disarming smile. That impish smile was a clue to his devilish, and sometimes scathing, sense of humour, which Voytek learned to love.

The pair met up in Rawalpindi on June 1, 1988, less than a month after Voytek's marriage to Halina Siekaj. He had met Halina in the Krakow Mountain Club years before, but they had only reconnected thanks to a chance meeting on the train from Warsaw to Krakow in 1987. The trains were slower in those days, so the two had several hours in which to get to know each other. "I remember it as a very positive experience," Voytek said. "I learned a lot about Halina: her work in London, her passion for horses, her sensitivity to animals, her honesty and fairness." They met again, and often. Both were at a stage in their lives where they were keen to start a family, so one year later they decided to make a life together. Since Halina knew and understood that Voytek was a climber and that his passion would take him away on a regular basis, it was no surprise to her when he headed back to Trango.

Voytek and Erhard stayed at the modest Gatmells Motel; Voytek's motto on expeditions was to sleep cheap and eat well. He suggested they indulge in the extensive buffet at the Oberoi Hotel. It was too far to walk, so they called for a taxi. When they arrived at the Oberoi, Voytek handed the driver the agreed-upon fare of 50 rupees. The driver accepted, saying, "*Shukriya* [thank you]." After Voytek and Erhard returned to their hotel later that night, they decided to play a game with their taxi driver the next day. A devilish, black, dastardly game. "Pakistanis are quite dignified people," Voytek explained. "If they ask a price, and if there is any delay in agreeing, they will say, 'Don't worry, my friend. Let's go.' We decided to play with this noble tradition."

The next night they headed back to the Oberoi for dinner. Voytek handed the driver his fare. This time it was 45 rupees. No words were exchanged, except "*Shukriya*." It was as if the fare had miraculously changed overnight. Voytek described the ensuing nights: "And this continued for something like three or four days. We grew fascinated. Every night I was paying five rupees less." When they reached 35 rupees, there was a slight crisis. The taxi driver took the rupees, but, for ten or fifteen seconds, he stared at Voytek. This time it was Voytek who said "*Shukriya*" before walking away. The silent partner in this childish and callous game was Erhard, but as soon as they were beyond hearing distance, he broke into an "indecent cackle," according to Voytek.

The game came to an end at 30 rupees. With a great show of dignity, the taxi driver finally protested: "Friends, this isn't fair. This isn't the price." Voytek agreed immediately and handed over significantly more than the original price of 50 rupees. Years later, when telling the story, Voytek admitted with a sheepish laugh, "We were bastards. Real bastards."

The two alpinists had other, more important games to play in Rawalpindi: games that could threaten their entire climb. Unbeknownst to Voytek, sometime during the previous winter the Pakistani officials had introduced a new rule prohibiting expeditions with teams smaller than four.

Voytek Kurtyka on Broad Peak in 1982, an acclimatization exercise that resulted in an "unofficial" ascent of the mountain with Jerzy Kukuczka. *Jerzy Kukuczka.*

Bivouac on the Broad Peak Traverse at the col between the North and Central summits in 1984. *Voytek Kurtyka collection.*

K2 from Broad Peak. *Voytek Kurtyka.*

Porters on the old approach to the Baltoro. *Voytek Kurtyka.*

Broad Peak Traverse, Karakoram, Pakistan.
Traverse of the North (7490 metres), Central (8011 metres) and Main (8051 metres)
summits via a new route, alpine-style, by
Voytek Kurtyka and Jerzy Kukuczka in
1984. *Voytek Kurtyka collection;
route outline by Piotr Drożdż.*

Austrian climber Robert Schauer, Voytek's
partner on Gasherbrum IV. *Voytek Kurtyka
collection.*

Voytek enjoying a
bit of bouldering at
Gasherbrum IV base
camp. *Voytek Kurtyka
collection.*

Voytek Kurtyka and Robert Schauer at Gasherbrum IV base camp.
Voytek Kurtyka collection.

Climbing the West Face of Gasherbrum IV in 1985.
Robert Schauer, Voytek Kurtyka collection.

Voytek climbing high on the West Face
of Gasherbrum IV. *Robert Schauer, Voytek
Kurtyka collection.*

Gasherbrum IV, 7932 metres, Karakoram, Pakistan. New route on the West Face (without reaching the summit); 10-day alpine-style ascent by Voytek Kurtyka and Robert Schauer in 1985. *Voytek Kurtyka collection; route outline by Piotr Drożdż.*

Noboru Yamada, Robert Schauer and Voytek Kurtyka at K2 base camp, enjoying some "medical purifier." Noboru has just consumed enough to be convinced to join Voytek on Trango Tower the following year. *Voytek Kurtyka collection.*

Voytek Kurtyka at the Trento Film Festival, Italy, in 1985. *Bernard Newman.*

Voytek Kurtyka and Noboru Yamada at Trango Tower in 1986 for their East Face attempt. *Voytek Kurtyka collection.*

Climbing on Manaslu in 1986. The red-helmeted climber is Artur Hajzer; next is Carlos Carsolio; and last is Jerzy Kukuczka. *Voytek Kurtyka.*

Voytek Kurtyka and Jerzy Kukuczka discussing the avalanche hazard on Manaslu in 1986. *Artur Hajzer.*

Voytek on his way to the South Face of Shishapangma in 1987 with his wife, Halina. *Voytek Kurtyka collection.*

Swiss alpinist Erhard Loretan. *Voytek Kurtyka collection.*

The magnificent crack systems on Trango Tower, 1988. *Voytek Kurtyka collection.*

Shimmering granite on the East Face of Trango Tower, 1988. *Voytek Kurtyka collection.*

Preparing the bivouac on the East Face of Trango Tower.
Erhard Loretan, Voytek Kurtyka collection.

Voytek Kurtyka on the East Face of Trango Tower.
Erhard Loretan, Voytek Kurtyka collection.

Erhard Loretan at the highest bivouac on the East Face of Trango Tower. *Voytek Kurtyka.*

Erhard Loretan nearing the summit mushroom on the East Face of Trango Tower. *Voytek Kurtyka.*

Trango Tower, 6239 metres, Karakoram, Pakistan. New route on the East Face, capsule-style, by Voytek Kurtyka and Erhard Loretan in 1988. *Voytek Kurtyka collection; route outline by Piotr Drożdż.*

Voytek Kurtyka and Erhard Loretan at the base of Trango Tower.
Voytek Kurtyka collection.

Voytek the gardener. *Jacenty Dędek, Voytek Kurtyka collection.*

When Voytek and Erhard entered Mr. Muriyamu's office to pick up their permit for Trango Tower, a French expedition was in the process of being refused a permit. Why? Because they were a team of two. Voytek looked at Erhard with a frown creasing his brow. Erhard stared back with a question in his eyes. Voytek described the horrifying moment. "We sat in total silence and watched the two French guys, completely depressed, being sent back home."

Mr. Muriyamu explained to the French climbers how important it was to understand and respect the regulations. "We can't afford to get foreigners killed in the mountains," he said with a patient smile. "For that reason, we have this rule." He turned to Voytek with his arm outstretched: "Here is Mr. Kurtyka, who has been an expedition leader for many years in our country and who understands our rules perfectly."

Voytek nodded back with a wan smile.

"Please, Mr. Kurtyka, explain to these young French climbers how it works."

"Yes, yes, I understand and support these rules completely," Voytek agreed, looking at the French with compassion. He and Erhard were in the same position, however: two climbers hoping to pick up a permit for Trango. They excused themselves and slunk out into the 46°C heat.

"*Merde*," said Erhard.

"*Scheisse*," muttered Voytek.

They now had just four days to find two more climbers to go with them to Trango Tower. Voytek suggested approaching some of his Hunza friends and adding them to their permit. Erhard had a better idea. "Listen, Voytek. I know of a Swiss expedition heading to Nanga Parbat. They have some trekkers with them. That's what we need – trekkers! We can ask to borrow their trekkers. They're going more or less the same way. No one will know that they're not along to climb the mountain with us."

Voytek agreed it was worth a try, so Erhard tracked down the Nanga Parbat team and explained the problem. Indeed, there were trekkers attached to the group. Two lovely Swiss girls. Blonde and blue-eyed. Within an hour, to his great joy, he had convinced them to pretend to join the Trango team. They seemed quite keen to do so, except for one small problem. Their expedition was leaving in three days, and Voytek and Erhard's next meeting with Mr. Muriyamu wasn't for four. They would be on their way to Nanga Parbat before Voytek and Erhard could negotiate a permit. What to do?

Voytek sprang into action. He gathered the two Swiss girls and Erhard and bundled them off to Mr. Muriyamu's office, two days early. "Hello, kind Mr. Muriyamu, here we are with our full team, and all of our paperwork. I'm sorry I didn't send it earlier."

"Ahhh, good to see you," said the smiling Mr. Muriyamu. "Welcome, welcome. So nice to meet you," he said to the two Swiss girls, who radiated health and happiness. "You can leave the papers and in three days, please come back and everything will be done. You can pick up your permit then."

"Thank you so much," offered Voytek, a phony smile plastered on his face.

The following day the four appeared once more. "Hello, again. How are you today?" asked Mr. Muriyamu, beaming at the Swiss ladies.

"Oh, sir, not well," said Voytek with a sad look. "We are suffering with this heat. And the girls ... they simply can't handle it." The girls wiped their dripping brows and fiddled with their limp braids, seemingly on the verge of tears. "Please, Mr. Muriyamu, can the girls go to Skardu? Truly, they are not used to this heat. It will be a disaster for them to stay here any longer. We can catch up with them in Skardu in a couple of days' time. It would be so good of you to allow this."

Voytek was convinced that a Pakistani gentleman would be unable to refuse two beautiful blonde Swiss girls who were close to fainting. He was right. Mr. Muriyamu agreed with the suggestion and off they went. To Nanga Parbat.

Two days later, Voytek and Erhard met once again with Mr. Muriyamu. "How are the girls doing?" he asked.

"Much better. Thank you so much for your consideration," Voytek replied, nodding his head in appreciation while picking up his permit.

They never saw the girls again.

On June 20, 1988, they arrived at the Dunge Glacier after a six-day march. They set up base camp, safely this time, atop a moraine feature at just over 4000 metres. Fantastic towers surrounded them, creating a wild jumble of granite fingers reaching toward the indigo sky. The most beautiful of all was Trango Tower. Their tower. It was Erhard's first glimpse, and his eyes glittered with anticipation. Liaison Officer Sajid's eyes glittered, too, but from terror. A large man who hailed from the plains of Punjab and hated every moment of this crazy alpine assignment, he pleaded, "What's the point of all those cliffs? ... Couldn't one somehow dispose of all those glaciers? Maybe melt them away?"[74]

Although it triggered fear in Sajid, the dramatic landscape instilled in Voytek a sense of unity with the place. His description of the approach to the tower reveals his receptivity to the power of Trango's splendour.

> The seemingly flat and bland surface of the glacier was furrowed with innumerable ice runnels in which clear streamlets shimmered. Every now and then deep-muffled moans came up from deep inside the glacier. In the deadly silence the purl of water blended with the glistening light which skimmed zigzagging along the glassy streams. This vast, clear space, hemmed in on all sides with bright barrier walls, was quickened by a pale flickering which filled the emptiness around us the way vegetation fills a rich garden. Two thousand metres above us hovered the great golden obelisk of Trango. Incalculably higher, a small stray cloud enveloped the upper walls of the peak, tirelessly trying to shake loose from the grip of that sheer mass of rock ... Somewhere inside me a trembling started, followed by a sense of quiet despair. I felt close to something extraordinary, and yet I could not even reach out with my hand toward it.[75]

His yearning to touch the source of this emotional flame echoed his experience at Bandaka base camp eleven years earlier, when he said of the mountain, "I was so close, but it wasn't responding to me."

They tried to calm their nerves as all climbers do – by sorting gear. One hundred twenty kilograms of food and equipment spread out in neat little rows atop a giant granite boulder stared back at them. But the base of the tower was still 1200 metres above their camp, and there was no one to help the two of them lug it all up there. Voytek was lean as a knife; Erhard was even thinner, 60 kilograms at most. When they considered the loads they would need to carry, Voytek realized that each of them would have to heft more than 30 kilograms onto his back. And Erhard's back had already been broken, twice. Nevertheless, shortly after midnight on the morning of June 24, they loaded up the "beasts" – their packs – and headed up.

Erhard was silent as he trudged along, maintaining a steady pace. To distract himself from the discomfort, he reviewed the last couple of years of his life: the death of his partner Pierre-Alain Steiner on Cho Oyu, directly in front of his eyes; the first fracture of his back while attempting to enchain thirteen north faces in the Alps; then a second back injury from paragliding. It had been a dark period for Erhard. But now he was in the Karakoram, poised to climb an exquisite granite obelisk. Voytek plodded along, squirming with the pain and fatigue and thirst. "How strange it was to find they tasted so much alike," he mused. In fact, it was tiny Erhard with the damaged back who reached the base of the wall first, his training and countless days of guiding in the Alps pulling him through the pain and drudgery.

Having arrived at the foot of the first buttress at around 9 a.m., they rested until noon. Erhard described the object of their desire: "Imagine a granite cathedral, with a forest of bell towers rising to 6257 [more recent measurements indicate 6239] metres, and 4000-foot-high organ pipes. And to better appreciate its proportions, two men strolling around the nave."[76] Once they had touched the rock, they couldn't resist its lure; they had to start climbing that same day. Who would start? They flipped a coin and Voytek won. He led the first pitch, Erhard the second. They fixed the rope to make a connection to the mountain and rappelled down to set up a bivouac. To celebrate their first contact with the rock, Voytek opened a can of caviar he had brought from Poland. The tiny eggs popped in their mouths, and they "gobbled it down like pigs," Voytek recounted.

The next day, June 25, they climbed up a series of awkward, slanting cracks, which, when they weren't seeping with water, hid glassy ribbons of ice. Voytek remembered this section of cracks from his previous attempt: slippery, mud-choked and tough to protect. And now he needed to do it all over again. "To the left of us, streams of water cascaded down a gloomy black and yellow chimney," he wrote of the climb.[77] The rock gleamed with thin, rippling sheets of water, which soaked them to the core. Dripping with moisture, Voytek made it to a generous ledge, where he discovered the bolts left behind when he and the Japanese had retreated off the tower. It was on this ledge that he and Erhard planned to set up their main bivouac for their attempt on the wall. From here they could push the route up, pitch by pitch, rappelling down to their nest on the ledge each night, an approach known as capsule style. But on this first arrival at the ledge, they merely dropped their loads and slid down the lines to base.

On June 26 they jumared up the slippery ropes, hauled loads up to their nest and then fixed one pitch above the snow ledge. They were now on the main vertical body of rock that soared, uninterrupted, to the top of the tower. By July 2 the unstable weather cleared and they were ready to start the climb proper. This time they left base camp with 25-kilogram loads on their backs. The two little men had managed to transport a total of 113 kilograms up to their bivouac over the two carries, yet according to Erhard, they were "fresh and enthusiastic for the final sprint, which should last ten to fifteen days – a sprint reserved for marathoners."[78]

Once again, they began at midnight. And by late the first day, they had scraped out a roomy platform on the snow-covered ledge and were firmly established with all their gear and enough food to climb the tower. That night, as they peered upward at the East Face spreading its soaring walls before them, their spirits ricocheted between nervousness and excitement.

The climbing was physically demanding, as crack climbing tends to be. Narrow finger cracks tested their technique; fist-sized cracks gobbled up their protection; slanting cracks pushed them off balance; widening cracks sapped their strength. Bulging roofs blocked out the sun. Occasionally, shards of ice shot past their heads, lethal daggers set free by the warmth of the sun from somewhere far, far up the tower. The golden-hued rock offered fantastic and elegant geometric shapes and a texture that was consistently rough, studded with shimmering crystals.

"We weren't pushing the limits of free climbing," Voytek said. "Whenever it became too hard, we used aid." Most of their aid climbing was done with Friends and nuts, along with the occasional piton. Every second day one of them went out front and lead climbed all day. This way, on alternate days, the belayer could relax, dressed warmly in down. Each pitch presented an unknown adventure. Every move was one more piece in a giant puzzle. Voytek explained that, once he was on the wall, his fear dissipated. "The abstract structure of the huge crystal tower with its angles and edges and its glimmering surfaces was so appealing and mysterious that each move up was not about facing unknown danger but rather an encounter with enthralling beauty. Every move, even when I was exhausted, was worth it."

Voytek spied something grey and hairy lurking in the shadows, wedged deep in a crack. It seemed alive. His first impulse was to jerk back away from it. Upon closer inspection, he realized it was an alpine flower. "I had the impression it was looking at me," he laughed. "It was immensely warm and encouraging – this meeting." Voytek was encouraged by his partner too, enjoying his sometimes perverse sense of humour. He valued Erhard's attentive attitude even more. "He seemed concerned for me," Voytek explained. "He was protective of me, and this was something new for me. If I was lagging behind, he waited. If I was having trouble with a move, he encouraged me. It was nice."

On one of Voytek's leading days, high on the tower amid an area of dihedrals, he fell. Twice. Erhard described the experience from the belayer's perspective. "The rope that moves through the belayer's hands reveals everything about the leader's climbing: hesitations; bursts of speed; comfort or unease. Sometimes sudden slack in the line tells the belayer that the leader has taken flight and that in a few split seconds, catching the fall will truly be in his hands."[79] Voytek's first flight occurred immediately after surmounting a roof. Atop the overhang, he inched up a smooth granite slab, placing sky hooks on tiny edges to use as aid, and then weighting the sky hooks with his etriers as he moved up to the next minuscule edge. One of the edges was brittle, and it fractured, tossing him off the wall like an autumn leaf. As he tumbled down, he scraped his hands on the rough, crystalline rock. After slowing the bleeding – and his heart rate – he continued up, fretting about his hands.

On the next pitch, he placed a camming device in a crack and weighted it with his etrier. Pop. It fell out in an instant, throwing him back down another three metres. Two falls in one day. He was justifiably rattled. Their position was so remote and the face was so committing that the smallest accident could be catastrophic. "We weren't on the Eiger or the Matterhorn; we weren't messing around across from hotel balconies," Erhard explained.[80]

That evening Voytek was in pain with a bruised elbow, a sprained thumb and skinned knuckles. Most of all, he was demoralized. "My pride was punished," he reflected years later. "It felt like I had lost my climbing virginity. Never had I taken a fall when climbing in serious mountains. And here it happened twice in one day." Feeling completely defence-less on this intimidating face almost 2 kilometres above the valley floor, Voytek gazed out into the fading light of the melancholy hour and con-cluded, "This is absolute madness."

Erhard sensed his despair and took over. "You take it easy," he said. "I'll do the cooking tonight. Just sit here." The cooking was pretty basic. After a typical sixteen-hour day of climbing, of living on adrenalin, their ap-petites were skittish at best. Before Erhard began cooking up the simple cheese fondue, he took out his Walkman and placed the headphones over Voytek's ears. After adjusting the volume, Erhard switched on the music. Voytek almost dissolved in tears when the Dire Straits lyrics washed over him.

These mist-covered mountains
Are a home now for me ...
You did not desert me
My brothers in arms.

"Thank you, Erhard," he whispered.

The next day was Erhard's turn to lead. Each time he discovered a per-fect hold hidden beneath an imposing overhang, he swore in ear-splitting French jubilation, much to Voytek's amusement. The day after, Voytek, with taped and swollen fingers, took the lead, finally reaching the section of the tower that resembled a pyramid. "I couldn't see anything except a smooth sheet of headwall," he explained. "Like in Yosemite. A blank shield. I rappelled back to Erhard full of concern because this was the greatest unknown of the tower. If this shield didn't have any climbing fea-tures, we might not be able to climb it." They had used up all their fixed ropes, so they now had to retrieve their lines and move their bivouac higher up the wall to continue.

While rappelling down, Voytek discovered that his locking carabiner had jammed shut. He was trapped in his harness. When he reached the bivy he tapped it and twisted it this way and that, with no result. Frus-trated, he crawled into his sleeping bag, hoping he wouldn't need to go to the toilet that night. Just then, a snowstorm moved into the valley, plas-tering Trango Tower and burying their little nest on the ledge. Before the night was over, the humidity had crept into every corner of their tiny bivy. Now what?

Erhard was all for descending, but Voytek couldn't decide. Erhard walked over to the ropes to start preparing the rappels, convinced that Voytek would soon see the wisdom in going down. When he returned to the bivouac he found Voytek nestled in his sleeping bag. An incredulous and somewhat amused Erhard later described what happened next. "He placed an order for a drink. I don't know if my four-day beard and my rock-manicured fingers anointed me the sommelier, but Voytek wished to have something to drink – something hot, if possible. I explained to him that the breakfast buffet wasn't open just then, that today the house was serving only iced Isostar, and that it would be nice if he could make up his mind: Up or down?"[81]

Voytek eventually agreed to descend. As they slid down the lines, he worried about ever getting past their high point again. He was also concerned about his bowels: he was still a prisoner of his harness. His imagination ran wild with terror as he imagined walking all the way to base camp with his pants full of crap.

Base camp presented a different climate. The air was thick with warmth and moisture as clouds wrapped around the tower, obscuring its immensity. Now they could relax. But first, Voytek had to escape from his wretched harness. He hit the carabiner with his hammer. He squeezed it with metal grips. He tried heating it over the stove, hoping to expand the metal and release the iron purchase. Nothing worked. He eventually found some pliers and a saw and sawed through the carabiner, destroying it in the process. Freed at last, he could go to the toilet, enjoy the leisurely meals, sleep and rest. "I sat silently with Erhard, absorbed in our favourite music. I could feel a quiet joy, inspired by his company," Voytek wrote of that time waiting out the storm.[82]

Although Erhard's recollection of those days was darker and full of angst, he too appreciated the break.

This return to base camp gave us a three-day reprieve from the law of gravity. That law was burdening us; we were obsessed with falling, and we could not drop anything. The void surrounded us and inhaled anything we didn't hold onto. Losing a stove, a boot, or a crampon would be extremely serious. Everything that we handled had to first be attached to something, and that required our constant attention. Behind this fear of loss, of course, hid the fear that we ourselves might fall. If a piton pulled out, a rock came loose, our strength failed us, or we dropped our guard, then – like the stove or the boot – we would be swallowed by the void. The void was a black hole.[83]

At midnight on July 9, rested and well-fed, they left base camp for the third time. As they hiked up through the gloom, their world brightened when the clouds split open and the tower shimmered from the faint light of a sky wild with stars. Twelve hundred metres of hiking brought them to their fixed lines. Six hundred metres of jumaring brought them to their previous high point.

Erhard took over the lead. He moved behind a small leaning tower, squeezing between it and the wall. As soon as he disappeared, the rope stopped moving. Not one sound from Erhard. Was he stuck?

"Erhard, how does it look?"

Still nothing.

Finally, Erhard reappeared around the edge of the tower, a wide grin plastered on his face and his arms raised in victory. "This is fantastic! This is fantastic," he cried.

"What is fantastic?" Voytek yelled back.

"It's a crack. A fantastic crack, and a bivouac site too."

It was true. Erhard had squeezed through a tight, chimney-like corridor between the separated flake of the pyramid and the wall, which led to a perfectly flat piece of rock. Detached from the face, it was 2 metres by 1.5 metres: the ideal size for a bivouac. "Fantastic nest for two," Voytek raved. "Incredible. Two kilometres above the ground on this vertical terrain, and we found this perfectly comfortable bivouac rock." This became their new room with a view as they began their final assault on the tower.

The details of the next few days are sparse in Voytek's journal, but there is enough to describe what they faced on the summit headwall, which was split by parallel cracks that rarely continued.

10 July – starting the headwall. I climb the first two pitches. 80 metres.

11 July – Erhard leads the next two long pitches, something like 90 metres…He starts the fifth pitch above the bivouac but he stops on the smooth wall…he discovers a chance for a pendulum.

12 July – I finish Erhard's pitch – the fifth one – which is complicated because of a shortage of equipment and a risky belay. Stance as usual is hanging…I pendulum to the dihedral and, 20 metres higher, fix a belay. Seventh pitch is very bad. Two bolts and delicate aid climbing on Polish "one" [figure-of-one] pitons.

13 July – summit day. Erhard is leading two pitches almost free. Then two pitches on the snow and ice – very easy. And then finally, almost without equipment because everything is on the wall, the last 25 metres to the summit.

It's revealing, and sometimes amusing, to see two versions of an event or action, since nobody sees an experience the same way. Voytek's succinct account of summit day, "two pitches almost free, very easy," contrasts sharply with Erhard's recollection, possibly because it was Erhard's day to lead.

The crack was difficult; where it wasn't clogged with ice, it was ice-rimed…The ambiance was changing; we were above 6000 metres, ice was replacing rock, and I felt as if I were in my pyjamas in a walk-in freezer…The air swirled from all directions, and I knew that I was close to the point where all of the cracks, dihedrals, and grooves that we had used during our fourteen days of climbing converged…Then, horror of horrors: a 100-foot rock bulge blocked our access to the summit. It was 3:00 p.m. and my arsenal consisted of three pitons hanging from my harness, and a handful of nuts. There must have been a moment when David faced Goliath and regretted having only a slingshot…Above me there was a piton, a relic from a previous Yugoslavian expedition. If I could get to it, I would be saved. I hammered in a pin behind a granite flake, threaded a cordelette through the eye of the piton, and stood up, at which point the entire flake broke off…It was time to activate the so-called springs of action – hope and fear…To me, that meant that I was risking it all, staking my life on one or two nuts that didn't look like they were being held by much…Then I made it up the crack! The last ten feet were ice, and completely vertical. I revived a great mountaineering tradition, whereby one ice axe can triumph over any difficulties. A half hour later, we were together on the summit of Trango Tower.[84]

Not exactly easy.

Voytek smiled at their choice of summit day: July 13. His lucky day. He began Gasherbrum IV on the 13th, started the Broad Peak Traverse on the 13th, and finished Trango on the 13th. "Son of the devil – lucky 13. Since I'm not fond of Christianity, I am in good favour with the devil," he joked.

A feathery layer of clouds scudded above them while they sat on the top, enjoying the unprecedented view of the Trango Group and the surrounding glaciers, the wildest landscape on Earth. As a bluish-grey ring snaked around the sun they grew leery of a storm, so, after snapping a few more photos, they began rappelling down. Using two ropes to increase the length of each rappel, they were soon at their highest bivouac.

On the last day, they continued down in the inevitable snowstorm. With 100-metre rappels, the thin lines snaked off into emptiness as the overhanging wall left them dangling in space. Loaded down with 10-kilogram packs and an additional 20 kilograms of gear hanging on their harnesses, they kept descending, 100 metres at a time. It was a nerve-racking business. By mid-afternoon they were in base camp, drenched and depleted and perfectly sated.

Voytek was more than sated; he felt relieved. It was his second attempt on the tower, and for an alpinist who was used to succeeding, this climb felt extra-sweet. In his journal, he wrote, "Two years have passed without success. It makes me think about how badly I need success and a bit of admiration. Otherwise I will go mad." Years later, when pressed to come clean about this seemingly sarcastic and self-mocking entry, he insisted, "I wasn't joking. I was honest. Okay, maybe a little bit of joking, but truth in the joking."

Voytek and Erhard had etched an elegant, twenty-nine-pitch line on the 1100-metre East Face of Trango Tower; theirs was the first two-person ascent of the tower. They spent fourteen days of actual climbing on the wall and rated it 5.10, A3. Though both Erhard and Voytek were strict devotees of alpine-style climbing, regardless of height or difficulty, they ended up fixing about 600 metres of rope on Trango. Voytek later explained why, with some understatement. "It would be unwise to expect too long a stretch of fine weather in the Karakoram." This capsule-style method allowed them to descend to their two bivouacs on the wall, and all the way to base camp during the inevitable storms.

A couple of years later, Voytek was in Atlanta, Georgia, at the American Alpine Club's annual meeting. The keynote lecture was by American rock climber Todd Skinner. Todd's illustrated talk was about his free climb of the *Salathé Wall* on Yosemite's El Capitan. Voytek was intrigued by this young climber's tenacity and commitment to free climbing big walls. Later that evening, he elbowed his way through the crowds to approach him. "Hi, Todd, I have something to show you." Although Todd had immense respect for Voytek, he thought of him strictly as a Himalayan climber. Visions of snow and ice clouded his enthusiasm, but he reluctantly agreed to take a look at some photos Voytek felt he should see.

"What I remember most about that fortuitous meeting with Voytek Kurtyka was the wild look in his eyes," Todd said. "I recognized in him a kindred spirit."[85] Voytek hauled out several photos of the East Face of Trango and spread them on a table. Todd was stunned. "Beautiful sunlit granite, laser cracks, extreme exposure," he raved.

Voytek watched Todd's face light up at the images and casually threw out, "You should go and free climb it." Todd had no Himalayan experience, yet he knew enough to realize that this was a project for the future. What he didn't comprehend was that, once it had lodged in his imagination, it wasn't going to leave. It was a project for *his* future.

Seven years after their unexpected meeting, in 1995, Todd and his team spent sixty days on Trango, making the first free ascent of the tower. They started up the *Slovenian Route* on the South-Southeast Face and joined Voytek and Erhard's route above the shoulder. They rated the climb VII, 5.13a, and called it *Cowboy Direct*.

Voytek attached great value to his Trango Tower adventure. Later, when he compared it to his two-person ascents of 8000-metre peaks, he assessed the Trango climb as somewhat higher in quality, at least from a sporting perspective. The Trango climb presented more challenges, both physically and technically. Erhard appreciated it because he enjoyed the experience, and his famously underrating recollections of his climbs reflect that attitude. "I loved this first ascent of the East Face of Trango Tower because it didn't have the stressful aspect of an 8000er. Of course, the technical difficulty was far greater than on my Himalayan summits, but this time the altitude was hospitable and merciful. It was nothing like the death zone, which cannot be ventured into with impunity. This was a relaxed, chilled-out expedition – a vacation that I could have spent almost without taking off my (climbing) slippers."[86] In his autobiography, he flippantly called his Trango chapter "My Vacation in Slippers on Trango Tower."

For alpinists such as Voytek and Erhard, both experts on rock and perfectly comfortable on ice, experienced at altitude and eager for a challenge, it's hard to imagine a better climb than Trango Tower. Voytek later described an ascent such as this as "an aesthetic art working in the magic play of light and space – is there a more impressive engraving than the one drawn by a climber on an immense wall or a ridge?" A photograph of their line on the tower suggests not. And Voytek, the devotee of aesthetics, could never have escaped Trango. It was simply too beautiful.

THIRTEEN

Night Naked

Once you are my friend, I am responsible for you.
  —Antoine de Saint-Exupéry, *The Little Prince*

Voytek's nose was buried deep in a book when he came across a photo that completely captured him – the mysterious Southwest Face of Cho Oyu. He couldn't take his eyes off its maze of rock buttresses and hidden ice couloirs. *Cho Oyu: By Favour of the Gods*, the book by Austrian climber Herbert Tichy, wasn't about the Southwest Face but rather about the story of Tichy's first ascent of the 8188-metre mountain back in 1954. Tichy's motivation to climb it came not from the Austrian climbing establishment but from Pasang Dawa Lama, his Sherpa travelling companion. They had hatched the idea while sitting around a campfire during an exploratory trip through Nepal the previous year. When Pasang suggested climbing Cho Oyu, Tichy, who was a keen smoker and drinker but only a moderately accomplished alpinist, said why not and left most of the team's makeup to Pasang.

As Voytek devoured Tichy's words, it became clear that this bespectacled man's love for his companions was stronger than his desire for the summit. After years of climbing with various people, Voytek understood the value of a great partner. A partner who was also a friend. The more he read, the more his respect for Tichy grew. He was astonished that this first ascent of the mountain had been done without supplemental oxygen and in alpine style. Way back in 1954! There was still another appealing aspect to their climb: it was illegal. They had crossed the Nangpa La illegally from Nepal into Tibet to reach the West Face, their chosen route. Good friendship, alpine-style and illegal – so much to admire.

"Tichy intrigued me," Voytek explained. "He was one of the first men who was going for total adventure, relying on himself and his partners and nothing else." The story of their unorthodox climb, the Nangpa La and the captivating photo of the Southwest Face remained with Voytek. He was repeatedly drawn to it. "Looking at this picture was like watching a mystery," he said. "It was not explored. Very beautiful. Impressive. It stayed in my mind and my heart forever – for my entire climbing career. It was something mysterious, secret and beautiful. Sometimes dreams are never realized, and you die with them unfulfilled. They are only a pleasant part of you. Sometimes you approach them, and then you see what happens: either disappointment – or a relationship."

Eventually, no longer able to resist the mountain, Voytek approached Erhard, his Trango partner. "Erhard, take a look at this picture. It's beautiful, don't you think? So wild and unknown. We could climb this face together."

"Oh, yes, I know that place," Erhard replied nonchalantly. "I've been there. I crossed the Nangpa La illegally, too."

Voytek was stunned. This face he had been living with and dreaming about – Erhard had already been there! It was true. Erhard had made an illegal attempt of a line on the left side of the face with another Swiss alpinist, Pierre-Alain Steiner, who had died on the mountain. Voytek had a literary relationship with the face, and Erhard had a physical relationship with it. It seemed inevitable that the two would climb it together. So, even though Erhard was still deeply distressed by the tragedy accompanying his attempt on the face, he and Voytek began to plan for the summer of 1990.

As their plans took shape, Voytek thought, why limit their undertaking to the Southwest Face of Cho Oyu? Why not climb two 8000ers in one go? Both Voytek and Erhard knew it was possible; acclimatizing completely on one 8000er would allow them to continue easily to another. Voytek had once jokingly suggested that climbing all fourteen of the 8000ers in one season was possible if you had enough money for helicopter approaches and a little luck with the weather. But for 1990, two

8000ers would have to suffice. Voytek proposed a couloir to the left of centre on the Southwest Face of Shishapangma as their second objective. Both faces reared 2000 metres from their bases and 2500 metres from their respective base camps.

Erhard and Voytek were well-matched, not only in their style of climbing but also in their ironic sense of humour, often self-directed. A tongue-in-cheek interview between the two, published in *Mountain*, gives a sense of it.

> VK: "Do you train for your climbs?"
> EL: "No, the best training is here," tapping his forehead.
> VK: "Do you smoke or drink?"
> EL: "No to the first, yes to the second."
> VK: "Any medications taken?"
> EL: "Only mild sleeping pills, never anything to improve blood supply."
> VK: "What do you want most in high altitude mountaineering?"
> EL: "As difficult, high and quick as possible, alpine-style of course."[87]

Erhard's most frequent climbing partner was fellow Swiss alpinist Jean Troillet. The pair had already climbed Dhaulagiri, Everest's North Face and K2 together. Voytek and Jean had tried K2 twice (once with Erhard) and were good friends, as well. The three of them would form the dream team for Cho Oyu and Shishapangma. When Voytek had first met them in a Kathmandu café back in 1986, he could see that their motivation for climbing far surpassed the element of sport. "I saw in my imagination two spirits travelling in dangerous communion with space and darkness," he later wrote in his foreword to Jean's autobiography. He could see on their faces and in their stories that the dangerous journey they had chosen in the mountains had made their lives works of art. They were like him. It was rare to find such common ground.

From the beginning, they knew they would climb fast and, for the most part, solo. After acclimatizing, they would bolt up in one push: no tent, no sleeping bags and very little food. They would only bring their clothing and a limited amount of equipment. And they would climb mostly at night. Climbing at night eliminated the need for sleeping bags and extra cold-weather clothing because they would be moving. Voytek admitted the concept required the complete deconstruction of accepted climbing behaviour and mentality. In fact, the concept was almost absurd. But he was convinced that reaching a new state of any art form often requires toying with the absurd. Only then could climbing break free from the established order and enter another level of creativity. Voytek described this new state-of-the-art climbing as "lightness, defencelessness and confidence…usually preceded by a torment of doubt and fear."[88] He called their strategy "night naked." He knew that these great faces were perfect for night-naked climbing since neither had major barriers that would slow them down. It was almost impossible to find such lines in the Himalaya that had not already been climbed.

On August 28 the three arrived at the Cho Oyu base camp, at 5700 metres. They were in high spirits. The mood soon changed when Jean became strangely ill. "On Thursday, August 30, he was no longer identifiable as any race that exists on Earth," Erhard recalled. "He was neither white, nor pink, nor black, nor yellow, nor red; he was green like a science fiction Martian. Without a doubt, he had altitude sickness."[89] The trio moved down to the Chinese base camp, more than 1000 metres lower. Jean hired a jeep to descend even lower to completely recover, and Voytek and Erhard moved back up to their base camp.

This was Voytek's first expedition after the birth of his son, Aleksander (Alex), and he noticed some new and unsettling sensations as he contemplated the job ahead of him. The smallest events could trigger a wave of emotions. Whenever he drank from his water bottle, a curious burbling sound emerged, reminding Voytek of his baby son sucking on his milk bottle. His mind would fill with visions of little Alex, or "Chubby," as Voytek liked to call him. It was a disquieting reminder of home. Of family. Of responsibility. Voytek struggled to return to his former identity as a climbing "beast."

Their plan moved ahead when a fully recovered Jean returned to base camp. After acclimatizing on the normal route, they began packing for the Southwest Face. Erhard was famous for his super-lightweight tactics, but Voytek felt he occasionally went too far. In fact, he was sure that Erhard and Pierre's unfortunate retreat from their previous attempt on Cho Oyu was due to having taken only one piton. And now the issue of equipment arose again. Voytek wanted to take a handful of pitons; Erhard wanted only one or two. Voytek scoffed at the idea. "One piton is useless, Erhard. Come on, be reasonable."

"This is a lightweight climb, Voytek. This is a modern climb. Even on my last time on Cho Oyu, I took only one piton."

"Yes, that's true. And look what happened to Pierre," Voytek threw back. "You couldn't climb a rock step with just one piton, and you had to retreat. And Pierre died."

The remark stung. Erhard stormed off, yelling back, "Do what you want, then. You will anyway. You never listen."

Although the argument was about pitons, the problem was much greater than that, causing the tension to grow between the two stars. Voytek and Erhard were both climbing luminaries, and they shared a similar approach to alpinism, but this situation was different. Erhard, who was twelve years younger than Voytek, was at a different stage of his career. His trajectory was up, up, up. He was on fire, climbing higher and faster and setting unimaginable records in the Himalaya. He was as fit as he could possibly be; few could keep up with him on a mountain. Voytek too had set incredible records, but not quite so recently. He was also extremely fit, but he freely admitted that he was not quite as fast as Erhard. Erhard was a professional climber, in the mountains every day. Voytek was no longer a full-time alpinist. He was a busy man back in Poland, with Halina, a baby son and a thriving import business.

Another issue was communication. Jean's first language was French, as was Erhard's. Multilingual Voytek had not yet mastered French, the "language of diplomacy." He felt lonely as the other two prattled away in their Swiss-accented French. Jean tried to include Voytek in the conversations by providing instant translation, but Erhard seemed strangely remote. When Voytek expressed his opinion about something, Erhard listened but rarely replied. His only response was to turn to Jean and continue speaking in French. Was he disputing Voytek's suggestions? Voytek didn't know.

"Erhard was a totally different guy than when we were on Trango," Voytek said with a note of sadness in his voice. "Completely different. I don't know what was going on in his private life, but it doesn't matter. I loved the guy. And it was reciprocal. We had experienced such nice times in the mountains together. But now there was tension."

Despite the strain, they resumed packing. Although they planned to solo most of the climb, each man moving at his own pace and rhythm, they packed 30 metres of double 7-millimetre rope that they could use if required on the upper rock barriers. They added three nuts, and, finally, Voytek threw a few pitons into his pack in case they needed to rappel. Two ice axes, a ski pole and not much food. Erhard described their rations. "We could have fit the food in an eyeglasses case: four Ovo Sport and two Mars bars."[90]

The annoying weather pattern added to their stress: good weather for a few hours each morning, snowfall starting at around noon and continuing well into the evening, stars appearing in the late evening, and clear skies throughout the night. The steady accumulation of snow from those daily snowstorms presented a real problem. The face was immense and, in some places, concave. Snow was piling up in dangerous slabs, and the avalanche hazard was becoming unmanageable.

They waited: one week, two weeks, three weeks – not as long as on some expeditions but long enough to grow impatient. Finally, they were fed up. They decided to outsmart the aggravating weather pattern. They would start their climb in the evening just as the weather was beginning to clear. They would climb throughout the night over terrain they had memorized from base camp. By the time dawn arrived, they would be high on the face and would be able to navigate the unknown ground. By noon they would be at the top of the mountain and could descend the other side via the original route on much easier ground, where the daytime storms wouldn't affect them as much. It was a brilliant plan, but it meant getting up and down Cho Oyu in twenty-four hours.

Late in the afternoon of September 14, they left camp and hiked up to the base of the wall. They found a comfortable spot and settled in to wait for dusk and for the daily snowstorm to let up. They cooked up a cheese fondue, monitoring the weather with every mouthful of the hot, stringy cheese. The temperature felt dangerously warm, increasing the likelihood of avalanches. "Whenever I put a piece of fondue to my mouth, I ate it with snowflakes," Voytek recounted. "But much worse, I heard the rumble of avalanches with every single bite." Erhard and Jean spoke quietly together in French. The rumbling continued. Voytek was silent, but his emotions were in turmoil. He felt incredibly lonely as his teammates conversed in

French. He sat there at the foot of the face, shaken by the avalanches, assessing the danger, growing annoyed at their incessant chatting. Finally, the feeling of helplessness morphed into something else entirely. Angry now, he announced, "Hey, guys, I want to tell you something. I'm not going."

Erhard ignored the blunt statement. Jean looked surprised. They continued eating their fondue and Erhard and Jean resumed their conversation. Voytek was already organizing his pack for the hike back to camp when Jean asked, "Do you have some kind of bad premonition?"

"No premonition, Jean. It's just dangerous. Obviously dangerous. You can hear these avalanches all the time." The two Swiss continued talking. About what, Voytek had no clue. Finally, he asked, "Are you going up?"

"Yes, we are," Jean said.

Voytek turned and started the long walk back to base camp. He remembered the feeling, many years later. "I was not happy. This climb was my idea. I proposed it. And here I was, going down. And these two brilliant, brave guys were going up. My good friends. Can you imagine how I felt? Shitty." He trudged down through the scree, his headlamp slashing the darkness, illuminating the snowflakes as they floated in front of his face, dancing in fantastic patterns. Dizzy from the snowflakes, he stumbled in the scree. One hour passed. A second hour passed. He struggled with his emotions, trying to come to terms with this defeat, knowing he must. For his own dignity and his peace of mind, he must accept the decision he had made, regardless of Erhard and Jean's resolve to continue. He grew weary as the descent stretched past the two-hour mark. He couldn't believe how exhausted he was. It was as if he were coming down from the summit. How could he have ever imagined climbing that face? Now he was not only exhausted but destroyed, both in body and in spirit.

He turned off his headlamp and spied two distant lights. Probably base camp, hopefully only a few hundred metres away. Seconds later, he heard a terrifying roar immediately in front of him. He leapt back and fell to the ground. What on earth? Sprawled on the boulders, he turned on his headlamp. There, standing on the trail, was a giant shaggy face. A yak stared back at him. His glittering eyes explained those mysterious lights, and, looking around, Voytek realized that he wasn't a few hundred metres from base camp, he was *in* it. Nothing more to fear.

He started laughing. A liberating, gut-massaging laugh. He felt an explosive release of tension from the paralysis of fear, almost as if he'd undergone shock therapy. "I realized that everything up to this point was an illusion," he explained. "Just a second before, I thought I was going to be killed by a monster far from home, and now I saw this was a friendly yak and I was in the middle of my home." Still sprawled on the rocks, he looked back toward the face of Cho Oyu with a completely new attitude. "I no longer minded that I had retreated. I had been suffering, feeling beaten, feeling like a coward. In a second, it all changed."

Voytek stood up, shook himself off and walked a few steps to the mess tent. He removed his pack and lit the stove. He would enjoy a cup of tea while savouring this peaceful state of mind. "Okay, I am defeated. It is my great pleasure to be defeated. I am free of ambition. Of all these obsessions. This is good."

As he started on his second cup of tea, he heard noises outside the tent. Since it was already well after midnight, he wondered who might be approaching the camp at such a late hour. Could they be robbers? The door flap opened. There stood Jean and Erhard. Surprised, Voytek asked, "Hey, guys, what are you doing here?" They took off their packs and leaned them up against the wall of the tent but said nothing. He pressed them for an explanation. "What happened?" No answer. Not a single word.

Frustrated and fed up, Voytek turned away and continued with his tea. He refused to allow his feelings of peace and contentment to be destroyed by these two guys. Erhard left the tent. Jean remained, removing some of his outer clothing. Voytek tried again. "Please, Jean, tell me. Why did you leave the face?"

"Well, actually, an avalanche came down, and we barely held on with our axes. We hardly survived. After the avalanche, we decided to come down."

Voytek pressed for details. "Where did it happen?"

"Just about 100 metres after crossing the bergschrund."

The following morning, they agreed to try again when the mountain was in a safer condition. Five days later, on September 19, they made the same approach to the bottom of the face. Erhard later wrote that Voytek was in much better spirits. "Voytek seemed to have gotten over his attack of the blues, and he hit his stride, looking like Gene Kelly in *An American in Paris.*"[91] They ate an equally delicious Swiss fondue, placed their tiny packs on their backs and started climbing.

The climbers soloed through the night, vaulting up the face, holding on with their axes when spindrift hunted them, threatening to sweep them off. It stopped snowing at around midnight, and a starry night emerged. They continued racing up in the wan starlight, through the plunging temperatures. Just before dawn they encountered their first serious obstacle, a steep rock barrier furrowed by 60° snow gullies. In the early morning hours, after traversing an airy knife-edge, they reached another rock barrier. Voytek asked Jean to throw the rope down for a belay. Jean seemed a little irritated about having to slow down for the belay, but Voytek didn't care. They were partners, after all, and he had done the same for his climbing partners many times in the past. As soon as the challenging section was over they dispensed with the rope.

They navigated up through a couple of linked snowfields hemmed in by rock. Just as they were approaching another rock barrier, they had to cross a snowfield; Voytek suggested roping up because the avalanche hazard was high due to the slope's concave shape. He faced another distinct lack of enthusiasm from his partners, but he insisted that the few minutes saved by climbing solo weren't worth the risk. So he pulled out the rope and led through the short section, followed by Jean and Erhard.

They reached one last, Grade IV rock band at around noon. When Voytek soloed up first, followed by the others, Jean complimented him on his effort, perhaps trying to atone for his earlier impatience. But there was little conversation, since they climbed independently and at their own pace. "On a big wall, there is no talking," Voytek explained. "You just climb."

Eventually, they reached a slanting snowfield that led up to the summit ridge. Despite their plan for a rapid ascent, it was evening before they arrived at this ridge separating the Khumbu side of Cho Oyu from the Tibetan side. A damp mist had crept in, creating a featureless pallor that obscured their visibility. They knew that a gentle, snowy plateau was all that lay between them and the summit, but they worried about continuing, because there would surely be wind on the open expanse. Given the current whiteout conditions, they could wander around up there for hours, trying to find the highest point and, more critically, the descent route. There was only one solution. They dug out a ledge in the snow, protected by a large boulder, sat down on their packs and covered themselves with their paper-thin bivouac sack. They were at around 8130 metres and would sit out the rest of the night, waiting for the dawn.

There were three positions on the tiny ledge: one on the left, one on the right and one in the middle. The one in the middle was clearly the preferred position, with protection from the elements and body warmth from both sides. Jean, Erhard and Voytek looked awkwardly at the ledge, then at each other. No one dared move. Finally, Voytek took one of the outside seats, but Jean then pushed him into the middle of the ledge. Voytek tried to resist; Jean was bulkier than him and wouldn't let him move. He spent the rest of the night sandwiched between the two climbers and awoke refreshed, ready for the next day. It was Jean who suffered most that night; his toes were black with frostbite by the end of the trip.

They reached the summit after an hour of climbing the following morning. As they started down the normal route, Voytek felt buoyed by the climb and motivated for Shishapangma. They raced down the mountain and were in base camp by 6 p.m. Voytek immediately started talking about the logistics of shifting their camp over to Shishapangma, hiring porters and firming up dates. Erhard was strangely silent. Years later, he admitted to Voytek that he had grave misgivings about Shishapangma at this point. "I didn't want to go," Erhard confided. But he said nothing about his concerns, and after only one day, they walked down to the valley and piled into a Jeep to head over to their second mountain. Voytek's exuberance swept the party along. He hardly noticed Erhard's reticence, so excited was he about the next stage of the expedition. Jean neither objected nor showed much enthusiasm.

Two days later they arrived at the Shishapangma base camp. Voytek knew the area, since he had been there in October 1987 with Halina, intent on soloing the same route they were about to try. Heavy snowfall had almost buried them in camp, and the couple had fled the area. But this year was different. Voytek described the scene: "In the morning hours of September 29, we set up base camp at a peaceful lake at 5400 metres. The weather was perfect and the moon was about to be full. Moss and dry grass gave comfort and big boulders sheltered us from the wind. The face appeared to be in perfect condition."[92]

Unfortunately, the rapport between Voytek and Erhard was still not ideal. Erhard, when he later wrote about the expedition, showed signs of excluding Voytek, even on Shishapangma. "Jean and I were now planning to climb a strikingly simple line – the most direct line that had ever been climbed on an 8000er. I knew that we only needed two days of good weather to finish this first ascent."[93] No mention of Voytek.

On this second 8000er they would again climb night-naked – one single push with just four chocolate bars, three bottles of liquid, 30 metres of 7-millimetre rope and four pitons. They even left their harnesses behind. They set out from base camp at 9 a.m. on October 2 and hiked up toward the bottom of the face, where they ate another fondue, now a pre-climb tradition. "We attributed all sorts of powers to this dish: it improved energy, vigor, and digestion, and maybe it even had a placebo effect on our morale and performance," Erhard explained.[94] At 6 p.m., just as the last rays of the sun were caressing the upper section of the wall, they began climbing. They sped up the face throughout the night and, near the top, came up against a steep, narrowing section of the couloir. Jean and Erhard were ahead of Voytek and chose the most obvious weakness. Voytek spied a steeper line that he thought might provide a quicker route to the col between the West and Central summits. He felt strong and confident and thought the shortcut might allow him to catch up with the Swiss. Besides, it looked "interesting."

It proved more than interesting. Before long Voytek was stuck. He tried straight up and then a little to the left, but both were the same. He moved up a bit more and then realized it led nowhere. He was forced to downclimb this technical ground – much harder than going up. After 100 metres he made it down, albeit somewhat shaken. Chastened by his bad decision, he headed over to the line that Jean and Erhard had already climbed. They were now a couple of hours ahead of him, and once again, he felt alone on the mountain.

When he finally met up with the others, they were already on their way down. They had reached the top of Shishapangma's Central Summit at 10 a.m. after sixteen hours of climbing, but, strangely, no details were exchanged between them and Voytek. Voytek simply told them he would carry on up. "He's a bit like a tanker truck that, once it gets going, can go for miles on just its kinetic energy," Erhard later observed.[95] They wished him luck and continued down.

Voytek arrived at the Central Summit in a strong wind at 4 p.m. and began trudging on to the col between the two summits. He was headed for the Main Summit, which is only 19 metres higher but much further along the long, undulating ridge. The fierce wind whipping across the ridge discouraged him. He changed strategy and tried to continue up on the Tibetan side, but the snow was knee-deep under a breakable crust. It was hopeless to try and break trail alone after having climbed non-stop for a full night and a day. So, like Erhard and Jean, he made do with the Central Summit and began descending.

He was still a long way from the base when night began closing in. Tired now, he sat down in an armchair-shaped depression in the snow at around 7800 metres and wrapped up as best he could in his down jacket. "Just a few hours," he thought. The hours stretched into the entire night. It was a warm night, so he didn't suffer but rather enjoyed a comfortable rest, alone with his thoughts. What a wonderful place. Such magnificent solitude. After dreaming for so long about this face and this beautifully direct line, now it was almost over. "It was the strangest bivouac of my life," he later said.

But when Voytek continued down the following morning he was surprised to note that he was moving more and more slowly with each step. So tired. So thirsty. A crazy, overpowering thirst. He began to imagine different ways of producing some water. He tried to light a bit of toilet paper with his lighter to melt the snow with its heat, but the toilet paper refused to burn. He rubbed sun cream onto the toilet paper, hoping the lotion might have some magical chemical to promote ignition. No change. Finally, he rammed his water bottle full of snow and attached it to the top of his pack while he front-pointed down the 50° slope, counting on the sun to melt the snow. Slowly and carefully, he made his way down to 5800 metres, where he found a pond and drank greedily.

Down at base camp Erhard and Jean were worried. They scanned the face, looking for any sign of life, dreading the worst. "I didn't want to believe that a mountaineer of Voytek's caliber had been defeated by that face," Erhard wrote later. "With every passing hour, I grew less certain of a happy outcome. Finally, pessimism injected me with its poison; tears fell on the scenes in my imagination."[96] Jean tried to reassure Erhard, but with little success.

Still two or three hours from base camp, Voytek stretched out and slept again: his second bivouac on descent. This was an unusually sluggish pace for Voytek. He carried on the next morning and arrived at base camp after a few hours of slow, laboured walking. It was deserted. Voytek crawled into his tent and fell into a deep sleep.

When Erhard and Jean had become overcome with concern for Voytek, they had headed back up toward the glacier to look for him. Upon reaching the snow and discovering their descent tracks, they almost fainted in relief, for there were three sets of tracks. "Voytek had just walked there, wearing those Adidas boots that belonged only to him and that we loved," Erhard explained.[97] Because Jean and Erhard had chosen a slightly different route up to the base of the wall, they had somehow missed him. Relieved, they sped back down to camp.

Voytek eventually emerged from his slumber when he heard someone calling, "Is that you, Voytek? Are you okay?" Voytek mumbled yes and dozed off again. When he finally woke, the three gathered to exchange their stories. Erhard noticed that Voytek had some difficulty talking, so depleted was his body. It had been two days since he had eaten or drunk anything, and the two nights of open-air, high-altitude bivouacs had taken their toll. "Voytek's emaciated face and hollow eyes, his stupor and lethargy, all gave his story a sense of having come back from the grave."[98] Voytek couldn't have anticipated it, but Shishapangma had given him the chance to perfect the art of suffering.

Jean, Erhard and Voytek had reached the Central Summit of Shishapangma a mere thirteen days after climbing Cho Oyu. Both were new routes. Both were done in night-naked style. A new standard of alpinism in the Himalaya had been established. And for Voytek, Shishapangma was his twelfth new alpine-style route in the Greater Ranges, six of which were on 8000ers.

Back in Kathmandu, they met for a final meal together. Despite the arguments, Voytek longed to bring some emotional closure to the trip. He decided to make a little speech to the Swiss duo. "Guys, we had a good expedition, right? Yes, we did. And I must say, it was an extremely hard expedition for me. It was a tough time socializing with you, but I want to say that, still, I enjoyed this expedition enormously. I am proud to be your partner, precisely because this trip was so difficult. We survived and we are what we are. We have come back and we are still friends." The fragile moment passed and the tension eased.

Voytek's emphasis on friendship went back – way back – to his painful split with Jurek. He had been, for a time, almost like a brother to Voytek. It baffled Voytek that Jurek had flitted from one large expedition to another, barely aware of who he was climbing with, solely to claim another 8000-metre summit. Voytek was sure this had increased the risks exponentially, and history proved him right. He was convinced that the best relationships were with partners on small teams. "The event of an alpine-style ascent has a very deep, ethical reason. I would go only with someone very dear to me," he said.[99] It was only then that partners truly cared about each other and watched out for each other. That's what Voytek valued above all, and why he was so hurt by Erhard's behaviour on the Cho Oyu expedition.

He may have been hurt as well by Erhard's assessment of the climbs, which could be interpreted as an indication of either modesty or arrogance. About the Southwest Face of Shishapangma: "It's walking; you do it with an ice ax in one hand and a ski pole in the other." The Swiss alpinist saw Cho Oyu as only slightly harder: "It's walking, with one or two rock sections." And when he was shown a climbing book in which the two climbs were described as important milestones in Himalayan climbing, Erhard scoffed, "I'm going to tell you honestly – that's rubbish."[100] Voytek agreed with Erhard's assessment of the Shishapangma route but added, "This is exactly what constitutes its value. It is the quickest and shortest line existing on an 8000-metre peak. It fulfills the climber's dream of rising to the sky in the span of a few hours." About the Southwest Face of Cho Oyu, he felt differently. "The Cho Oyu line is much more difficult and complex. The degree of difficulty is easy to express: Grade IV rock and 60° ice. But the value of this route far exceeds the numbers. This is truly a line of character. It is simply beautiful and bold. I consider it one of the smartest lines on an 8000er in the Himalaya to be climbed in alpine style. For the experienced eye, it's obvious just from the photo." Voytek suspected that Erhard's deprecating comments were likely motivated by their mutual dislike of the "omnipresent, tacky media tendency to evaluate everything and everybody in terms of milestones and legends and other meaningless things."

The rift between Erhard and Voytek disappeared as mysteriously as it had appeared, and in a couple of years they were climbing together again. Erhard later publicly stated, "I would go to hell with Voytek: if Voytek calls me, I will go with him anywhere." Even now, Voytek remains puzzled about what happened on the expedition. "It is strange. A great relationship before – and later. But not during." He wonders if he was too pushy on the trip, forcing his opinion too hard on the boys.

Despite everything, their Cho Oyu and Shishapangma ascents raised high-altitude climbing to a new standard. No camps. No sleeping bags. On Shishapangma, not even a harness. For Voytek, night-naked style took freedom to the next level. "Climbing in this way means dancing with continuously changing situations. Your entire self takes part in this dance. Dancing is pure creation. That's why it's so terribly appealing."

A leading alpinist from the next generation, American Steve House, reflected on this and other climbs of this period, placing them in perspective. "Historically, the best barometer of the state of climbing has been alpinism. And the last stylistic climax in alpine climbing came in the mid- to late 1980s when many of the 8000-meter peaks were climbed in single-push style, often by new routes. Such climbing was termed 'night-naked' by Voytek Kurtyka; he, Jean Troillet, Pierre-Alain Steiner and Erhard Loretan were at the center of adapting this bivouac-less style to the peaks of the Himalaya."[101] Slovenian alpinist Andrej Štremfelj agrees and wonders how future alpinists will deal with the bar being set this high. "This generation climbed in the Himalaya incessantly until the end of the century and so brought alpine style to such extremes that the future will require a twist in psychology in order to enable even greater deeds and more difficult routes to be done."[102]

Cho Oyu and Shishapangma were both beautiful and painful for Voytek. He experienced the full range of emotions: anger, humiliation, loneliness, triumph and, finally, redemption. "After finishing a climb like this you feel a sort of catharsis," Voytek explained. "You are just a happy creature." This expedition was his farewell to the 8000ers and a fitting and elegant departure from the Himalaya: he managed to save a friendship; he pushed the concept of lightweight climbing to an unusually high standard; and everyone survived.

FOURTEEN

Dance of the Underclings

To lose something, or everything, sharpens our vision and gives us an acute awareness of what remains.
— Stephen Alter, *Becoming a Mountain*

By the following summer, Voytek had more on his mind than Himalayan summits. Poland had a new, freely elected president; Voytek's business was growing; and Halina was pregnant with their second child, due that autumn. The situation created considerable stress. "It was like being caught in a trap," he wrote.[103] He clearly needed to "feed the rat," a term British climber Mo Antoine so aptly used in describing the drive that climbers have for flushing out their systems with a good old alpine sufferfest.

Voytek was out climbing in the Kościeliska Valley in the Western Tatras when he spied something interesting – the Raptawica Spire. It rose above the dark spruce forest like a gleaming beacon. One hundred metres of perfect limestone, it beckoned. He was hypnotized by the spire, drawn to it like a moth to light. Although it had already been climbed by several routes, Voytek wondered if a new line might be drawn on this extraordinary piece of rock. Maybe an exciting new route would compensate for his lack of a Himalayan expedition this season.

He began to search for partners. This one was too busy with his studies. Another had recently started a new business. A third was out of shape. The summer was slipping by and Voytek was becoming anxious. He tried infiltrating a clique of young sport climbers full of swagger. "No way," they said. "We need to keep our skills up for the crags. We don't have time to develop a long route with you." He finally found a climber half his age, twenty-two-year-old Grzegorz Zajda, who was willing to help him. They ascended the spire on an already established route and rappelled down, searching for a clean piece of undeveloped rock. Voytek was excited as he examined the spire up close. "You Pretty – I spoke to myself and caressed the white rock covered by tiny Karst spikes."[104]

The wall was mostly vertical, with a few overhanging sections. When Voytek discovered that the lower part was smooth as marble, he began to doubt the sanity of his plan. But upon closer inspection, he could see potential holds. Unfortunately, they were all inverted. Climbing it would mean using underclings as handholds, repeatedly. As he dangled in the air, being lowered down the spire, it appeared that this climb – if it could be done – would be defined by underclings.

The two began working on the route, driving three hours from Krakow to the spire, climbing for a few hours and then driving back. It was a brutal schedule. Not as committing as going to the Karakoram but still all-engaging. Then a new problem emerged. Since the spire was located within a national park, drilling bolts was forbidden. The park rangers had a hunch something was up, so they began monitoring the pair.

Crafty Voytek changed tactics. He and Grzegorz would rise at 3 a.m., drive to the tower, climb between 6 and 8 a.m., and then shut down all activity during the park rangers' normal working hours. After dozing under a shade tree for most of the day, they would start again at around 5 p.m. They could climb another three or four hours, then hop in the car and drive back for a late-evening arrival in Krakow. Driving back was the most harrowing part of each day. "After 20 hours of efforts and excitement I was shrinking before every charging headlight," he wrote. "Hands clamped on the wheel, on the verge of sleep, twice I avoided a ghostly truck by inches. No 8000-metre peak was as dangerous as the Zakopane Highway between 21:00 and 23:00..."[105]

Halina was not amused by the new schedule. Her stay-at-home husband, who had supposedly remained in Krakow because of the expected baby, was rarely at home. And when he *was* there, his mind was elsewhere. He stared absently into space, mimicking strange jerky movements to the left, throwing an arm above his head, grunting with the effort he knew that move required, then staring at his fingers as the "magic pump" – those tiny beads of perspiration he claimed had ruined his first marriage – appeared. Halina shook her head in bewilderment. Little Alex shrieked in laughter at his dad's strange, spastic movements and his wonderful grimaces.

Voytek was fixated on the route, focused now on fingernail-width edges, sharp underclings and dynamic lunges. Discouraged by their glacial progress on the climb, he concluded that the only appropriate name for the line was *Breaker*. "I knew the name was right – I felt that in every particle of my tortured flesh," he wrote.[106] His hands became torn as he fought for every centimetre of upward movement, rehearsing each move over and over, ripping his fingertips to shreds in the process.

Now that the (potential) route had a name, they proceeded to name each pitch. Pitch one became "Arrival of the Underholds." The second was dubbed "Underholds Are Feeling Very Good." And pitch three was christened "Farewell to Underholds." Clearly, a theme was emerging.

When Voytek fell asleep at the wheel on the commute home one night, almost crashing, he decided to change tactics once again. They would drive to the spire during daylight hours, work the evening shift and then spend the night in the nearby mountain rescue headquarters building. In addition to this being safer, they would be much closer to the spire for the early-morning shift. Before long, they decided they were wasting too much time walking to and from the spire, so they camped in a nearby cave. Their commitment to the climb had reached a fanatical level. Almost a comical one.

The summer slipped by, week by week. Voytek's fingers wore down, millimetre by millimetre. Halina grew larger each day. In the middle of the night on September 1, Halina shook Voytek awake. "Voytek, I think the baby is coming. Take me to the hospital."

Unbelievably, Voytek reacted with indignation. "What? You said it would be in two weeks." He needed at least two more weeks to finish his climb.

Agnieska (Agnes) was born the following day, and Voytek spun in a swirl of noisy domesticity: crying Agnes, shouting Alex, exhausted Halina. Yet his mind was still on the Raptawica Spire. Halina finally dismissed him with "Just go. Finish it."

Shortly after Agnes's birth, Voytek was back at his climb. (Time estimates vary between one and a few days, depending on the source.) After two more weeks of effort, they finished their route on September 17. "And that Sunday, between 1 and 3 p.m., we climbed *Breaker* RP, that is – as Riko would say – in 'prrr... [pure] style'. But who save us knows what it really means?"[107] The three-pitch route was graded Polish VI.5- (French 7c+) and has only one confirmed repeat, partly due to its location in a restricted area.

Voytek was consumed with shame after the climb. Not because he had left his family so soon after his daughter's birth but because he had bolted the beautiful new route. He had previously stated that climbing bolted sport routes was a kind of "consumption." But actually *placing* the bolts? That was inexcusable. "I blame myself and point the finger at myself," he later explained. "I am distressed by all that steel being put into the rock. I wouldn't mind it if there were lots of rocks – as in Spain or Greece. It's different here. We have hardly any crags, and they are degraded by the great number of people visiting them every day. They are so crowded. Yes, of course I go there, too. But if I'm a bastard, I always say it loudly – I am a bastard. But it doesn't mean I accept it." Then, laughing, he concluded, "Okay, I am a bastard. And I enjoy it! Yes!"

Despite his post-climb regrets, photos of Voytek working the route reveal a shameless, broadly smiling face that radiates happiness. He had salvaged the season; he had done something interesting. And he was proud that he had managed, at least in his opinion, to be a good and responsible husband and father. Halina, in an interview a few years later, was asked about how Voytek's behaviour had changed once he became a father. She laughed at the camera. "Voytek didn't change at all," she said, shaking her head. "He was exactly the same."

Halina's statement had a ring of truth. Despite his vow to give up on expeditions to the Greater Ranges, Voytek was not quite finished with K2. He returned unsuccessfully in 1992 with Erhard and again in 1994 with Krzysztof Wielicki and American alpinist Carlos Buhler, still hoping for a route on the elusive West Face. His obsession with the West Face was part of the problem, since it was such an ambitious objective. In 1994 their strategy was to fix lines on the lower ice slopes to facilitate a speedy ascent, and to climb the upper part of the mountain in alpine style. Despite the new tactics, the West Face wouldn't co-operate. The powerful August sun baked down on the ice-covered face, which soon ran with water. "I had never seen an 8000-metre mountain change into a waterfall like that," Voytek recalled. Their fixed-line strategy was hopeless. The ropes dangled in the running water during the daytime, and the cold alpine nights froze them in place. When their chances on the West Face slipped away, they traversed to the *Basque Route*. Voytek wasn't remotely interested in the route, but he climbed with them to Camp IV all the same. The wind blew with hurricane force all night. At 2 a.m. it was so strong that no one stirred from their tents. By 5 a.m. the wind had lost a bit of its fury. Buried deep in his sleeping bag and half asleep, Voytek detected sounds of movement in the camp. He sat up and saw that Krzysztof was quietly putting on his outer clothing, gearing up for a summit attempt. "Do you think it makes sense?" Voytek asked.

"The others are moving. So I'll try," Krzysztof answered.

Voytek sat there, watching. Should he go? Follow the flock? "The tent was still flapping in the wind," he recalled. "It felt aggressive, and it was annoying me. It was late for a summit bid, and the wind was troubling." No, he would not go. He would stay in camp and provide backup for the others. He burrowed back into his bag.

Krzysztof left with Carlos and New Zealand climber Rob Hall, along with two others: Australia's Michael Groom and Veikka Gustafsson from Finland. By 7 a.m. the wind had died down completely and the Shoulder on K2 was basking in sunshine. Voytek felt foolish. "What's wrong with me?" he wondered. "Why am I staying here in camp?" To entertain himself, he went for a leisurely stroll 200 metres from the tents, trailing his bootlaces, which he had carelessly left untied. The walking was easy and exhilarating. He felt fantastic: fit and acclimatized, strong and healthy. The situation was absurd. For a while, he considered gearing up and following their trail up the mountain. But, no way. It was 8 a.m., much too late to begin.

As he watched their progress below the Bottleneck, Voytek had a strange sensation that something was amiss. Years later, he recalled his thought process that day.

Gradually, I grasped it. I was shamelessly devoid of any ambition. I didn't feel any distress or disappointment that I was not with the others. Their quest seemed irrelevant to my situation. For the first time in my climbing life I clearly perceived a certain change within me. Some part of my life was coming to an end. I realized that pushing to my limit one more time wouldn't reveal anything new to me. On the contrary, at this stage of my life, the obsessive pursuit of the art of suffering was obstructing the vista. Was I then a wasted, decadent person? I didn't feel so. Okay, I guessed I would be receding from the public show, but I felt like I was in the middle of a huge galactic crystal. I knew I was a part of it. My presence here made sense. I remained on my path. The obsessive journey to the edge of the crystal had lost its appeal because I had the premonition that the final challenge was the journey inward, into the crystal.

He watched the others as they continued climbing, more slowly the higher they went. All but one turned around close to the summit. The one who persisted turned out to be Rob Hall, using bottled oxygen. Shortly after midnight Carlos and Krzysztof piled into Voytek's tent, where hot tea awaited them.

Years later, Voytek pondered his behaviour on K2 that day. "If I had wanted to summit K2, that was the day. I should have done it," he said. "But it wasn't the route I wanted, and it didn't interest me." Once again, the path proved more important than the destination. Occasionally, when he reflected on his decision, he wondered if it had been a mistake. Perhaps he should have just climbed it. But when he was perfectly honest with himself, with his values and with his chosen path, he knew that failure on the West Face was more important to him than success on the *Basque Route*. The path...each time the path. The cost of staying on that path was turning out to be quite high.

This was particularly true given the success of other Polish alpinists only slightly before this time. After Jurek and Artur climbed Manaslu in 1986, the pair made the first winter ascent of Annapurna. And Jurek finished off his 8000-metre quest the following year with a new route on Shishapangma, again with Artur. Krzysztof too was on fire, having made the first winter ascent of Lhotse on the last day of 1988 and a very fast ascent of the East Face of Dhaulagiri. He climbed both these routes solo. Wanda had made the first female ascent of K2, among her many climbs. But the list of successes ended in 1989 when five of Poland's best alpinists – Eugeniusz Chrobak, Mirosław Dąsal, Mirosław Gardzielewski, Andrzej Heinrich and Wacław Otręba – were killed on the West Ridge of Everest, and the indestructible Jurek fell to his death on the South Face of Lhotse. It seemed as if the Poles were climbing themselves into extinction.

By the early to mid-1990s, Voytek noticed a change in his Himalayan track record: the failures now outnumbered the successes. Not that he was a stranger to failure, far from it. But after 1991 the disappointments came more frequently. "It was strange, and quite striking, that at this stage of my climbing, I had a series of failures." He became almost paranoid. "Maybe it was time for me to pay back for the extreme luck in my life," he mused. "Maybe failure would now be pursuing me." When he added up the time spent at K2 – 110 days, only eight of them without snowfall – he was puzzled. "I started suspecting it was time to repay my debts," he admitted.

He tried one more time on K2, this time in 2000 with Yasushi and Taeko Yamanoi on the East Face, declared by Voytek to be another "masterpiece on the planet." He forgot all about his reflections resulting from his last attempt with Krzysztof and Carlos; the image of the East Face had stolen his heart. "I was addicted to it for ages, and as in all love affairs, the new partnership with Yasushi and Taeko awoke hope in me." Despite clever fresh tactics, they experienced the same weather patterns as before: weeks of useless snowstorms and wasted hopes. "At one point, I understood I was finally fed up with K2," Voytek said, laughing. When Yasushi decided to make another attempt at the summit via the *Basque Route*, Voytek knew he couldn't face days of toiling up fixed ropes. He excused himself. "K2 had finally confirmed itself as my great failure," he said. "It was a tremendous chapter in my life. It rejected all my approaches, but it consequently established one of the most important reconciliations of my life."

Instead of going back to Poland, he set off on a solo trek, prolonging the transition from the mountains to his other life. One week in the Hushe and Nangpa valleys swept away his sad farewell to K2. "The mountains regained their grandeur," he said. "I continued my journey into the crystal."

Yasushi later reached the summit alone via the *Basque Route* on the South-Southeast Rib. One year later, the trio returned to the Karakoram to try Latok I but climbed the magnificent Biacherahi Central Tower instead.

Voytek tried to analyze the experiences of failure – and his reaction to them. "After each failure, I had returned home like a sad puppy that had fallen out of a running sled. The mountains had a stranger and stranger meaning for me. My climbing grew in significance and turned into a pilgrimage. I continued to believe that next time a veil would lift, and the strange, unremitting internal tension would dissolve."[108]

The pilgrimage continued. There was an attempt on the long and committing Mazeno Ridge on Nanga Parbat with Doug Scott in 1993; another attempt on the same ridge with Doug Scott and party in 1995; and a third attempt with Erhard in 1997. The latter was perhaps the strangest expedition of all. Voytek later admitted the weather was perfect. The conditions were perfect. His partner was perfect. But at some point, they both agreed to retreat from all this perfection. He tried to explain. "At the last stage of my climbing in the Himalaya, everything had changed. The reasons changed. I confessed to my own weakness. This was the case on Mazeno. We were happy to be defeated and to leave," he laughed, remembering that curious Mazeno day.

After each failure, he reminded himself that it was essential to retain the ability to accept defeat. He knew life was full of failure and not only in the mountains: failure with finances, failure in love, failure in artistic endeavours. He wanted to be prepared. "I knew I had to be utterly immune to these failures. If I couldn't find a way to be immune, then real problems would begin in my life. That would signify total failure." With time, he grew to value and take pride in his defeats, knowing he had discovered a new source of strength.

Voytek needed every bit of that strength because his life was now bursting with responsibility. He had a demanding business. He had a house and a massive garden. He had a wife and two children. He felt responsible for his family and was convinced he needed to continue making changes to his lifestyle in order to be a better father. Halina didn't notice any changes. In a film about Voytek called *Way of the Mountain*, she said, "I don't think Voytek's approach to the mountains changed much…I don't think he ever hesitated when he had to choose between staying with us or going on an expedition."

His daughter, Agnes, was a little more generous in her assessment, attributing much of his absenteeism to his work. "A trip somewhere with my father to some exotic islands would definitely have been fun...but on the other hand I realize that for him there was no such thing as a holiday. He was constantly thinking about work." Agnes rarely saw her father, but being a practical girl, she accepted his long absences as normal. He was fully engaged in his import business, and his schedule was complicated, with frequent trips abroad. "I didn't worry," she said. "He was travelling a lot to India and Indonesia for work, and I didn't see the difference between those trips and his climbing trips."

Alex, Voytek's son, did differentiate between the types of trips and remembered the preparation for climbing expeditions as exciting. "It was fun for us to see all that gear." Even more memorable for Alex was when Voytek would return. "He always seemed fresh and happy after an expedition," he said.

Agnes's image of Voytek during this time was as neither a climber nor a businessman but as a gardener. "It seemed more important to him than anything," she said. "One of my favourite memories of my father is of him on cold, misty autumn mornings. He would take his coffee cup and go out to the garden, walk three steps and stop and look at a plant. Then three more steps and examine another plant. I think he was happy there in his garden."

Alex recalled the occasion of his First Communion, when the family was preparing for the celebration, carting tables and chairs around, preparing food and drinks. Voytek was nowhere to be found. When he finally appeared, he was carrying a ladder and a camera, on his way to the garden to capture an image of one of his beloved trees. "He was in his own world," Alex said, laughing, with some generosity.

Voytek was slowly beginning to understand that alpinism was no longer the great challenge and creation of his life. He realized it wouldn't help him discover anything more in himself. "It didn't make sense anymore," he explained. "To suffer and suffer, for what?" Now, Voytek saw more clearly the flip side of the art of suffering, which Polish alpinists, in particular, had perfected. He knew from experience that to survive in intensely cold conditions, with little food or water, with fear gnawing constantly, all the while expending tremendous physical effort, required a certain stolidness. In Himalayan climbing, this was seen as a virtue. Voytek agreed that this indifference was considered an admirable trait, or at least a necessary one. But what did it look like from the outside? Often selfish callousness. It was much easier to focus on one's own battle with exhaustion and terror than to empathize with a less able partner. "I am sadly convinced that ego-centricity and a kind of inner deafness are common personality blemishes in our climbing community, more so than many care to admit," he said.[109]

It was no longer imperative for Voytek to do yet another climb. He knew exactly what he would experience. "It would be the same story: the same pitons, the same plodding, the same guessing, the same mystery, nothing – absolutely nothing – new. I loved the mountains but I lost interest in repeating the same story," he explained.

Even more fundamental was his change in attitude to landscapes other than mountains. "I began to see the same marvels in the forest," he said, gazing out his window into the nearby woods. His daughter agreed, re-calling their long walks in the woods. "My love for nature comes from him," she said. His words reflected a maturity, a mellowing, a more open mind to softer landscapes and a less intense lifestyle.

But Voytek, the rock animal, was not quite done with risk.

FIFTEEN

Chinese Maharaja

Find beauty; be still.
—W.H. Murray in *The Sunlit Summit* by Robin Lloyd-Jones

The Krakow Mountain Film Festival was in full swing. Over a thousand people thronged the stadium to hear climbers tell their stories and to watch nail-biting adventure films. When the program had ended and the audience was streaming out into the lobby, a couple of young climbers were overheard discussing a film they had seen about Voytek.

"Really intelligent guy," one of them commented.

"Yeah, super-rad climber too," replied his friend.

"I didn't know Voytek climbed in the Himalaya," the first mused, somewhat puzzled. "I thought he was a rock climber."

"Yeah, that was news to me too. Cool. Pretty well-rounded guy. But rock was his main deal. For sure."

Such was Voytek's reputation among the younger generation of climbers in Poland. He was known for his bold rock climbs, many of them solo. In fact, by the 1990s, his Himalayan career had been somewhat forgotten – or perhaps had never been fully known – by young Polish rock climbers. By this time, sport climbing was firmly established in the country. Climbing at the crags was no longer done exclusively on top-ropes, since bolted routes were everywhere. Young climbers were pushing the standards to extremely high levels, as in the rest of Europe.

And there, at the local Krakow crags – with the twenty-somethings, all lean as hounds – was Voytek, now in his late forties. He still moved with a kind of negligent grace, like a dancer. He fit in well with this special tribe of crag rats. He called them "believers" and admitted he was one of those believers: contact with the rock was such a necessary part of his life that it had the makings of a cult. "It isn't difficult to spot a believer in the crowd," he wrote. "Often they are strikingly skinny... But more to the point: if you ever notice flighty, almost independently alive fingers, searching every nook and crevice to hook onto, take a closer look... If the pads are covered in a leathery layer, hard like a nutshell, the joints visibly swollen, endowing the palm with the look of a bird-of-prey claw, you can be sure you're looking at a believer."[110] He could have mentioned their club-like forearms, their hunched and bulging shoulders and their skinny, underdeveloped legs, as well. "Look this person in the eye," he continued. "If, in that vacant stare, he is wandering through space, looking for something indefinite, and meanwhile, peculiar movements and facial grimaces ensue, you can be sure – he's a true believer."[111]

Voytek climbed hard alongside the other believers – often at the level of French 7c+ and 8a (North American 5.13a and 5.13b) – sometimes solo. His motivation for dispensing with the rope was the same as it is for all soloists: the fewer restraints, the better. Despite his domestic and business responsibilities, he was still intent on pushing his own limits, and soloing was a way to do so without spending months on end in Asia. He understood the inherent danger in solo climbing but insisted that it was much less than on many of his big-wall ascents. Climbing unroped was all about freedom, something Voytek never stopped craving. And in a weak (and brutally honest) moment, he admitted he enjoyed the shock effect that his hard climbs had on those rock jocks young enough to be his children. Routes such as *Shock the Monkey* (Polish VI.5+/6; 8a/8a+; 5.13b/5.13c RP), possibly his hardest sport climb, which he climbed in 1993 at the age of forty-six. His most notable rock climb, however, was undoubtedly his solo climb of *Chiński Maharadża* (*Chinese Maharaja*) (Polish VI.5; 7c+; 5.13a), which he climbed the same year.

From his earliest days on rock, Voytek had shown a natural talent for soloing. He had a spontaneous, animalistic need to move up, and he climbed quickly, with a sense of urgency and excitement. "Because it gives me a thrill," he gushed. But it wasn't only about darting up the rock like a gecko. Solo climbing was also a head game. Whenever the animalistic urge to move up faltered, the mental challenge would begin.

Voytek wanted to solo *Chinese Maharaja*, a bolted rock climb not far from Krakow, but more important, he wanted to do so in a completely relaxed manner. In fact, this was his one self-imposed condition for soloing it. "I will manage to preserve an absolute calm," he promised himself. "The same level of calmness as taking a cup of coffee in my garden. It will be a kind of test for myself."

He knew exactly what he wanted to avoid. Back in 1985, when he had soloed *Filar Abazego* (French 7a+), a strange thing had occurred. He had floated up through the lower difficulties and was nearing the crux. "My left hand reached for the key undercling," he explained. "In this position, the body forms a tense, wound-up ball of energy, concentrated in the fingertips hooked high overhead on a precarious, small undercling. With my left foot on a slippery bulge, I began, on the verge of a delicate balance move, pulling on the undercling, only to feel an oddly familiar weakness. It wasn't a normal lack of strength, and I recognized it immediately: it was a jelly-like weakness." Voytek began to lose the tension in his body, and with that loss of tension his strength melted away. His body became limp. "In a panic, I felt the void under my feet and the rocky meadow beneath *Abaz*. Somewhere off to the side I could hear the gurgle of a stream."[112]

All of this happened in a fraction of a second: the concentration on the undercling, the slippery foothold, the loss of body tension, the awareness of the void beneath him. And what happened next? He regained control. He *demanded* control. "That command, like a Great Broom, swept away the fragments of my frightened thoughts – thoughts that flew away past the babbling brook, taking with them a fledgling despair. In their place came emptiness; in the emptiness, I pulled again."[113]

This was not the experience he wanted on *Chinese Maharaja*. Voytek wanted no lapse in concentration, no slippery footholds, no loss of body tension and, certainly, no fear. He insisted on absolute calm. He told no one about his intentions. Even Halina didn't know what he was up to. When she eventually became suspicious of his regular, mysterious disappearances, she squeezed a partial truth out of him. Yes, he did intend to solo something. But he wouldn't say what.

Voytek knew he needed to rehearse the moves many times before daring to solo it. The climb was devilishly difficult, particularly solo. The problem was not one of steepness but of delicacy. *Maharaja* was covered in shallow divots large enough for one finger but not deep enough for one to gain traction with that finger. And when the divots petered out, all that remained were maddening sloper holds. Divots and slopers. What a nightmare. He needed an entire dictionary embedded in his hands to pull it off: pinching, palming, squeezing, crimping, pushing and pulling.

The only way to tackle such problems was with the imagination. Luckily, Voytek was not short on imagination. He was sure he could solve the puzzle with a combination of perfect balance and controlled momentum. Perfect balance while climbing is obviously a good thing: careening wildly on a wall with flailing arms and flapping legs is not an elegant sight. Controlled momentum is particularly useful on steep rock with widely spaced holds, since the climber can use momentum to make a dynamic move up to a large, secure hold and then regain his sense of balance. But on *Maharaja*, it wasn't a case of just one dynamic move. And even more problematic was the absence of large, secure holds. Voytek would need to link several dynamic moves between shallow, slippery divots.

That's where the aspect of control became so critical. The dynamic nature of the moves could not be too energetic, or Voytek would propel himself out of the next divot and off the wall. He needed to move dynamically with just the right amount of pressure to glide upward like liquid, divot by divot, not sliding out and never popping off, until he could reach a solid stance. The sequences were complex and ever so delicate. When he rehearsed them in his mind, his fingers were uncontrollably affected by his old friend, the magic pump. "The magic pump infuriated and perplexed me," he mused. "Somewhere in its workings resided the mysterious link between body and soul."[114]

Voytek called *Maharaja* a "feminine route," one that required more finesse than brawn. This kind of climbing took practice, and to rehearse the moves he needed a belayer. But he wanted to keep his project secret. How could he work on this thing over and over without revealing his plan?

As he visualized the climb, his mind sometimes wandered into unthinkable territory. What if a bee buzzed by? What if it thundered? What if someone yelled nearby, breaking his concentration? A leg cramp? A fart? An itchy nose? The possibilities were endless. Any one of these unforeseen occurrences could rip him off the wall and send him plunging to the ground. Voytek was turning into a nervous wreck as he contemplated soloing *Maharaja*. Halina, in turn, was becoming impatient and irritated with this neurotic husband of hers. All he did was worry and stare at his pathetic fingers. And when he wasn't worrying, he was training.

The essence of his training lay in achieving the perfect relationship in what he called the "crank to flank" – strength to weight – ratio. The objective was to have more crank than flank. It sounds simple, but it's not. Should he pursue more crank, or concentrate on losing more flank? He tried to explain the dilemma. "Too much effort towards strength (crank) invariably caused muscle growth, and consequently led to increased body mass (flank), and despite the significant gains in strength, I was disheartened to learn that, in the cosmos of crimpers and slopers, a ballast of flank robbed me of any grace and lightness."[115]

This sounded confusing. "Moreover, as a true believer, I understood that climbing really isn't about a body rising in space, but rather an attempt to rise above oneself. Where does that leave the flank? Why bother sculpting it with athletic training, since it is not the thing that is rising and, what's worse, is but a ballast in the whole endeavour?"[116] Now he seemed conflicted.

Voytek decided to focus on flank. He fasted. He cleansed. He became light as a feather. But as he carved away at his flank, he was horrified to see that the tools of his crank were wasting away at an identical pace. Perpetually tired, he became sluggish.

He shifted his focus to crank. He concentrated on bent-arm pull-ups. Day after day he positioned himself on the iron bar, forcing himself to keep slightly bent arms, pulling up his outstretched legs until his knees were level with the bar. The results were miraculous. "The chest becomes girdled in strength that binds soul to body. The waist is bound tight, promising lightness and beauty. And the shoulders, tensioned and poised, promise unbreakable strength."[117] He graduated to one-arm pull-ups and punished his fingers on the campus board training wall. He ran for hours in the forest. His body became a machine of efficiency, lightness and strength.

But while training was important, it was even more critical to rehearse the actual moves on the rock. He couldn't climb with any of his regular pals because they would soon realize his intention, so he found novice climbers who were happy to belay him. The rehearsals began. The first step was to top-rope *Maharaja*. It felt good on the first try. His confidence bolstered, he repeated the climb twice more, belayed by his patient and innocent belayer. Three repeats without a fall. Then five. Voytek was encouraged but only to a point. "Though it was close to perfection, I arrived at an alarming awareness that the crux section demanded such a delicate balance between upward dynamic momentum and body tension holding my body to the rock that even the slightest deviation from the perfect move would cause me to fall." He realized that all the rehearsing in the world couldn't change it, so why bother?

Still, week after week, he rehearsed *Maharaja*. As the months rolled by, unexpected circumstances foiled his plans for the final attempt: business trips to India, crowds at the crag, family responsibilities. And while he bustled about, preparing for this perfectly "contented" climb, he was inadvertently ensuring that he would never realize that level of serenity. "There's something wrong with you," Halina observed.

Finally, Voytek could put it off no longer. If he rehearsed any more, he would psych himself out to fail. Failing meant falling. The art of soloing is the art of removing this kind of thinking from your brain. It was time to climb.

The day was calm. Only one tiny cloud marred the summer sky. His concentration was intense. His perception of everything around him was magnified to an almost unbearable level. A nearby stream slurped loudly. A snail emerged from behind a rock and galumphed along the ground. He decided to top-rope it one more time. To be sure. "I don't find any traps. The pockets are snail-free. Slopers are in their place."[118]

He pulled the rope and took off his harness. He tightened his shoes. A young couple arrived at the crag, chatting together. As they prepared for their first route they glanced over at Voytek, standing alone at the base of *Maharaja*. In a flash, they grasped his intention. Suddenly there was total silence, intensified by their horror. Everything slowed to a dream-like pace; small images filled the screen, frame by frame, in achingly clear focus. He was wound up like a spring. This was not what he wanted.

With a Herculean effort, he forced himself to focus completely on the present. He needed to place his chalked-up fingers delicately, yet firmly, in each shallow divot. To make precise foot placements on each sloper. To move steadily upward without hesitation. He stepped ahead and touched the rock. "The feeling of the rock gave me a great, encouraging affect," he later said. "I held it stronger, pulled it a bit and then I started moving."

A few easy moves got Voytek up to the black roof. He bent back and reached above the roof for the hidden hold he knew was there. "I climb lightly above the roof – from here there is no return. And in this moment, I feel like I'm waking up from a nightmare. I feel relief. I'm filled with peace."[119] His body tension was good. His fingers were dry. His feet were quiet, moving with great precision from one tiny hold to the next. "The moves flow together with lightness and balance. I start feeling proud that I'm moving upward. My own audacity begins to please me. I want more of this satisfaction."[120]

Below, the couple watched wordlessly.

Voytek looked up toward the most difficult part of the climb. It was something he had never done before. In all his rehearsals, he had never looked up but rather had just reached up smoothly, without hesitation. There was no need to look. But now he did, and the crux looked strange. Different from what he expected. A quiver of fear radiated through him. "I was dumbstruck. Just behind that feeling crouched terror... I knew that if I wavered I'd hit the ground. But the body, a wise beast... doesn't ask what the feverish head is thinking. With one finger of my left hand hooked into a pocket, I fluidly climbed up to where there is no turning around, to those small grey bulges, to the tilted vertical rock outlined against the blue sky, and oddly enough, in front of my nose appeared an edge as thin as the skin on my fingers. Got it!"[121]

A few more moves brought him from the shaded wall to the sun-drenched ridgetop. "The brightness of the summer sky hit me like a wave. It released in me a joyful laugh. I laughed like a madman; every atom in me felt joyful."[122] He leaned back, the rock warming his body. He gazed across the valley toward his home. He thought of his family, his garden, his Christmas roses. "When I envisioned soloing *Chinese Maharaja*, I designed it as a perfectly safe state of mind," he later said. "This was my challenge, to climb it, but in this state of mind. And I was pretty confident I could do it. Later, unfortunately, it proved no chance. When I was approaching the last stages, no, I was anxious. When I faced the final assault, I was lucky that I didn't do something wrong."

In the following weeks, Voytek wallowed in an elevated state, a feeling of delicious freedom. But eventually that feeling faded, leaving a void and then a sense of agitation. Surely there were no more demons? He watched as his beloved plants withered in his garden, baking in a midsummer heat wave. He became depressed. Then, as if by a miracle, it began to rain and the shrubs and trees and flowers regained their tenuous hold on life. "It's hard to believe, and yet I feel that, drop by drop, goodness radiating nothing begins to pool within me. It fills me and tenderly envelops the charred garden."[123]

What could possibly have motivated Voytek to solo *Chinese Maharaja* at the age of forty-six? He had two children who were depending on him. His life was already full. It's true, he wanted to rise above his human limitations, to take "unleashed" to the ultimate level. But there may have been other reasons, as well. He admitted he was challenged by the "me" generation, the generation that could climb circles around the previous generation – Voytek's generation. "They do things that surpass past achievements and they treat us old guys like daddies," he said, laughing. "And then when Daddy comes and solos a top climb…well, this was a kind of motivation – a little bit – in the back of my mind. This was the part of vanity."

Voytek was rare because, despite his age, he participated in the younger generation's activities. Nobody else from his peer group did. When he returned from his Himalayan career, young Polish climbers were already sending routes graded 5.13 and higher. Voytek simply joined them. He climbed the same grades, opened *Breaker* in the Tatras and then – to top it off – soloed *Chinese Maharaja*. It was an irresistible challenge for Voytek, the man who said he abhorred competition. Up to this day, no harder route in Poland has been soloed.

Although he continued to climb at a high level well into his sixties, *Chinese Maharaja* was Voytek's last big solo climb. It signalled a changing time in his life – a time of new beginnings and sad endings. It was the beginning of a period of great creativity for him and a new burst of energy in his business activities. And it marked the end of his second marriage.

Voytek working his new route *Breaker* in the Western Tatras. *Voytek Kurtyka collection.*

Swiss alpinist Jean Troillet. *Voytek Kurtyka collection.*

The "night naked" team: Swiss climbers Jean Troillet and Erhard Loretan, and Voytek Kurtyka. *Voytek Kurtyka collection.*

Voytek Kurtyka at Cho Oyu base camp in 1990. *Voytek Kurtyka collection.*

Cho Oyu, 8188 metres, Himalaya, on the border between Nepal and Tibet. New route on the Southwest Face, alpine-style (night-naked), by Voytek Kurtyka, Jean Troillet and Erhard Loretan in 1990. *Voytek Kurtyka collection; route outline by Piotr Drożdż.*

Solo climbing on the Southwest Face of Cho Oyu with Jean Troillet and Erhard Loretan in 1990. *Voytek Kurtyka collection.*

Shishapangma, Central Summit, 8008 metres, Himalaya, Tibet. New route on the Southwest Face, alpine-style (night-naked), by Voytek Kurtyka, Erhard Loretan and Jean Troillet in 1990. *Voytek Kurtyka collection; route outline by Piotr Drożdż.*

Voytek and Halina Kurtyka in California. *Voytek Kurtyka collection.*

Voytek Kurtyka doing some backyard training. His weightlifting program is sponsored by his son, Alex, and his daughter, Agnes, both squirming and squealing in delight. *Halina Kurtyka, Voytek Kurtyka collection.*

Shock the Monkey, Polish VI.5+/6; 8a/8a+; 5.13b/c, one of Voytek's hardest climbs, in the Prądnik Valley near Krakow. He climbed it in 1993 at the age of forty-six.
Bernadette McDonald.

Voytek Kurtyka at K2 base camp in 1994. This was an attempt on the West Face with Carlos Buhler and Krzysztof Wielicki. *Krzysztof Wielicki, Voytek Kurtyka collection.*

Carlos Buhler in the bergschrund below the West Face of K2 during the 1994 attempt. *Voytek Kurtyka.*

Attempt on
the Mazeno
Ridge of
Nanga Parbat
in 1995.
Andrew Lock.

Andrew Lock on the Mazeno Ridge attempt in 1995, which included Voytek Kurtyka, Andrew Lock, Doug Scott, Sandy Allan and Rick Allen. *Voytek Kurtyka collection.*

Voytek the writer. *Voytek Kurtyka collection.*

Voytek Kurtyka ignoring the "No Entry for the Unauthorized" sign in front of *Shock the Monkey*. Mind you, he had soloed the climb twenty years earlier, so he may actually be authorized. *Bernadette McDonald.*

Chinese Maharaja, Voytek Kurtyka's famous solo climb, goes through the blank slab on the highest, 25-metre section of the cliff. He soloed the route in 1993 at the age of forty-six. *Piotr Drożdż.*

Voytek Kurtyka after his final attempt on K2 in 2000. This time he was aiming for the East Face, climbing with Yasushi and Taeko Yamanoi. *Voytek Kurtyka collection.*

Voytek Kurtyka and his daughter, Agnes. *Voytek Kurtyka collection.*

Voytek Kurtyka and Jean Troillet reunion in 2016 in La Grave, France. *Anna Piunova.*

Voytek Kurtyka
and his son, Alex.
Piotr Bujak.

Voytek Kurtyka
looking somewhat
intense at the 2016
Piolets d'Or in
La Grave, France.
*Voytek Kurtyka
collection.*

Voytek Kurtyka and Robert Schauer reunion in 2016 in La Grave, France. *Anna Piunova.*

Voytek Kurtyka with friends in La Grave, France. From l. to r.: Lindsay Griffin, Voytek Kurtyka, Bernadette McDonald and Mick Fowler. *Voytek Kurtyka collection.*

SIXTEEN

Metaphysical Think Tank

Death sentences are short and very, very manly. Life sentences aren't.
They go on and on, all full of syntax and qualifying clauses and con-
fusing references and getting old.
                              —Ursula Le Guin, *The Wave in the Mind:*
            Talks and Essays on the Writer, the Reader, and the Imagination

One of Poland's greatest exports in the 1970s and '80s was its Himalayan climbers. Each had their specialty. The charismatic Andrzej Zawada galvanized an entire generation of alpinists to expand the boundaries of what was considered possible by climbing 8000-metre peaks in winter. He made them proud to be Polish and helped them become the finest in the world. Krzysztof Wielicki was the cheetah, racing up the peaks. Jurek Kukuczka became the best man he could possibly be in the mountains, a symbol of courage and bravery for countless people, not only climbers. Equally driven, and years ahead of her time, Wanda Rutkiewicz earned a record on the 8000ers that wasn't matched by another woman for fifteen years. She inspired and mobilized a powerful team of female high-altitude alpinists. Voytek and Jurek, Wanda, Krzysztof, Andrzej, and the army of climbers who joined them, created a powerful Himalayan legacy. They lived vagabond lives rich in everything but money.

Voytek was unique within that group of climbers. He didn't seek 8000-metre peaks in the same way as Jurek and Wanda and Krzysztof. Nor was he a Himalayan winter specialist. Instead, his forte was technical big walls and high-altitude traverses. He was motivated by beautiful lines, difficult lines, futuristic lines. He turned his back on fixed ropes and large expeditions, preferring the flexibility, the independence and the intimacy of small teams. He remained somewhat aloof from the Polish climbing community, and for many, his path was difficult to understand. Piotr Pustelnik, a Polish high-altitude specialist who became the twentieth person to climb all fourteen of the 8000-metre peaks, explained: "How could we understand a man for whom it was more important to climb a certain wall, a particular route or a specific ridge than to reach the top? In the era of Wanda's and Jurek's mountain-collecting programs, Voytek's approach was so eccentric it was seen as not very serious. But now I tend to think that, for those reasons, Voytek's charisma 'shone' more brightly abroad than in Poland."

Elitist, intuitive and artistic, Voytek defined his freedom by the style and aesthetic qualities of his experiences, and by those climbs and risks he chose not to undertake. Ever the intellectual, he took the idea of freedom to another level, even if it was only a temporary state of consciousness. "There is no better anti-neurotic remedy that would restore the right proportion to the reigning social conventions and to our imaginary problems than the exquisite big wall. Therefore, the man coming back from a hard mountain trip is a wiser being, calmer and radiating inside. I'd say, momentarily liberated."[124]

Despite his maintaining a distance from the community, almost every alpinist in Poland, and far beyond, has an opinion of Voytek. Leszek Cichy, one of two Polish climbers who made the first winter ascent of Everest, described him as "the greatest personality in Polish rock climbing, in addition to his Himalayan achievements." Leszek added, "Voytek created an intriguing aura of mysticism around his climbing." American alpinist Steve House called him a "luminary of the high alpine world." He elaborated, "His ascents, some reaching the summit, others not, were always beacons of hard climbing in good style on the world's most difficult peaks … He's a legend, a giant of alpinism, and his climbs speak clearly for themselves."

Ludwik Wilczyński placed him within the context of the larger Polish scene: "While Zawada was working in the lounges of Polish and international alpinism, and Kurtyka, the community's metaphysical think tank, walked alone on the roof, the cellars were occupied by filthily dressed outsiders who, singing the no-passport-and-no-job blues and drinking low-quality spirits, gave us all the satisfaction of self-fulfillment and a feeling of independence."[125] Kacper Tekieli, a serious Polish alpinist who is almost forty years younger than Voytek, regards him as the most relevant role model from that golden era of Polish climbing.

Reinhold Messner said of Voytek, "No doubt he was the best. He made so many brilliant climbs." And when Reinhold reflected on the unstoppable team of Voytek and Jurek, he grasped the magic of their relationship: "It was Voytek who was leading Jurek Kukuczka to great challenges. Voytek realized what he was doing and Kukuczka was the man of power."

Voytek seemed to offer something for everybody. He could be kind and generous, yet he sometimes surprised with intolerance and impatience. He could be aggravatingly stubborn and set in his ways and then explode with some crazy, spontaneous act. Frighteningly bright, he could be equally mischievous. When he was "on," he was outgoing, even flamboyant, seducing the camera, inviting a sense of intimacy. But his need for privacy and solitude was sacred, making him unapproachable at times, protecting him with a serene veneer that could appear cool and haughty, dismissive. He could fluctuate wildly between egocentricity and humility. Many people spoke of their admiration for him; few described a closeness. Although he sought friendship – while abhorring recognition – in the end there was a sense of unknowability about Voytek that kept people at a respectful distance.

This applied even, for a time, to his family. "I wasn't close to him as a child," his daughter, Agnes, said. "He became interested in me when I was a teenager." He was not only interested but very much wanting to be involved in her upbringing, even though he was living apart from the family. "He visited almost every day," Agnes explained. "He tried to educate me, about philosophy and religion. Also about life. When he saw my unmade bed, he exclaimed, 'You have to make your bed or your life will be shit.'" She laughed, adding, "I rebelled."

Alex recalled Voytek being very critical about religion. Voytek agreed, saying that he felt compelled to share his wholehearted rejection of the frightening Judeo-Christian vision of God with the two people most important to him. "I considered the dogma that distributed fear and mercy and grace to be more harmful and painful than Communism." But Voytek was clear: it wasn't spirituality that he was rejecting. He encouraged his children to look further afield for spiritual guidance and to read, read, read. One day, when Agnes was sixteen, she approached Voytek, her eyes sparkling with amusement and a letter in her hand. "Will you sign it?" she asked.

"What's this?" Voytek responded, curious.

It was a letter, written by her to the school authorities, expressing Voytek's agreement to release her from attending religion lessons. "I'm proud the seed was sown," Voytek said. "The matrix gene got broken."

Agnes and Alex recalled that, when he wasn't lecturing them, Voytek took them trekking in the mountains, and even rock climbing. But Voytek's expectations were high. "His perfectionism was hard to live up to," Agnes admitted with a sigh. Alex remembers his father's disappointment with his school grades. "He said, 'Oh, so you just want to be mediocre?'" But Voytek later praised Alex for learning three languages on his own: French, English and German. His children's faces break wide open as they both remember discovering a small chink in their father's perfect armour. "He doesn't know anything about technology," Agnes gloated. "It's like talking to a blind person about colour."

It was the creative process that eventually provided a bond between father and son. Tall and idealistic and full of dreams, Alex today shares a strong creative affinity with his father. Alex, with his passion for literature, art history and film. Alex, whose only fear in sharing his filmmaking ideas with his father is that Voytek will get so excited he will want to take over the project. For more practical Agnes, it is work that has provided a link between her and her businessman father as they collaborate in the import business that takes them both into the world of fabulous fabrics and exotic furniture.

Voytek was always a reflective person – a "metaphysical think tank" – but his self-analysis became more discerning as he matured. He became brutally honest, berating himself for his indiscretions, particularly his egocentricity. In an interview published in 2015, he tried to explain, albeit with a leavening dose of humour. "I don't like egocentricity, which is something that I have arduously battled in myself my entire life.

It's tough, but I manage somehow; now and then a human being comes along whom I love more than myself, and my ego dissipates. Or I throw myself into some creative project, entertaining or insane, and my cowering ego dissolves. In the worst-case scenario, I get a glass of wine…and my ego goes away with its tail between its legs."[126]

Voytek has found many creative outlets to help with his ego management: hard manual labour in his garden; designing and constructing a stylish building for his business; studies in botany and architecture; and, most important, writing. Voytek writes constantly; it is an inexhaustible pleasure for him. Poems, short essays, long essays, stories and, finally, a book, *Chiński Maharadża* (*Chinese Maharaja*). Every sentence, every phrase, every word is chosen with care. And not surprisingly, he writes about climbing, even though he insists he doesn't want to. "My best climbing experiences tend to have a strong sense of intimacy about them. It's not easy to talk about them."[127] Yet his book is all about those intimate experiences: his solo climb of *Chinese Maharaja* provides the case in point. His descriptions of ambition, pride, fear, shame and pure, unfettered joy are unmatched. He has written very little about his Himalayan ascents, concentrating more on climbs closer to home. Exploring the meaning of climbing within the context of his daily life is what engages him most. "This is actually a much bigger challenge for me," he said.

At least as big a challenge for Voytek is letting go of his writing, finishing something, allowing it to be seen and read and published. Piotr Drożdż, who published *Chiński Maharadża*, recalled, "Voytek is like a Zen master when it comes to the written word. He polishes every sentence endlessly. Even his editor confessed that Voytek was one of the most 'language-sensitive' authors she'd ever met, aware and ready to discuss every single change that she made." Leonard Cohen's son, Adam, who produced his father's final album, *You Want It Darker*, once joked that his dad often took five, seven, even ten years to finish a poem. And even then, the words weren't final. Voytek is like that, fussing and fixing, editing and revising, changing his mind, fine-tuning his thoughts, rewriting, rewriting, rewriting.

His work is full of little nuggets of eccentric wisdom about climbing and about life. His opinion of climbing grades: "The nefarious cult of the number took the noble art of ascent and made it one-dimensional, robbed of its soul and artistry."[128] His benevolent judgment of those who use bottled oxygen at altitude: "Thou shalt not blame thy neighbour for using spectacles, condoms or oxygen." His thoughts on guiding in the high mountains: "The relations between man and woman and the relations between man and the mountains are better without guides." About perfectionism: "I don't like perfectionism. I am a perfectionist."[129] And his pronouncements about the aging process: "First commandment: thou shalt not pass by a toilet without due consideration. Second commandment: thou shalt not waste a hard-on. Third commandment: thou shalt not trust your own farts."[130] His thoughts on ambition: "If the dream turns into public ambition, it's very bad for the dream." His evaluation of compassion: "If true compassion for others is awakened, you start ignoring your own misery."

What Voytek fears above all else is to write about climbing in the pretentious or self-aggrandizing style that he knows is all too common. Back in 2003, he wrote in *Alpinist*: "I now see clearly that climbing is Art. I also see that advertising is poison, while self-advertising is the oldest disease of the human soul."[131] American alpinist and ice-climbing pioneer Jeff Lowe once wrote: "Do your own thing with integrity, and communicate the things you've experienced and learned with honesty and humility, humor and enthusiasm, and you'll end up influencing new climbers more than if you beat them over the head with the rightness of 'your' style and the 'wimpiness' of their style."[132] Voytek tries hard to avoid the hammer technique, using black humour and self-mockery to make his points. But despite knowing better, he can't help doing a certain amount of "preaching," offering involved opinions and bits of wisdom, then chastising himself for falling into the trap.

And Voytek can't resist speculating about the future of alpinism. He believes that modern climbers have different expectations and that something new is ruling their imagination: ideas about digital intelligence, gene creation, space and time travel, and immortality. These ideas have led to an almost virtual mental realm – a realm that, in Voytek's opinion, is not the imagination of the mountains. For Voytek, the imagination of the mountains is a romantic one. "The heart of romantic imagination is emotion. Its path is blood, sweat and tears. And its limitation is God."

On a path as long and rich as Voytek's, there are countless memories. Some evoke sadness, some disappointment, and others pride. Some, even anguish. His first brush with tragedy in the Polish Tatras, when Jurek's partner fell to his death a few rope lengths below him on the direttissima. His hours at the Bandaka base camp, tormented and terrorized by the constant rumble of rockfall. His refusal to climb up to Krzysztof Żurek on Changabang because of some unspoken and seemingly irrational fear. Even worse, the terror of watching Krzysztof trapped in a body over which he had no control, and not knowing what to do for him. The terrible argument with Jurek about the avalanche danger on Manaslu. The day he refused to join Erhard and Jean on the Southwest Face of Cho Oyu and the long, lonely walk back to base camp. These were soul-tormenting moments because each one involved partners and friends.

Even worse were the losses of his former partners, one after the other: Alex on Annapurna, Jurek on the Lhotse South Face, and then, in April of 2011, Erhard. When Voytek learned of Erhard's tragic death while climbing in the Alps, he was stunned by grief. He knew Erhard had endured many losses: his climbing partner, his life partner and his infant son. And now Erhard, who was most alive in the world of rock and snow and ice, was dead. "I'm feeling empty," he said after hearing the news. "I'm really confused. I hardly grasp the meaning of his death." Each loss left a wound. Each wound became a scar.

But there are an equal number of joyful memories. The day Alex discovered a way through the ice seracs atop Bandaka. The time on Changabang when he knew Krzysztof would survive. The moment when Alex gave him tapes for his brand-new Walkman. "These are brilliant," Voytek laughed as he held the tapes, decades later. "They are gifts from Alex, a fantastic memory." And the feeling on Trango Tower, when Erhard cared for him after his falls, cooking and offering music. His friendship with Jean: "When I memorize the friendly face of Jean and his strong figure, I regret I didn't climb with him more. I regret we didn't explore together other mysterious corners of the planet which often guide us to the most mysterious corners of our own self." Friendship in the mountains provided the best moments of all.

Perusing his journals and reliving those days and weeks – sometimes months – with his partners, Voytek felt occasional pangs of remorse. As he revisited those long-forgotten disagreements with the people so dear to him, he tried to explain the emotional struggle. "When I think of Erhard now, he is an angel. Jurek was something very, very fine, almost a brother. Also, Alex. But when I started digging into the stories, I realized there were moments that were terribly destructive for us." Remembering is a delicate process, one that selects and shapes for survival.

In the final account, Voytek's partnership with Jurek remains the most conflicted – in part because of their diverging philosophies of climbing and, almost certainly, because they were two of the biggest climbing stars in Poland. "It is true you are never completely free of your ego, but I can honestly say I directed no jealousy toward him," Voytek insisted. "I was pure in that case. And I think he was fair in his attitude to me. Probably in his heart he was more innocent than me, even though I was avoiding publicity and media and he was seeking it. My impression was that he was pure inside. Jurek was a real partner for me." It is true that, despite attaining international fame for his climbing, Jurek never lost his endearing natural attitude. "For this, I candidly admired and loved him," Voytek wrote. "On the other hand, his unreflecting readiness for blind charging annoyed me."[133] It more than annoyed Voytek. It eventually turned him away from Jurek; he was convinced that this "blind charging" contributed too much to his partners' tragedies.

Some of Voytek's memories give him pride, including his impeccable safety record. Apart from a few bruised knuckles and skinned fingers, he emerged without injury. Despite his penchant for extremely difficult and dangerous climbs, he avoided accidents and tragedy – not only for himself but also for his partners. "Even now, I still can't fully grasp it," he admitted, shaking his head in amazement.

At times, he credits his safety to luck or some idealistic notion of a reciprocal love between the mountain and him. But when he is in a more analytical mood, the truth emerges. Voytek was extremely receptive to danger signals, probably more so than most. In some cases, the dangers were obvious, such as the avalanche hazard on Cho Oyu and on Manaslu. He refused to climb in those conditions. There was no miracle in this. Even then, however, there was a part of him that second-guessed and doubted his rational decisions because others around him were often ignoring those danger signals – and sometimes surviving.

Voytek knew this kind of behaviour wasn't sustainable. The most obvious example of charging ahead into danger was Jurek. "After Jurek was acclimatized, he was indestructible," Voytek explained. "He could stay two months in base camp and not deteriorate. He was still moving well." The problem was that his partners *were* deteriorating. "Other people couldn't keep up with him under those conditions. They were dying. It's that simple. He just didn't realize it. It doesn't require much to notice if your partner is weaker than you. When I noticed something going wrong with my partner, I changed into a radio receiver collecting signals from the guy, watching, watching all the time. Of course, the climbing experience was spoiled, much worse than if I was in trouble myself." Despite the ruined experiences, Voytek and his partners came back alive every time.

Although he sometimes likened Jurek to a brother, Voytek qualified the statement: "When you fight three or four hard wars with your partner, he automatically becomes a kind of brother. But it doesn't mean that your relationship is perfect." Voytek explained how his disrespect for Jurek intensified after their final split in 1986. "When I watched him peak-bagging and losing his partners, one after the other, I knew too well what was driving those climbers to their deaths."

Voytek's disdain finally grew to encompass much more than Jurek's relationship with his partners. "His climbing eventually became for me a kind of dull art. What kind of inspiration could there be if he arrived at base camp and received, on a silver platter, an almost completely prepared mountain, perfectly equipped with fixed ropes and camps? Permanently acclimatized, all he had to do was clip in with his Jumars and trudge to the summit. Such were the winter ascents of Dhaulagiri, Cho Oyu and Kangchenjunga. This way of climbing misses the basic values of adventure, of technical challenge and of style."

Far beyond that, however, Voytek's conflict with Jurek represented an even broader struggle, one extending to a set of values that collided with his basic approach to life. Voytek tried to explain the painful discord – painful because Jurek was no longer alive to defend himself.

> Our climbing differences I could ignore. But the clash with Jurek essentially represented my clash with the world's values, which are embodied in a matrix system that is powerfully instilled in our

collective mentality. We are slaves of this system. Enslaved, we tend to accept these values as our own. I felt that Jurek eventually became a champion of this matrix when he and Messner competed for the Himalayan Crown, transforming the noble art of climbing into a worthless display. They ignored the most precious potential of the climbing tradition, with all its multi-layered values – its romantic, metaphysical and aesthetic values. They reduced it to just one mediocre dimension: a game for climbing stars. Through their competition, they degraded alpinism into a matrix web that enslaved and contaminated us. Climbing sensitivity values and freedom values were replaced by matrix values.

The strong, painful and emotionally charged opinion that Voytek now holds about Jurek seems hopelessly distant from all that was good and sound in their early partnership.

In addition to his loyalty to sensitivity and freedom values, Voytek is known for his commitment to safety. Many climbers credit Voytek's highly tuned intuition for his safety record in the mountains. Russian high-altitude specialist Valery Babanov wrote about how, at the most extreme levels of climbing, intuition becomes increasingly important. "For me, alpinism has always been a means to self-knowledge, and now I am traversing into the next evolutionary stage – into a sphere of human activity that maximizes unpredictability, where survival requires mobilizing all of a person's inner reserves, even his intuition."[134] The same could be said about Voytek.

One theory about his safety record that Voytek dismisses is that he had a low tolerance for risk. "Beginning the Broad Peak Traverse, entering the Gasherbrum IV West Face, the level of risk was exceptional. I accepted incredible danger by going onto that face, but I refused to do it in crazy conditions. The same was true on Bandaka." This was what frustrated him most about Jurek. "Jurek was taking too many chances, definitely. And the basic proof is that he lost so many partners." It was only during the four-year period when Jurek and Voytek climbed almost exclusively together that Jurek didn't lose a partner.

Although Voytek admired the creative aspect of Jurek's behaviour, his death on the South Face of Lhotse sickened him: it was a dead-end situation where Jurek kept pushing higher and higher on unprotected ground. When he fell, the 7-millimetre rope broke, as it inevitably would. "There was no retreat for him," Voytek said. "He would never back down. He was that kind of person." As Reinhold Messner once said, "The best climber is the one who does great things at the highest level and survives."

But it is Voytek's record of illegal ascents – his own version of a "collection" – that brings him some of his greatest pleasure. "Being illegal is part of a creative life," he insisted. "Restrictions are mostly imposed by the brutes of the world and they turn our lives into slavery. They ruin the sense of freedom. I'm not a natural-born hater, but sometimes I find it is my duty; I hate every kind of rule. I never had a problem ignoring customs regulations. Climbing royalties restrict our vocation; away with them. Permissions ration our freedom; I hate them too. Birth registrations label us and help to trace us down. If I could, I would install a virus into this registry and turn it into a mess."

He was gleeful as he rattled off his inventory of illegal summits. "Illegal for sure were Broad Peak North and Broad Peak Central. We only had a permit for Broad Peak Main. Oh, yes, and of course Broad Peak Main the first time, in 1982, was also illegal. But we climbed it for acclimatization, so maybe that doesn't count?" Of course, it does count, so (only mildly chastised), he continued with his list: "Gasherbrum II East between I and II was also illegal," he mused. Then, with a slight air of justification, "Again, it's not prominent – perhaps a kind of subpeak. Maybe not so illegal?" But then he remembered, "It's true, it was a first ascent." Reflecting on the Gasherbrum trip, he suddenly recalled he didn't have a permit for Gasherbrum I either. Or for his K2 attempt with Robert Schauer. Or for his Malanphulan attempts with Sandy Allan and Erhard. Or for his first attempt at the Southwest Face of Shishapangma. Or Bandaka. Or Trango (with a two-person team). Or for the Losar icefall above Namche Bazaar. "I was considering asking them for a permit," he explained, "but they would have been completely confused because there was no summit. How would I explain to them that I wanted to climb 700 metres of ice to a pasture?" So he didn't ask.

And how about the Slovakian Tatras? How many hundreds of times did Voytek and his partners sneak over the border, giggling as they crept through the forest one more time without being caught? Such sweet adventures.

The illegal aspect was but one part of those grand exploits. "On many trips, we were coming to the mountains not knowing if we would end up in jail or in the mountains. We were coming without money. We were coming without permits. We were coming just as two people." The unknowns far outweighed the knowns, which, of course, is the formula for real adventure.

Voytek's fondness for breaking rules extends far beyond climbing. His successful – and entirely legal – import business is based on the knowledge he gained through his illegal smuggling activities in the 1970s and '80s. All those pesky border officials and inspections gave him a priceless education in the art of importing. "Every simple man was smuggling; Lech Wałęsa saw this. People were so fed up not being able to develop in a simple way – not being free, not being able to grow their property, their money. This is normal. And this is how Poland freed itself."

Even now that Poland has freed itself, Voytek can't resist. He finds the most convenient parking spots in crowded cities, usually directly in front of a signpost saying NO PARKING. He weaves back and forth across the solid white lines on Poland's highways, and when asked why, he answers with a laugh, "Because it is forbidden." His son occasionally follows in his footsteps, too, recounting amusing stories about selling Tibetan jewellery for enormous profit on the streets of Cadiz, about himself and a handful of Senegalese entrepreneurs heading out onto the streets during siesta. "Because," as Alex explained, "the police are sleeping then."

Breaking the rules is, above all, a creative activity for Voytek. And he is obsessed with creativity, in all aspects of his life. Even his search for clarity, an answer to that age-old question "Why do we climb?" was the start of an intellectual journey that went deep into the meaning of creativity. The first hint of that journey was his essay "The Path of the Mountain," but that was just the beginning. As he continued thinking about the link between creativity and his reasons for climbing, he scoured the dictionary for words and phrases that best expressed his thoughts. When he couldn't find the words he needed, he created new language for his purposes. *Crea* became a word that came to represent a central force in his life, all life.

After years of deliberation, he has arrived at a concept of Crea that rules both his life and the universe. He believes that every aspect of nature, social life, the economy, the arts and even politics is a manifestation of the creative drive – Crea. "The bursting of buds on the trees in springtime, the potato shoots striving for the light. It is Crea that composes the musical motif, and Crea is what weaves the thought sequence. It is Crea that pushes climbers to ascend a mountain wall, and similarly drives the Masai to stand up and boldly approach the lions."

At a personal level, Crea is what allows Voytek to thrive. It sustains him. "You don't need anything else. Crea is the source of mental oxygen. A change occurs through the drive of Crea, and the manifestation of that change is creation." The creation – or end product – isn't nearly as important to Voytek as is the desire – the inner drive toward change, some kind of transformation. His writing sometimes results in a product, such as a book or an essay. But often the product is nothing more than a personal conclusion, a creative exercise. As Leonard Cohen said, "The cutting of the gem has to be finished before you can see whether it shines." Fulfilling Crea is, for Voytek, the highest form of happiness. "As long as Crea functions within us, we are alive. When it disappears, we are dying. We are deteriorating. And finally, the emptiness overcomes us and we become like a zombie. Like a shell. Boredom, depression, mental illness, and finally, nothing." Voytek is convinced that without Crea, he would die.

Even Voytek's attitude to death is creative. While in his fifties, he was diagnosed with cancer. After the first flush of grief, he began to accept his fate with grace. He searched for, and found, the power and the strength to prepare for this final battle. He turned inward, bracing himself for the inevitable. After returning from an extended business trip to India, he opened a letter from his doctor and could hardly believe what it said: the most recent tests indicated a perfectly clean bill of health. The original diagnosis had been a huge mistake; he did not have cancer. Incredibly, Voytek's first reaction was disappointment. He had been so prepared.

There isn't a single aspect of Voytek's life that isn't driven by Crea. His business, his house, his garden, his writing, listening to music and walking in the forest are all transformative experiences filled with curiosity and imagination. And to achieve this imaginative transformation, he needs stillness. As Pico Iyer wrote, "The need for an empty space, a pause, is something we have all felt in our bones; it's the rest in a piece of music that gives it resonance and shape."[135]

When Voytek ponders the big questions – What is most important to me? What can I not live without? – the answers, although maddeningly incomplete, ultimately lead him back to the space and light he first experienced in the mountains. "The view of Changabang is so beautiful. And that piece of rock – Trango. Same thing with the Shining Wall of Gasherbrum IV – all these beautiful places. I would do anything to be in these beautiful places." The mountains adopted Voytek, and he remained faithful to them.

In the end, his exploration of Crea brought Voytek back to climbing. "Human creativity is an example of Crea," he began. "Climbing is an example of human creativity; I believe it is one of the richest. My climbing is simply a manifestation of Crea, and once I grasped the concept, I was able to give a totally satisfying answer to the question of why we climb. Crea manifests itself in the human world as creativity, and climbing simply provides the climber with the richest form of creativity. A person who is endowed with a specific sensitivity to the sport of climbing and to the mountains naturally finds in climbing his richest creation, and therefore mental oxygen is supplied to his mind when climbing." He adds that the same answer is as valid for cellists and dancers – indeed, for every creative endeavour.

Climbing on those soaring walls was irresistible because it was a dance with beauty. Every line was a unique creation. Every moment of overcoming suffering was creative. As he moved higher into the unknown, sometimes a wonderful transformation occurred. "I discovered that this connection with the mountains was so strong I was getting access to the surrounding nature at a different level – as if united with it," Voytek explained. "It was almost a blessed state of mind."

The Crux

I have wrestled with the angel and I am stained with light and I have no shame.

—Mary Oliver, *Upstream: Selected Essays*

I was about to enjoy some toast and coffee when my phone rang. It was 7:30 a.m.

"Hello. Bernadette, it's me, Voytek. I'm sorry, is it okay to call you now?"

"Yes, of course. What's going on?"

"Well, it's a bit difficult. Are you busy? Could you come down to my hotel? We are having a meeting about tonight's ceremony, and it would be good if you could be here. But only if it's convenient for you."

I could hear anxiety in his voice. "Sure, I can come. Half an hour. Hang on."

We were both in La Grave, France, at the Piolets d'Or. Yes, the Piolets d'Or.

After all those emails back and forth, Voytek had assumed the Piolets battle was finally over. But Christian Trommsdorff wouldn't give up. In 2016 he decided to give the lifetime award to Voytek, regardless of whether he accepted it or not. He sent another message, this time making it clear the award *would* be given.

Now began an epic inner battle. Voytek caught the drift of the strategy, as Christian had drummed up public support for the announcement, hoping Voytek would cave in to the groundswell. Christian even modified his language a bit, mentioning "mountain spirit" and "heart of the mountains," trying to appeal to Voytek's aesthetic leanings. Voytek was caught in the middle of an impossible dilemma. If he rejected the award, it would probably look like pride and arrogance on Voytek's part and alienate him from the climbing community. They would never guess his reasons for refusing. But accepting the award was a clear betrayal of his ideals. Fame was something that other people determined, yet it could affect the way people behaved toward him. Even worse, he feared the real possibility of deluding himself into believing he was worthy of this inflated public image. This award would make that delusion much harder to resist. He might become enslaved by fame, addicted to it. He would lose both his dignity and his freedom. He well understood that fame is a pendulum and that it could be dangerous to be in the way of its downward swing. Or, as the Canadian author Alice Munro wrote, "Fame must be striven for, then apologized for. Getting or not getting it, you will be to blame."[136]

Voytek read the letter. He read it again. He delayed his reply, conflicted about his response. Was it better to offend or to be a traitor? "I don't mind if other people accept this thing; I just don't want it for myself," he wailed. "I realize this is my own personal problem. I'm sure Jurek would have accepted it. He didn't see anything wrong with accepting awards and recognition. He was completely at peace with his conscience, so why am I not? What to do?" Finally, Voytek wrote back.

> Dear Christian,
>
> The show goes on. Of course, it is not easy for me. I feel like a traitor. I used to say "no awards for prayers" and now I keep silent and the only thing I could do to stay faithful to myself would be rejecting this "axe" and thus, offend a lot of good people … And even worse – I would shed on myself a bad suspicion of tremendous pride and vanity … I would end up the vainest climber in the world.
>
> The only thing that remains is to believe that I'm taking part in the show with good intention … of course deep in my heart I enjoy the distinction of the Piolets d'Or and it is better to accept it. Thank you for making me a special member of our climbing community. Pass my thanks to the other members of the board.

Christian had finally won the battle. It was a remarkable victory, not only for Christian but for the entire mountaineering community. Chosen by his international peers, Voytek would be honoured for his years of pioneering minimalist, totally committing, alpine-style ascents in the world's Greater Ranges. This was the highest recognition and level of respect they could bestow on a climber.

And so here we were in La Grave on the morning of the big day. Voytek was unhappy – dishevelled, distraught, his blood pressure rising. He appeared decidedly uncomfortable with the attention, with the media and with the award. But the call that morning was not about this ongoing discomfort; Voytek, the perfectionist, was disturbed by the freewheeling structure of the award ceremony. If he was going to be part of it, it needed to be perfect.

He asked for several changes and the organizers agreed. Now everyone felt reasonably comfortable with the more tightly controlled choreography of the event. When we descended to the hotel lobby, however, a group of people thronged him. Voytek seemed twitchy. He looked trapped. Was this a case of nerves, I wondered, or a prima donna performance? I finally suggested that he escape the crowds for a long walk in the hills above La Grave. He leapt at the chance.

High above the village, the alpine meadow was studded with spring crocuses nodding in the sunlight. Staring across the deeply shaded valley at the brooding face of La Meije, Voytek again questioned his presence at this event. He wasn't meant to be in the media glare, on stage, in the limelight, he tried to explain. I could understand his distress as he differentiated between mutual acceptance – friendship – and recognition. He seemed worried that he didn't have the purity of soul to accept recognition with dignity. "Public gifts are difficult and problematic gifts," he said. I had heard these arguments from him many times before, but I listened while he worked his way through the dilemma, equating it to "the most difficult climb." As the lonely black walls and enticing ice gullies of La Meije beckoned, he must have felt like a traitor to himself.

And yet, here he was.

Later that evening, hundreds of people from around the world gathered in a cavernous tent. Mostly climbers, they milled about, glasses of wine in their weathered hands, exchanging fantastic stories of high-altitude bivouacs and splitter cracks. People were smiling, laughing. This was the Piolets d'Or celebration, the gathering of the tribe.

Voytek stood at the back of the room behind the crowd, waiting to be called on stage. His demons appeared tamed for the moment. Trim and fit and elegantly dressed, he looked the part of a world-class alpinist about to be honoured. As the introductions neared their end, I leaned over and asked, "Are you ready?"

He smiled. "The show goes on."

And with that, he bounded onto the stage with the grace of a gazelle. He dazzled the audience with his amusing stories, his smile and his gratitude. The public Voytek seemed well protected by his mask yet completely aware of his own masquerade. What an actor, I thought.

Voytek managed to have the final say, nonetheless, insisting that his climbing partners join him on stage so they could accept the award together. It was a touching gesture for his partners, and for the hundreds of climbers watching, all swept up in the happiness and generosity of the moment. He had taken the experience and responded to it in a way that transformed it. Even reluctant Voytek finally had to admit to a sense of gratification when all those weather-beaten hands clutched the golden axe. The hands of his partners from those glorious climbs: Bandaka, Gasherbrum IV, the Mazeno Ridge, Dhaulagiri, Cho Oyu, Shishapangma and Changabang. How wonderful if Jurek and Alex and Erhard could have been there, too.

Climbing gave Voytek the chance to rise above his limitations and to confront his weaknesses. Ultimately, coming to La Grave, reconnecting with his partners after years – sometimes decades – of being apart, mingling with climbing friends, answering questions from the media and stepping onto that stage, may have provided him the ideal opportunity to face other vulnerabilities head-on. Within that lonely dread of being a traitor to everything he believed in, he searched for – and found – a dignified way to accept the award.

I believe Voytek found dignity in the process of co-operating on this biography, as well. It wasn't always easy. The story of his life was a long time coming, and the silence, over the years, had become deafening. But the unspoken tends to strengthen and grow richer over time. There were many instances when, reading his journals for the first time in many years,

Voytek was genuinely saddened. When I asked him why, he mused, "I was hoping I was wiser now, but I think there isn't much difference." Then he laughed. "At least I have stopped the hunger days."

The journals reveal intense emotions from those days in the mountains: fear, disappointment, friendship, envy, joy, even anger. The flashes of irritation sometimes appearing on those pages seemed to surprise and disturb him. Anger, envy and hatred, if allowed to inhabit one's psyche for a prolonged period, are crippling, and Voytek appeared to want no part of them. As Ursula Le Guin wrote, "The longer a man stays in a form not his own, the greater his peril."[137] Voytek now seems much more focused on preserving the joys of life, of companionship, of being part of his children's lives, of being creative and sensitive to beauty. He seems happy: not in possession of some euphoric bliss but of a simple contentment, a release from sadness and melancholy. His son Alex worries about him, though. "He seems so isolated," Alex said. "He's in his own world."

His daughter worries, too. "When he was younger he gave up everything to climb," Agnes explained. "Everything for his freedom. Now he can't do that, so I think he should relax more, have some fun, not work all the time." Father and daughter have differing perspectives, however. Voytek countered, "I am definitely a bit more peaceful today, at least toward the final questions: life, aging, death. I get much greater satisfaction from the simple life. This is progress, I think."

Although he co-operated fully during the writing of this biography, the hardest thing for Voytek was the tedious process of reflecting on his past for days on end. "Why would I dwell on the past when the present is so much more fascinating, much more mysterious, and it has much more potential?" But he *did* make the effort to reflect on his life, through his journals, his photos and, of course, his memory. And what was revealed in that reflection was that his most intensely beautiful experiences in the mountains created a capacity within him to live life more fully, long after he had left the mountains. "Sometimes I think the awakening of that expanded sense of adoration – in a way, of nothing – has been the most important transformation in my life. It's definitely made me stronger. Isn't a person who can live on nothing much stronger? I try to nurture that transformation in myself."[138]

I am sure that for Voytek, the purest climbing experience exists in a realm beyond any form of communication. That story can never be told. But he understands the value in communicating his deeply personal epiphanies about beauty, companionship and – most of all – freedom. He knows that his conviction that alpinism is not only about ascending a mountain but about ascending above *yourself*, should be shared with others. "If you can't bring back the experience of power and love from the mountains to your normal life and to others, it is senseless to do it."

When he was asked if he would ever consider quitting climbing, Voytek's answer was clear. "It would be a travesty to abandon a love that is reciprocated. I don't have great expectations. The touch of warm stone, the feel of mountain space – that's enough for me. The mountains are my breath."[139]

Chronology of Selected Climbs

Unless otherwise indicated, all climbers are Polish.

1970

▲ *Kutykówka*, VI+, Mały Młynarz, Slovakian Tatras, East Face, first ascent, considered the first route harder than Grade VI made by Polish climbers in the Tatras, with Michał Gabryel, Janusz Kurczab.

1971

▲ *Ściek* (*The Sewer*), VI, A3, Kazalnica Mięguszowiecka Wall, Polish Tatras, first winter ascent, with Michał Gabryel, Marek Kęsicki, Janusz Kurczab, Andrzej Mierzejewski, Janusz Skorek.

▲ *Direttissima*, VI, A2–A3, Kazalnica Mięguszowiecka Wall, Polish Tatras, first winter ascent, with Michał Gabryel, Tadeusz Gibiński, Andrzej Wilusz.

1972

▲ *Pająki* (*Spiders*), VI, A3, Kazalnica Mięguszowiecka Wall, Polish Tatras, first winter ascent, with Kazimierz Głazek, Marek Kęsicki, Andrzej Wilusz.

▲ Akher Chioch, 7017 metres, Afghan Hindu Kush, Northwest Face and West Ridge, new route, with Adam Lewandowski, Jacek Rusiecki.

▲ Kohe Tez, 6995 metres, Afghan Hindu Kush, North Ridge, new route, with Alicja Bednarz, Ryszard Kozioł.

▲ Akher Chioch, 7017 metres, Afghan Hindu Kush, North Face, new route, alpine-style, with Piotr Jasiński, Marek Kowalczyk, Jacek Rusiecki.

1973

▲ *Voie Petit Jean*, TD, VI, A1, Petit Dru, French Alps, North Face, first ascent, with Jerzy Kukuczka, Marek Łukaszewski.

▲ *Superściek* (*The Super Sewer*), V, A2, ice 90°, Kazalnica Mięguszowiecka Wall, Polish Tatras, new route in winter, with Piotr Jasiński, Krzysztof Pankiewicz, Zbigniew Wach.

1974

▲ *French Direct*, Trollveggen (Troll Wall), Romsdal Valley, Norway, North Face, first winter ascent, with Kazimierz Głazek (partway only), Marek Kęsicki, Ryszard Kowalewski, Tadeusz Piotrowski.

1975

▲ Lhotse, 8516 metres, Himalaya, Nepal, member of the first winter expedition to an 8000er, led by Andrzej Zawada. Highest point reached by Kurtyka: 7800 metres; highest point reached by Zawada and Andrzej Heinrich: 8250 metres.

▲ *Polish Route*, TD, V+, 60°, 800 metres, Pointe Hélène, Grandes Jorasses, French Alps, first ascent, with Jerzy Kukuczka, Marek Łukaszewski.

1976

▲ K2, 8611 metres, Karakoram, Pakistan, member of a Polish K2 Northeast Ridge expedition led by Janusz Kurczab. Highest point reached by Kurtyka: 7900 metres; highest point reached by Eugeniusz Chrobak and Wojciech Wróż: 8400 metres.

▲ *Filar Abazego*, Polish VI.3+; 7a+; TR (top-rope), Dolina Bolechowicka, the hardest free ascent of a rock climb in Poland at the time.

1977

▲ Kohe Bandaka, 6843 metres, central Hindu Kush, Afghanistan, Northeast Face, new route, alpine-style, with Alex MacIntyre (British), John Porter (British).

1978

▲ *Czyżewski–Kurtyka*, VI+, A2+, Kazalnica Mięguszowiecka, Polish Tatras, new route in winter, with Zbigniew Czyżewski.

▲ Changabang, 6864 metres, Garhwal Himalaya, India, South Buttress, new route, alpine-style, with Alex MacIntyre (British), John Porter (British), Krzysztof Żurek.

1979

▲ Dhaulagiri, 8167 metres, Himalaya, Nepal, East Face attempt, with Walenty Fiut.

1980

▲ Dhaulagiri, 8167 metres, Himalaya, Nepal, East Face, new route, alpine-style. High point: 7500 metres on the Southeast Ridge. Later in the same expedition, reached the summit via the Northeast Ridge. With René Ghilini (French), Alex MacIntyre (British), Ludwik Wilczyński.

▲ *Kant Filara*, VII+, Kazalnica Mięguszowiecka Wall, Polish Tatras, first free ascent, with Władysław Janowski.

1981

▲ Spring: Makalu, 8485 metres, Himalaya, Nepal, West Face, alpine-style attempt, reached 6800 metres, with Kunda Dixit (Nepali), Padam

Gurung (Nepali), Cornelius Higgins (British), Alex MacIntyre (British). Only Alex and Voytek went onto the West Face.

▲ Autumn: Makalu, 8485 metres, Himalaya, Nepal, West Face, alpine-style attempt, reached a high point of 7900 metres, with Jerzy Kukuczka, Alex MacIntyre (British). After retreating, Kukuczka reached the summit by soloing the Northwest Ridge.

1982

▲ Broad Peak, 8051 metres, Karakoram, Pakistan, normal route, alpine-style, with Jerzy Kukuczka.

1983

▲ Gasherbrum II, 8034 metres, Karakoram, Pakistan, Southeast Ridge, new route, alpine-style, with Jerzy Kukuczka.

▲ Gasherbrum I, 8080 metres, Karakoram, Pakistan, Southwest Face, new route, alpine-style, with Jerzy Kukuczka. The expedition was named the Polish Alex MacIntyre Memorial Expedition: two new routes on 8000ers in one season by two men, alpine-style.

1984

▲ Broad Peak Traverse, Karakoram, Pakistan, Traverse of the North (7490 metres), Central (8011 metres) and Main (8051 metres) summits, new route, alpine-style, with Jerzy Kukuczka.

1985

▲ Gasherbrum IV, 7932 metres, Karakoram, Pakistan, West Face, new route, 10-day alpine-style ascent (without reaching summit), descent via unclimbed North Ridge, with Robert Schauer (Austrian).

▲ *Filar Abazego*, Polish VI.3+; 7a+, Dolina Bolechowicka, free-solo ascent.

1986

▲ Trango Tower, 6239 metres, Karakoram, Pakistan, East Face attempt, with Kasuhiro Saito (Japanese), Noboru Yamada (Japanese), Kenji Yoshida (Japanese).

1987

▲ *Kurtyka–Marcisz*, IV, A2, ice 80–90°, Kazalnica Mięguszowiecka Wall, Polish Tatras, new route in winter in twenty-six hours, with Andrzej Marcisz.

▲ K2, 8611 metres, Karakoram, Pakistan, West Face attempt, with Jean Troillet (Swiss).

1988

▲ Trango Tower, 6239 metres, Karakoram, Pakistan, East Face, ED+, VI, A3, 1100 metres, new route, capsule-style, with Erhard Loretan (Swiss).

1989

▲ K2, 8611 metres, Karakoram, Pakistan, West Face attempt, with Erhard Loretan (Swiss), Jean Troillet (Swiss).

1990

▲ Cho Oyu, 8188 metres, Himalaya, Nepal and Tibet, Southwest Face, new route, night-naked-style, with Erhard Loretan (Swiss), Jean Troillet (Swiss).

▲ Shishapangma, Central Summit, 8008 metres, Himalaya, Tibet, South Face (left of the *Yugoslav Route*), new route, in night-naked style, with Erhard Loretan (Swiss), Jean Troillet (Swiss).

1991

▲ *Łamaniec*, Polish VI.5; 7c+, Raptawica Tower, western Polish Tatras, new route, one of the hardest bolted rock climbs in the Tatras, with Grzegorz Zajda.

1992

▲ *Gacopyrz Now*, VIII+, Kazalnica Mięguszowiecka Wall, Polish Tatras, new route, with Andrzej Marcisz.

▲ K2, 8611 metres, Karakoram, Pakistan, West Face attempt, with Erhard Loretan (Swiss).

1993

▲ Nanga Parbat, 8125 metres, Himalaya, Pakistan, Mazeno Ridge expedition with Doug Scott (British). Scott was swept by an avalanche, seriously injuring his ankle before starting the route.

▲ *Chiński Maharadża* (*Chinese Maharaja*), Polish VI.5; 7c+, Dolina Bolechowicka, Polish Jura, free-solo ascent, done at the age of forty-six – one of the hardest free-solo climbs in Poland, even now.

▲ *Shock the Monkey*, Polish VI.5+/6; 8a/8a+, RP, Pochylec, the Prądnik Valley.

1994

▲ K2, 8611 metres, Karakoram, Pakistan, West Face attempt, with Carlos Buhler (American), Krzysztof Wielicki.

1995

▲ *Losar*, 700-metre ice climb above Namche Bazaar, Himalaya, Nepal, ascent, with Maciej Rysula.

▲ Nanga Parbat, 8125 metres, Himalaya, Pakistan, Mazeno Ridge attempt, with Sandy Allan (Scottish), Rick Allen (Scottish), Andrew Lock (Australian), Doug Scott (British).

1996–2002

▲ Malanphulan, 6573 metres, Himalaya, Nepal, attempts on the North Face with various partners.

1997

▲ Nanga Parbat, 8125 metres, Himalaya, Pakistan, Mazeno Ridge attempt, with Erhard Loretan (Swiss). They climbed almost half the ridge in a day and a half, then turned back in perfect weather.

2001

▲ Biacherahi Central Tower, 5700 metres, Karakoram, Pakistan, South Face, new route, 5.9, A2, with Taeko and Yasushi Yamanoi (Japanese).

2003

▲ *Imperium Kontratakuje* (*The Empire Strikes Back*), Polish VI.5+; 8a, Łaskawiec, Prądnik Valley, at the age of fifty-six.

▲ *Poniekąd Donikąd*, V+, A2+, 250 metres, Jarząbkowa Turnia, Slovakian Tatras, new route in winter, with Marcin Michałek.

Acknowledgements

I've heard it said that it takes a village to raise a child. I believe it's the same for a book, and in the case of *Art of Freedom*, that village was global.

I couldn't have even considered tackling this project without the support of many whose previous research and established scholarship in mountaineering history have been priceless. Thank you to Bob Schelfhout Aubertijn, Michael Kennedy, Cameron McNeish, David Simmonite, Victor Saunders, the Whyte Museum of the Canadian Rockies, Greg Child, Rodolphe Popier, Janusz Majer, Jacek Trzemżalski, Jan Kielkowski, Lindsay Griffin, Eberhard Jurgalski, Gabi Kuhn and Carlos Buhler for your enthusiasm, your time and your knowledge.

I spent many hours in fascinating interviews with climbers from around the world. Some of these I conducted years ago for *Freedom Climbers*, but they remain relevant to this book. Thanks to Jean Troillet, René Ghilini, Robert Schauer, John Porter, Sandy Allan, Greg Child, Carlos Carsolio, Doug Scott, Reinhold Messner, Kacper Tekieli, Ludwik Wilczyński, Steve Swenson, Raphael Slawinski, Christian Trommsdorff, Steve House, Leszek Cichy, Krzysztof Wielicki, Artur Hajzer, Bogdan Jankowski, Celina Kukuczka, Janusz Kurczab, Janusz Majer, Krystyna Palmowska, Anna Okopińska, Aleksander Kurtyka and Agnes Kurtyka.

I was fortunate to have a truly wonderful collection of photos from which to choose. Thanks to Voytek for opening his entire photographic archive, and to John Porter, Robert Schauer, Bernard Newman, Bogdan Jankowski, Piotr Drożdż, Anna Piunova, Halina Kurtyka, J. Barcz, Krzysztof Wielicki, Andrew Lock, Piotr Bujak and Jacenty Dędek, as well as to those who gave me permission to use the image archives of Danuta Piotrowska, Ewa Waldeck-Kurtyka, Jerzy Kukuczka, Erhard Loretan, Alex MacIntyre, Wanda Rutkiewicz, Janusz Kurczab and Artur Hajzer.

My good friend and climbing and ski-touring buddy Julia Pulwicki once again performed translation miracles for this project. Building on all the work she did for *Freedom Climbers*, Julia stepped up to the plate, translating numerous essays and one really interesting book authored by Voytek. Thank you, Julia.

It's impossible to overstate the value of editing; on this project, I have had some fine editing support. Interested friends offered critical reads: thank you to Jon Popowich, Harry Vandervlist, Mary Metz and Bob Schelfhout Aubertijn. Jennifer Glossop helped me early in the project, and I so admire her ability to create order out of chaos. Thank you, Jennifer. I was fortunate to be admitted into the Banff Centre Mountain and Wilderness Writing program and to benefit from five co-participants, along with two world-class editors. I've worked with both Marni Jackson and Tony Whittome on previous projects and can only scream from the rooftops about how wonderfully supportive they are. If anyone reading this is considering a writing project that fits within the parameters of this program, I would strongly suggest that you look at the website and apply: www.banffcentre.ca/program-tags/wilderness-writing. Three weeks of concentrated work with a small group of like-minded writers and two wonderful faculty editors at the Banff Centre. What more to ask for?

Rocky Mountain Books has become my Eastern European mountaineering history champion publisher. They just keep saying yes. Thank you again to the entire RMB team: publisher Don Gorman, editor Meaghan Craven, designer Chyla Cardinal, eagle-eyed proofreader Anne Ryall, marketing guru Rick Wood, Joe Wilderson, Cory Manning and everyone else at RMB who had a hand in the book.

A huge thank you goes to my mountaineering and writing friends who have supported me so loyally on this project. And to my husband, who has once again shown amazing patience and support throughout this journey.

And finally, to Voytek. Writing a biography, particularly of a living climber, sometimes feels as difficult as climbing an 8000er. And to write that biography of a climber as complex as Voytek felt like doing it night-naked-style. Without his tolerance, trust, honesty, generosity and good humour, this book would not exist. Thank you so much, Voytek.

Notes

1   Sylvie Simmons, *I'm Your Man* (Toronto: McClelland & Stewart, 2012), 459.

2   Voytek Kurtyka and Zbyszek Skierski, "View from the Wall," *Alpinist* 43 (Summer 2013): 68.

3   Bernadette McDonald, *Freedom Climbers* (Calgary: Rocky Mountain Books, 2011).

4   Ludwik Wilczyński, "The Polish Himalayan Boom 1971–91," *Taternik* 3 (2012): 33.

5   J.A. Szczepański, "Dekalog," *Bularz* 91 (1991): 39.

6   The elevation of Kohe Tez was previously estimated at 7015 metres. Elevations quoted in this book are provided by Eberhard Jurgalski, whose website is 8000ers.com. His sources include the Gerald Gruber Survey and Finnmap.

7   Marek Brniak, "Troll Wall in Winter," *Climber and Rambler* (March 1976): 22.

8   Brniak, "Troll Wall in Winter," 25.

9   John Porter, *One Day as a Tiger* (Sheffield: Vertebrate Publishing, 2014), 107.

10 Ibid., 109.

11 A0 refers to an aid-climbing move that pulls on equipment – sometimes pitons – to gain upward progress.

12 Porter, *One Day as a Tiger*, 146.

13 Ibid., 148.

14 Alex MacIntyre, "Broken English," *Mountain* 77 (January 1981): 36.

15 Porter, *One Day as a Tiger*, 179.

16 MacIntyre, "Broken English," 37.

17 Ibid.

18 Ibid.

19 Ibid.

20 Jerzy Kukuczka, *My Vertical World* (Seattle: The Mountaineers Books, 1992), 36.
21 Ibid.
22 Porter, *One Day as a Tiger*, 179.
23 Doug Scott and Alex MacIntyre, *Shisha Pangma* (Seattle: The Mountaineers Books, 2000), 21.
24 Oswald Ölz, "Cho Oyu, South Face Winter Attempt," *American Alpine Journal* 25, no. 57 (1983): 233.
25 Wojciech Kurtyka, *Chiński Maharadża* (Krakow: Góry Books, 2013), 25.
26 Voytek Kurtyka, "The Polish Syndrome," *Mountain Review* 5 (November–December 1990): 44.
27 Voytek Kurtyka, "The Gasherbrums Are Lonely," *Mountain* 97 (May–June 1984): 38.
28 Kurtyka, "The Polish Syndrome," 46.
29 Kurtyka, "The Gasherbrums Are Lonely," 38.
30 Ibid., 42.
31 Ibid.
32 Valery Babanov, "Karakoram Doubleheader," *American Alpine Journal* 51, no. 83 (2009): 70.
33 Kei Taniguchi, "Being with the Mountain," *Alpinist* 52 (Winter 2015): 63.
34 Voytek Kurtyka, "Broad Peak North Ridge," *Climbing* 94 (February 1986): 41.
35 Ibid.
36 Ibid.
37 Ibid.
38 Ibid., 42.
39 Ibid.
40 Ibid., 40.
41 Voytek Kurtyka, "The Art of Suffering," *Mountain* 121 (May–June 1988): 35
42 A.V. Saunders, "Book Reviews," *Alpine Journal* 94, no. 338 (1989): 281.
43 Kurtyka, "The Art of Suffering," 35.
44 Kurtyka, "Broad Peak North Ridge," 40.
45 Taniguchi, "Being with the Mountain," 63.
46 Michael Kennedy, "Gasherbrum IV," *Alpinist* 2 (Spring 2003): 22.
47 Walter Bonatti, "Gasherbrum IV," *Alpinist* 2 (Spring 2003): 26.
48 Voytek Kurtyka, "The Shining Wall of Gasherbrum IV," *American Alpine Journal* 28, no. 60 (1986): 3.
49 Robert Schauer, "Shining Wall," *Climbing* 95 (April 1986): 42.

50 Ibid.

51 Ibid., 41.

52 Kurtyka, "The Shining Wall of Gasherbrum IV," 3.

53 Greg Child, *Mixed Emotions* (Seattle: The Mountaineers Books, 1993), 186.

54 Kurtyka, "The Shining Wall of Gasherbrum IV," 5.

55 Taniguchi, "Being with the Mountain," 63.

56 Voytek Kurtyka, "The Shining Wall," *Alpinist* 2 (Spring 2003): 31.

57 Kurtyka and Skierski, "View from the Wall," 71.

58 Lindsay Griffin, "Playing the Game," *Alpine Journal* 115, no. 359 (2010/11): 89.

59 Andrej Štremfelj, "Observations from the Roof of the World," *American Alpine Journal* 43, no. 75 (2001): 158.

60 Dave Dornian, "Mixed Messages," *American Alpine Journal* 46, no. 78 (2004): 122.

61 Erhard Loretan, *Night Naked* (Seattle: Mountaineers Books, 2016), 130.

62 Kurtyka and Skierski, "View from the Wall," 69.

63 Ibid., 66.

64 Kurtyka, *Chiński Maharadża*, 21.

65 Artur Hajzer, *Atak Rozpaczy* (Gliwice, Poland: Explo Publishers, 1994).

66 Kukuczka, *My Vertical World*, 156.

67 Wilczyński, "The Polish Himalayan Boom 1971–91," 43.

68 Dornian, "Mixed Messages," 122.

69 Kurtyka, "The Polish Syndrome," 46.

70 Bernadette McDonald, *Tomaž Humar* (London: Hutchinson, 2008), 235.

71 Martin Boysen, "Last Trango," *Mountain* 52 (November/ December 1976): 32.

72 Voytek Kurtyka, "Nameless Tower Attempt, Trango Towers," *American Alpine Journal* 29, no. 61 (1987): 283.

73 Kurtyka, "The Polish Syndrome," 47.

74 Voytek Kurtyka, "Trango Extremes," *Mountain* 127 (May/ June 1989): 22.

75 Ibid.

76 Loretan, *Night Naked*, 129.

77 Kurtyka, "Trango Extremes," 25

78 Loretan, *Night Naked*, 133.

79 Ibid., 134.

80 Ibid.

81 Ibid., 136.

82 Kurtyka, "Trango Extremes," 26

83 Loretan, *Night Naked*, 137.

84 Ibid., 139.

85 Todd Skinner, *Beyond the Summit* (New York: Portfolio, 2003), 61.

86 Loretan, *Night Naked*, 140.

87 Kurtyka, "The Art of Suffering," 36

88 Kurtyka, "The Polish Syndrome," 44.

89 Loretan, *Night Naked*, 146.

90 Ibid., 148.

91 Ibid.

92 Voytek Kurtyka, "New Routes, Cho Oyu and Shisha Pangma," *American Alpine Journal* 33, no. 65 (1991): 16.

93 Loretan, *Night Naked*, 149.

94 Ibid., 150.

95 Ibid., 151.

96 Ibid.

97 Ibid., 152.

98 Ibid.

99 Child, *Mixed Emotions*, 184.

100 Loretan, *Night Naked*, 141.

101 Steve House, "Divided Interests and the Hope for American Alpinism," *American Alpine Journal* 42, no. 74 (2000): 57.

102 Štremfelj, "Observations from the Roof of the World," 156.

103 Voytek Kurtyka, "Breaker," translated by Jurek Kopacz, Lone Sail Far Away website, accessed January 2015. Originally published as "Łamaniec," *Góry* 1 (1991).

104 Ibid.

105 Ibid.

106 Ibid.

107 Ibid.

108 Voytek Kurtyka, "Losar," *Alpinist* 4 (Autumn 2003): 68.

109 Kurtyka, "The Art of Suffering," 32.

110 Kurtyka, *Chiński Maharadża*, 12.

111 Ibid.

112 Ibid., 11.

113 Ibid.

114 Ibid., 31.

115 Ibid., 52.

116 Ibid.

117 Ibid., 54.

118 Ibid., 115.

119 Ibid., 119.

120 Ibid., 120.

121 Ibid.

122 Ibid., 121.

123 Ibid., 129.

124 Voytek Kurtyka, "The Path of the Mountain," *Bularz* 88–89: 43.

125 Wilczyński, "The Polish Himalayan Boom 1971–91," 36.

126 Kurtyka and Skierski, "View from the Wall," 67.

127 Ibid.

128 Kurtyka, *Chiński Maharadża*, 70.

129 Kurtyka and Skierski, "View from the Wall," 66.

130 Kurtyka, *Chiński Maharadża*, 81.

131 Kurtyka, "Losar," 79.

132 Dornian, "Mixed Messages," 121.

133 Kurtyka, "The Polish Syndrome," 46.

134 Babanov, "Karakoram Doubleheader," 65.

135 Pico Iyer, *The Art of Stillness* (New York: Simon & Schuster, 2014), 53.

136 Alice Munro, *My Best Stories* (Toronto: Penguin Random House, 2009), xvii.

137 Ursula Le Guin, *A Wizard of Earthsea* (Boston: Houghton Mifflin, 1968), 127.

138 Kurtyka and Skierski, "View from the Wall," 67.

139 Ibid., 75.

Select Bibliography and Sources

BOOKS

Alter, Stephen. *Becoming a Mountain*. New York: Arcade Publishing, 2015.

Buffet, Charlie. *Erhard Loretan: Une vie suspendue*. Chamonix: Editions Guérin, 2013.

Child, Greg. *Mixed Emotions: Mountaineering Writings of Greg Child*. Seattle: The Mountaineers Books, 1993.

Davies, Norman. *God's Playground: A History of Poland*. Rev. ed., Vol. 2, *1795 to the Present*. Oxford and New York: Oxford University Press, 2005.

Hajzer, Artur. *Atak Rozpaczy*. Gliwice, Poland: Explo Publishers, 1994.

Kukuczka, Jerzy. *My Vertical World: Climbing the 8000-Metre Peaks*. Seattle: The Mountaineers Books, 1992.

———. *Mój Pionowy Świat, Czyli 14 x 8000 Metrów*. London: Wydawnictwo Arti, 1995.

Kurtyka, Voytek. *Chiński Maharadża*. Krakow: Góry Books, 2013.

———. *Trango Tower*. Warsaw: Wydawnictwo Text Publishing Co., 1990.

Loretan, Erhard. *Night Naked*. Seattle: Mountaineers Books, 2016.

McDonald, Bernadette. *Freedom Climbers*. Calgary: Rocky Mountain Books, 2011.

————. *Tomaž Humar*. London: Hutchinson, 2008.

Pawłowski, Ryszard. *Smak Gór. Seria Literatura Gorska na Świecie*. Katowice, Poland: Grupa Infomax, 2004.

Porter, John. *One Day as a Tiger*. Sheffield: Vertebrate Publishing, 2014.

Porter, John. *One Day as a Tiger*. Calgary: Rocky Mountain Books, 2016.

Scott, Doug. *Up and About: The Hard Road to Everest*. Sheffield: Vertebrate Publishing, 2015.

Skinner, Todd. *Beyond the Summit*. New York: Portfolio, 2003.

Tichy, Herbert. *Cho Oyu: By Favour of the Gods*. London: Methuen, 1957.

Wielicki, Krzysztof. *Korona Himalajów: 14 × 8000*. Krakow: Wydawnictwo Ati, 1997.

JOURNALS, NEWSPAPERS AND MAGAZINES

Alpine Journal, years: 1989, 2001, 2008, 2010–11.

American Alpine Journal, years: 1983–84, 1986–87, 1989, 1991, 2000–01, 2004.

Brniak, Marek. "Troll Wall in Winter." *Climber and Rambler* (March 1976): 22–25.

Child, Greg. "Between the Hammer and the Anvil." *Climbing* 115 (August–September 1989): 78–86.

Kurtyka, Voytek. "The Abseil and the Ascent." *The Himalayan Journal* 42 (1984–85): 121–126.

————. "The Art of Suffering." *Mountain* 121 (May–June 1988): 32–37.

————. "Breaker." Translated by Jurek Kopacz. Lone Sail Far Away website. Accessed January 2015. Originally published as "Łamaniec" in *Góry* 1 (1991): 8–11.

———. "Broad Peak North Ridge." *Climbing* 94 (February–March 1986): 40–42.

———. "Die Leuchtende Wand (12/85)." *Der Bergsteiger* (June 1986): 30.

———. "The East Face of Trango's Nameless Tower." *American Alpine Journal* 31, no. 63 (1989): 45–49.

———. "Gasherbrum II and Hidden Peak: New Routes." *American Alpine Journal* 26, no. 58 (1984): 37–42.

———. "Gasherbrum IV: Świetlistą Ścianą." *Taternik* 2 (1985): 61–62.

———. "The Gasherbrums Are Lonely." *Mountain* 97 (May–June 1984): 38–42.

———. "Losar." *Alpinist* 4 (Autumn 2003): 66–81.

———. "New Routes, Cho Oyu and Shisha Pangma." *American Alpine Journal* 33, no. 65 (1991): 14–18.

———. "The Path of the Mountain," *Bularz* 88–89: 37–43.

———. "The Polish Syndrome." *Mountain Review* 5 (November–December 1993): 36–47.

———. "The Shining Wall." *Alpinist* 2 (Spring 2003): 31–33.

———. "The Shining Wall of Gasherbrum IV." *American Alpine Journal* 28, no. 60 (1986): 1–6.

———. "Trango Extremes." *Mountain* 127 (May–June 1989): 22–26.

———. "The Trango Tower." *Alpinism* 1 (1986).

———. "Troje." MEM 3. Accessed January 2015. www.facebook.com/chinskimaharadza.

Kurtyka, Voytek, and Zbyszek Skierski. "View from the Wall." *Alpinist* 43 (Summer 2013): 65–75.

MacIntyre, Alex. "Broken English." *Mountain* 77 (1981): 36–37.

Porter, John. "Changabang South Buttress." *Climbing* 55 (1979): 2–6.

———. "South Side Story." *Mountain* 65 (1979): 44–47.

Rogozińska, Monika. "Góry Pod Powiekami." *Gazeta Wyborcza*, March 7, 2009.

Schauer, Robert. "Erstdurchsteigung der Westwand des Gasherbrum IV." *Der Bergsteiger* (December 1985): 26–29.

———. "The Shining Wall." *Climbing* 95 (April–May 1986): 41–44.

Szczepański, Dominik, and Łukasz Ziółkowski. "Wojciech Kurtyka: Igrzyska Śmierci." *Gazeta Wyborcza*, May 15, 2014.

Szczepański, J.A. "Dekalog." *Bularz* 91 (1991): 39.

Taniguchi, Kei. "Being with the Mountain." *Alpinist* 52 (Winter 2015): 62–63.

Wilczyński, Ludwik. "The Polish Himalayan Boom 1971–91." *Taternik* 3 (2012): 32–44.

FILMS

Kłosowicz, Marek. 2007. *Himalaiści: Ścieżka Góry – Wojciech Kurtyka.* TVN S.A., Poland.

Porębski, Jerzy. 2008. *Polskie Himalaje: The First Conquerors.* Artica, Poland.

———. 2008. *Polskie Himalaje: The Great Climbing.* Artica, Poland.

———. 2008. *Polskie Himalaje: The Great Tragedies.* Artica, Poland.

———. 2008. *Polskie Himalaje: The Ice Warriors.* Artica, Poland.

———. 2008. *Polskie Himalaje: Women in the Mountains.* Artica, Poland.

Index